THE AMERICAN COLONIAL CRISIS

THE
AMERICAN COLONIAL
CRISIS

The Daniel Leonard-John Adams
Letters to the Press 1774–1775

Edited by

Bernard Mason

HARPER TORCHBOOKS
Harper & Row, Publishers
New York, Evanston, San Francisco, London

THE AMERICAN COLONIAL CRISIS

First TORCHBOOK edition published 1972.

LIBRARY OF CONGRESS CATALOG NUMBER: 75–178972

STANDARD BOOK NUMBER: 06–131636–9

For Jennifer, Derek and Valerie for whom the American Revolution may be as much their handiwork as it was that of their predecessors.

CONTENTS

INTRODUCTION

"Should you be told that acts of high treason are flagrant through the country, that a great part of the province is in actual rebellion, would you believe it true? . . . Are not the bands of society cut asunder, and the sanctions that hold man to man, trampled upon? Can any of us recover a debt, or obtain compensation for an injury by law? Are not many persons, whom once we respected and revered, driven from their homes and families, and forced to fly to the army for protection for no other reason but their having accepted commissions under our King? Is not civil government dissolved?" With these words, Daniel Leonard, writing in 1774 as "Massachusettensis," sought to shock the readers of the *Massachusetts Gazette* into an acute awareness of the consequences of the escalating provincial conflict with the imperial government. The author's shrill tone was a reflection of the fact that 1774 had become a nightmare for many people, Tory and Whig, as Parliament, in response to the Boston Tea Party, had opted for a series of severely repressive measures which touched off waves of determined resistance. On the one hand, as General Thomas Gage confessed with chagrin to Lord Dartmouth, "Nobody here or at home could have conceived . . . that the Country People could have been raised to such a pitch of Phrenzy. . . ." But on the other hand, by the winter of 1774–75 the Whigs had circumvented General Gage's royal government and were building effectively revolutionary organizations on both the provincial and local levels. It was the very success of these activities that provoked Daniel Leonard to take up his quill in defense of King and empire.

Leonard, as the pseudonym "Massachusettensis" implied, was indeed a native son of the Bay whose ancestors had migrated to this colony in the seventeenth century. From iron production, a family tradition, the Leonards had fashioned a leading position for themselves among the local elite of Bristol County. After graduation from Harvard in 1764, Daniel applied himself to the law in the Taunton office of Samuel White, Speaker of the Massachusetts House of Representatives and his future father-in-law. Prospering in the legal profession, young Leonard entered politics and won election to the House where he served several terms. When the North ministry, implementing the coercive Massachusetts Government Act of 1774, appointed the Taunton barrister to the new governor's council that was heretofore elective, it gave him membership in a legislative body that was now wholly Tory and highly unpopular. News of Leonard's selection as councillor provoked the local Whigs to drive him from his home into the provincial capital. Adherence to the Friends of Government would cost Leonard his citizenship and his property when he joined the loyalist refugees from Boston in 1776.

The barbs of Massachusettensis elicited a powerful vindication of the Whigs by a lawyer who had defended the British soldiers in the Boston Massacre trials and who with the Massachusetts delegation had recently returned from the Continental Congress. John Adams, selecting the Latin equivalent for New Englishman as an appropriate nom de plume with which to reply to a local Tory, undertook a detailed rebuttal and counteroffensive in the *Boston Gazette*, January 23, 1775. "Novanglus" brought to his task top-flight credentials, since he represented Braintree in the House of Representatives, had been chosen to the Provincial Congress, was intimate with the revolutionary leadership and was a practicing lawyer with a flair for political theory. In important respects Adams was the mirror image of Leonard.

The effect of the Revolution on social relations was often shattering and the Tory-Whig alignments of these two men illustrated what had become a feature of the crisis: individuals with similar socio-economic status often joined opposing camps. Kinfolk of both men who were craftsmen or tradesmen and landowners were among the towns' elites. Leonard and Adams were Harvard graduates, lawyers, served in the provincial legislature, and were driving men who were anxious to move upward in society. However, their perceptions of the kinds of socio-political communities in which they preferred to live diverged fatefully in 1774–75. Perhaps one way of understanding this divergence is to remember that, as Massachusettensis remarked, the penalty for rebellion was death and the confiscation of property, and that at this juncture few Europeans would have granted the colonials any possibility of successful insurgency. Therefore, the rebels were the risk-takers, the most venturesome elements in colonial society.

Both authors contrived to write on several levels. Each was anxious to shape public opinion through appeals to fear, anger, honor, pride, virtue and communal and imperial loyalty. Factional politics appeared and reappeared throughout these essays as Tory and Whig each charged his opponent with responsibility for the crisis, each seeing in the other side a horrid conspiracy against virtue and the virtuous. The two men assiduously sought assistance from Clio whom they employed didactically and prophetically as they ranged over the time from the ancient past to the eighteenth century. Lastly, on the conceptual level, three important sets of ideas emerged from the welter of words that the writers produced in the space of four months. Adams and Leonard formulated opposing views of the British constitution, of imperial relationships and of the colonial political structure. Although most of the one-sided pleading and accusations proved ephemeral, these ideas have a more enduring distinction because they were central to the problem of ideology's role in the onset of the Revolution.

When Massachusettensis began his exposition of essential

ideas, he turned back to the origins of the body politic. Leonard believed that in its delineation of the reciprocity between the people and the rulers the constitution mirrored the original social compact because government sprang from voluntary agreement. The Taunton counsellor wrote that within the framework of law, the citizens owed obedience and in return the government guaranteed security, legally through the courts, of the individual and his property, of "the poor . . . against the rich, the weak against the strong, the individual against the many." Another element of this security was defense against foreign invasion. Notably absent from his formulation was the broadly held notion that the object of government included the preservation of liberty as well as life and property. Leonard's stress upon the people's obligations rather than their rights is a theme which permeated the entire series. The shaping of the constitution along the lines of order and security was calculated to produce social stability rather than innovation and dynamic change.

Nowhere in the Massachusettensis essays will the reader encounter a precise definition of the British constitution. It is true that in number five Leonard expounded a "cursory view" of the subject, but his outline was largely a statement that the British form of mixed government was the constitution. Here he developed the familiar observation that the best system wisely balanced the three ingredients of monarchy, aristocracy and democracy. Furthermore, in Britain the aristocracy was the "bulwark" of the constitution because it checked the Crown on the one hand while it withstood the "sappings" of the Commons on the other. As his remark implied, the Massachusetts Tory harbored an aristocratically oriented conception of society that appeared in other places in his discussions of provincial politics. Elsewhere in the series, Leonard intimated that in his opinion the fundamentals of government included the judiciary, but he omitted any reference to the role played by the common law. A further ambiguity in Massachusettensis's understanding of the constitution was his indirect reference to the English Bill of Rights when he discussed Parliamentary taxation. In the context of his rationale the Bill appeared to be within the constitutional framework but its relationship was not explicitly acknowledged.

"Two supreme or independent authorities cannot exist in the same state," the Taunton authority posited in expounding the most widely held British theory of the empire, and, therefore, Parliament must be the center of authority for the kingdom. Even though the colonies had subordinate rights and privileges, these in no way impinged upon the jurisdiction of Parliament because settlements were merged into the colonizing state, according to the law of nations. The relationship of the American colonies to Britain was similar to that of Ireland, Jersey and Guernsey, all of which were subject to the hegemony of Parliament, although the precise nature of the connection varied from case to case. Furthermore, seventeenth-century Englishmen and settlers both assumed that colonial subservience to the legislature was the natural state of things. Leonard substantiated this view by referring to sections of the Massachusetts charters, to Parliamentary statutes and to expressions of acquiescence by the provincial legislature. One consequence of Parliament's supremacy was the right to determine the allocation of taxes for all parts of the empire notwithstanding that the exercise of this authority contravened a basic British liberty, the colonial subject's agreement through his representative to the appropriation of his property. Although Massachusettensis accepted in principle the idea of colonial representation in the British Commons, he asserted that the reality of geography made it impracticable and the Americans must accept their exclusion from the seat of government. As a counterweight to the loss of representation Leonard pragmatically accepted the colonists' distinction between internal and external taxation in order to find an acceptable basis for relations with the mother country.

The Massachusetts Tory accentuated the material benefits of the imperial system as the main question for British Americans. Nowhere on the globe was there a level of affluence comparable to that in British North America, or another dominion where the people luxuriated in the benefits of mild government. Leonard admitted that the royal government, acting through the trade laws, limited colonial enterprise, but on balance the Americans always received a generous quid pro quo, occasionally even at the expense of British interests. But most important of all, Britain maintained military and naval security for its maritime possessions and indeed had fought the last major war primarily in behalf of the American colonists. In the face of these blessings, Whig grievances were imaginary, the desperate fulminations of a conspiratorial junto that would stop at nothing to gain power.

The subjection of the provincial political structure to the extraordinary strain of the quarrel with the mother country had revealed to the Tories the inherent instability of the local government. Massachusettensis lamented the Whig domination of the upper house because he conceived that body as playing a role in support of the governor against the House of Representatives. Only if the councillors were men of wealth and "first abilities," and crown appointees, could the Council effectively buttress the king's vicegerent and contribute to the security of lives and property.

The charter prescription of House nomination of the Council had led directly to the current difficulties since it had allowed the Whigs to establish domination over the upper house thereby undercutting the governor's power. Moreover, another bulwark of social order, the judiciary, had fallen under the sway of the popular legislative branch through the House's authority over judicial salaries. When "democratical" influence spread through political society in this manner, it was impossible to maintain stability. Leonard further aired his elitist sensibilities when he deplored the office-seeker's efforts to ingratiate himself with the voters, a method understood to be the cardinal means of winning power. He implied that the wooing of the electorate at the expense of the representative's independent judgment constituted a sacrifice of public virtue in order to cater to the "multitude." Massachusettensis thus hammered together the basic framework to which he attached his detailed arguments against the Whigs.

When Adams took up the problem of constitutional origins, he explained contractual government as an enduring relationship in which the rights of the people were matters of greater sensitivity and gravity than obligations to authority. The seventeenth-century English revolutions, notwithstanding Cromwell's authoritarianism, had so underscored these aspects of the compact for the Massachusetts Whigs that the New Englanders thought of them as first principles. Nevertheless, as Adams warned, in the eighteenth century government possessed the power and institutions with which to command obedience whereas the citizenry lacked the organizations and capability to react quickly in order to prevent incursions upon their liberties. Novanglus, linking his fears of antipopular ministerial conspiracies and political venality with the threat to freedom, justified resistance to any authority that sought to destroy the objectives of government by curtailing the citizen's rights and enslaving him.

Although Adams in his "Clarendon" letters of 1766 had sketched with broadstrokes his understanding of a constitution, in this series of polemics he employed the word in varying and ambiguous contexts. In truth neither Tories nor Whigs had precisely defined, not to say reached a consensus on, their usage. In one breath Novanglus debated with his opponent as though the constitution were simply the mixed form of government but in another he reverted to elements in his 1766 exposition by emphasizing middle class ascendancy in representation and the people's role in the judicial process through the jury system. Furthermore, when Adams included in his description the powers of the three branches of British government, he insisted repeatedly that these had derived in large part over the last century from "revolution principles." The attorney from Braintree was transferring the disputation, however, to even more familiar terrain when he implied the existence of an analogy between the British constitution and the Massachusetts charter. The latter was a "charter constitution," a discrete body of fundamental law which prescribed the institutions of colonial government. Perhaps the most brilliantly perceptive of Adams's comments on constitutional relations was his characterization of the intrinsic nature of British government as "nothing more nor less than a republic," "a government of laws and not of men." With these words Novanglus not only lucidly summed up, perhaps with greater clarity than most British leaders, the consequences of the English Revolution but he also predicted by implication the later movement to limit further the political activity of the crown. Whigs of the Adams stripe had a more innovative notion of constitutionalism than did the Hutchinsonian Tories and applied it imaginatively to the debate over imperial sovereignty.

Acrimonious arguments over colonial subordination between Britons and Americans in the preceding decade had stimulated thought about ideas that were relatively new or vaguely delineated but that grew in significance with the quickening tempo of events. One of these was the connotation of the word "empire," a word whose earlier meaning of trade and oceanic colonization British leaders and American Tories were transforming into one of territorial and governmental centralization. When Novanglus dissected the structure of the empire, he challenged his opponents' views by ridiculing their attribution of imperial authority to Parliament. Colonials "are to be conjured out of [their] senses by the magic in the words of British Empire" but this was the "language of newspapers and political pamplets," and did not derive from the foundation of Parliamentary power which never extended beyond the "four seas."

As for the "imperial crown of Great Britain," these were the phrases of "court sycophants." Indeed, the mother country was not an empire at all, since such a government was by definition a despotism, whereas Britain was a limited monarchy. Moreover, there was a crucial question of historical process to be confronted; when had the people created this British Empire and the supremacy of Parliament? The 1707 Act of Union that established the Kingdom of Great Britain was subsequent to the founding of most of the colonies and was enacted without consultation of the colonials who were thus effectively denied any benefit from their supposed connection with the House of Commons. Obviously, Adams declared, Parliament did not elicit American opinion because it did not believe that it possessed hegemony over the settlers.

Having disposed of Parliamentary supremacy as a consequence of a theory of imperial suzerainty, the Massachusetts Whig passed on to another facet of the problem: the claim of universal sovereignty of Parliament which it acquired through the governance of the realm of England. Here Adams fell back on the common law in order to deny Parliament's power outside the home islands because he reasoned that this body of law was the source of legislative jurisdiction over the kingdom but that such law never carried beyond English tidewater. Therefore, if Parliament ruled the colonies it was not through the sanction of common law. Still another origin of legislative supremacy, by Leonard's account, was colonial incorporation into the realm, but Novanglus denied that the King-in-Parliament had ever enacted the requisite statute or that the Americans had ever entered into any compact for that purpose. Nonetheless, the first colonizers were citizens outside the kingdom even though they came to the wilderness without English laws, because they brought with them royal charters and instructions in addition to their natural rights. When the settlers forged their polities, they voluntarily adopted portions of the common law and claimed the heritage of English rights. Adams also pointed out that the Stuart kings had neither intended to institute colonial subordination to their royal legislature nor formulated their overseas policies on this principle. Seventeenth-century attitudes and official actions demonstrated that Americans believed themselves free to shape their institutions without interference from Parliament, subject only to the restraints of the crown. To be sure, Novanglus could not blink the fact of Parliamentary regulation of trade; however, he insisted that the colonials had acquiesced in this action as necessary for the general welfare. Although the colonies were not within the jurisdiction of Parliament, they were British dominions whose link to the nation was the king. Ireland and Wales in times past were examples of this type of relationship until both peoples had voluntarily acceded to Parliamentary power over them. Adams exposed the core of the intricate system when he commented pragmatically: "That Britain has been imprudent enough to let Colonies be planted, until they are become numerous and important, without ever having wisdom enough to concert a plan for their government, consistent with her own welfare."

Novanglus was sensitive to the problem of local political stability, but he approached it within the milieu of a popular representative structure rather than an aristocratic one. Social tensions diminished when the people could take an active part in government through their deputies. One of the implications of the broad franchise was the legislature's exercise of the power of the purse in the matter of the governor's and judges' salaries in order to operate as a check on the executive. But even this was not sufficient because elected delegates might stray from the path of virtue. Adams, therefore, urged the necessity of the publication of legislative voting records to inform the citizenry and stipulated that voters should press their opinions upon their delegates. Legislatures in turn ought not to enact an "unpopular measure." An important component of the system was the elective council which was to be preferred to a crown-designated body, since the latter as well as the governor would be under royal dominion and thus the king would be master of two branches of the legislature. If independence of influence was a virtue, then the only alternative to an hereditary house of lords was an elected council.

Adams and Leonard in the exposition of their ideology were crossing swords over two antithetical models of society. For the Tory the basic elements were order and an imperial stability; only within this framework could colonials expect to thrive. But the crisis had eroded these fundamentals and aroused Leonard's anxiety. Fear of mounting restiveness among hitherto passive classes, fear of a spreading tendency to resort to mob action to achieve social ends evoked in Leonard's mind a vision of the social structure's collapse. For the Whig, liberty and innovation were the key ingredients of the model. Adams, then, was responding to his perception of the need for greater flexibility in order to avert the explosion of pent-up hostility to a deferential society. His remedy was widespread involvement of the electorate and modification of the empire. Consequently, Adams faced toward the future, Leonard toward the past. This was the American Revolution.

This edition of the polemics contains about four-fifths of the original wordage and comes from two sources. A 1775 Boston pamphlet, *To the Inhabitants of the Province of Massachusetts Bay,* supplied Leonard's essays while the *Boston Gazette and Country Journal,* January 23–April 17, 1775, furnished those of Novanglus. In addition the Massachusetts Historical Society has generously permitted me to include portions of the Novanglus manuscript number 13 which is in the Robert Treat Paine papers. I have altered the spelling only in those cases where clarification was necessary.

Bernard Mason,
State University of New York at
Binghamton

To the Inhabitants of
the Province of Massachusetts Bay

Massachusettensis
[Daniel Leonard]

LETTER I

When a people, by what means soever, are reduced to such a situation, that everything they hold dear, as men and citizens, is at stake, it is not only excuseable, but even praiseworthy for an individual to offer to the public any thing that he may think has a tendency to ward off the impending danger; nor should he be restrained from an apprehension that what he may offer will be unpopular, any more than a physician should be restrained from prescribing a salutary medicine through fear it might be unpalatable to his patient.

The press, when open to all parties and influenced by none, is a salutary engine in a free state, perhaps a necessary one to preserve the freedom of that state; but, when a party has gained the ascendency so far as to become the licensers of the press, either by an act of government, or by playing off the resentment of the populace against printers and authors, the press itself becomes an engine of oppression or licentiousness, and is as pernicious to society as otherwise it would be beneficial. It is too true to be denied that ever since the origin of our controversy with Great-Britain, the press, in this town has been much devoted to the partizans of liberty; they have been indulged in publishing what they pleased . . . while little has been published on the part of government; the effect this must have had upon the minds of the people in general is obvious; they must have formed their opinion upon a partial view of the subject, and of course it must have been in some degree erroneous. . . .

We have been so long advancing to our present state, and by

such gradations, that perhaps many of us are insensible of our true state and real danger. Should you be told that acts of high treason are flagrant through the country, that a great part of the province is in actual rebellion, would you believe it true? Should you not deem the person asserting it an enemy to the province? Nay, should you not spurn him from you with indignation? Be calm, my friends, it is necessary to know the worst of a disease, to enable us to provide an effectual remedy. Are not the bands of society cut asunder, and the sanctions that hold man to man, trampled upon? Can any of us recover a debt, or obtain compensation for an injury, by law? Are not many persons, whom once we respected and revered, driven from their homes and families, and forced to fly to the army for protection, for no other reason but their having accepted commissions under our King? Is not civil government dissolved? Some have been made to believe that nothing short of attempting the life of the King, or fighting his troops, can amount to high treason or rebellion. If, reader, you are one of those, apply to an honest lawyer (if such an one can be found) and enquire what kind of offence it is for a number of men to assemble, armed and forceably to obstruct the course of justice, even to prevent the King's courts from being held at their stated terms; for a body of people to seize upon the King's provincial revenue; I mean the monies collected by virtue of grants made by the general court to his Majesty for the support of his government within this province; for a body of men to assemble without being called by authority, and to pass governmental acts, or for a number of people to take the militia out of the hands of the King's representative, or to form a new militia, or to raise men and appoint officers for a public purpose, without the order or permission of the King or his representative; or for a number of men to take their arms, and march with a professed design of opposing the King's troops; ask, reader, of such a lawyer, what is the crime, and what the punishment; and if per chance thou art one that hast been active in these things, and art not insensibility itself, his answer will harrow up thy soul. . . . However closely we may hug ourselves in the opinion that the parliament has no right to tax or legislate for us, the people of England hold the contrary opinion as firmly; they tell us we are a part of the British empire; that every state from the nature of government must have a supreme uncontrolable power coextensive with the empire itself; and that, that power is vested in parliament. It is as unpopular to deny this doctrine in Great-Britain as it is to assert it in the colonies; so there is but little probability of serving ourselves at this day by our ingenious distinctions between a right of legislation for one purpose and not another. We have bid them defiance, and the longest sword must carry it, unless we change our measures. . . . Had we been prudent enough to confine our opposition within certain limits, we might have stood some chance of succeeding once more, but alas we have passed the Rubicon. It is now universally said and believed, in England, that if this opportunity of reclaiming the colonies, and reducing them to a sense of their duty is lost, they in truth will be dismembered from the empire, and become as distinct a state from Great-Britain as Hanover; that is, although they may continue their allegiance to the person of the King, they will own none to the imperial crown of Great-Britain, nor yield obedience to any of her laws but such as they shall think proper to adopt. Can you indulge the thought one moment, that Great-Britain will consent to this? For what has she protected and defended the colonies against the maritime powers of Europe from their first British settlement to this day. . . . Perhaps you are as fatally mistaken in another respect, I mean as to the power of Great-Britain to conquer; but can any of you that think soberly upon the matter, be so deluded as to believe that Great-Britain, who so lately carried her arms with success to every part of the globe, triumphed over the united powers of France and Spain, and whose fleets give law to the ocean, is unable to conquer us. Should the colonies unite in a war against Great-Britain (which by the way is not a supposeable case) the colonies south of Pennsylvania would be unable to furnish any men; they have not more than is necessary to govern their numerous slaves, and to defend themselves against the Indians. I will suppose that the northern colonies can furnish as many, and indeed more men than can be used to advantage, but have you arms fit for a campaign? If you have arms, have you military stores, or can you procure them? When this war is proclaimed, all supplies from foreign parts will be cut off. Have you money to maintain the war? Or had you all those things some others are still wanting, which are absolutely necessary to encounter regular troops, that is discipline, and that subordination whereby each can command all below him from a general officer to the lowest subaltern; these you neither have nor can have in such a war. . . . Your new-fangled militia have already given us a *Specimen* of their future conduct. In some of their companies, they have already chosen two, in others three sets of officers, and are as dissatisfied with the last choice as the first. I do not doubt the natural bravery of my country men, all men would act the same part in the same situation. Such is the army with which you are to oppose the most powerful nation upon the globe. . . . I have hitherto confined my observations to the war within the interior parts of the colonies, let us now turn our eyes to our extensive sea coasts, and that we find wholly at the mercy of Great-Britain; our trade, fishery, navigation and maritime towns taken from us the very day that war is proclaimed. Inconceivably shocking the scene; if we turn our views to the wilderness, our back settlements a prey to our ancient enemy, the Canadians, whose wounds received from us in the late war will bleed a-fresh at the prospect of revenge, and to the numerous tribes of savages, whose tender mercies are cruelties; thus with the British navy in the front, Canadians and savages in the rear, a regular army in the midst, we must be certain that when ever the sword of civil war is unsheathed, devastation will pass through our land like a whirlwind, our houses be burnt to ashes, our fair possessions laid waste, and he that falls by sword will be happy in escaping a more ignominious death.

I have hitherto gone upon a supposition that all the colonies from Nova-Scotia to Georgia would unite in the war against Great-Britain, but I believe if we consider cooly upon the matter, we shall find no reason to expect any assistance out of New England. . . .

I have as yet said nothing of the difference in sentiment among ourselves; upon a superficial view we might imagine that this province was nearly unanimous, but the case is far different; a very considerable part of the men of property in this province, are at this day firmly attached to the cause of government; bodies of men compelling persons to disavow their sentiments to resign commissions, or to subscribe leagues and convenants, has wrought no change in their sentiments, it has only attached them more closely to government, and caused them to wish more fervently, and to pray more devoutly for its restoration; these and thousands beside, if they fight at all, will fight under the banners of loyalty. I can assure you that associations are now forming in several parts of this province for the support of his Majesty's government and mutual defence; and let me tell you, when ever the royal standard shall be set up, there will be such a flocking to it, as will astonish the most obdurate. . . .

December 12, 1774.   Massachusettensis

LETTER II

. . . At the conclusion of the late war, Great-Britain found that
though she had humbled her enemies, and greatly enlarged her
own empire, that the national debt amounted to almost one
hundred and fifty millions, and that the annual expence of keeping her extended dominions in a state of defence, which good
policy dictates no less in a time of peace than war, was increased
in proportion to the new acquisitions. Heavy taxes and duties
were already laid, not only upon the luxuries and conveniences,
but even the necessaries of life in Great-Britain and Ireland. She
knew that the colonies were as much benefited by the con-
quests in the late war, as any part of the empire, and indeed
more so, as their continental foes were subdued, and they might
now extend their settlements not only to Canada, but even to
the western ocean. The greatest opening was given to agriculture, the natural livelihood of the country, that ever was known
in the history of the world, and their trade was protected by the
British navy. The revenue to the crown, from America,
amounted to but little more than the charges of collecting it.
She thought it as reasonable that the colonies should bear part
of the national burden, as that they should share in the national
benefit. For this purpose the stamp-act was passed. The colonies
soon found that the duties imposed by the stamp-act would be
grievous, as they were laid upon custom-house papers, law proceedings, conveyancing, and indeed extended to almost all
their internal trade and dealings. It was generally believed
through the colonies, that this was a tax not only exceeding our

proportion, but beyond our utmost ability to pay. This idea, united the colonies generally in opposing it. At first we did not dream of denying the *authority* of parliament to tax us, much less to legislate for us. We had always considered ourselves, as a part of the British empire, and the parliament, as the supreme legislature of the whole. Acts of parliament for regulating our internal polity were familiar. We had paid postage agreeable to act of parliament, for establishing a post-office, duties imposed for regulating trade, and even for raising a revenue to the crown without questioning the right, though we closely adverted to the rate or quantum. We knew that in all those acts of government, the good of the whole had been consulted, and whenever through want of information any thing grievous had been ordained, we were sure of obtaining redress by a proper representation of it. . . . Some few months after it was known that the stamp-act was passed, some resolves of the house of burgesses in Virginia, denying the right of parliament to tax the colonies, made their appearance. We read them with wonder —they savoured of independence—they flattered the human passions—the reasoning was specious—we wished it conclusive. The transition, to believing it so, was easy and we, and almost all America, followed their example, in resolving that the parliament had no such right. It now became unpopular to suggest the contrary; his life would be in danger that asserted it. The news-papers were open to but one side of the question, and the inflammatory pieces that issued weekly from the press, worked up the populace to a fit temper to commit the outrages that insued. A non-importation was agreed upon, which alarmed the merchants and manufacturers in England. It was novel, and the people in England then supposed that the love of liberty was so powerful in an American merchant, as to stifle his love of gain, and that the agreement would be religiously adhered to. It has been said, that several thousands were expended in England, to foment the disturbances there. However that may be opposition to the ministry was then gaining ground, from circumstances, foreign to this. The ministry was changed, and the stamp-act repealed. The repealing statute passed, with diffi- culty however, through the house of peers, near forty noble lords protested against giving way to such an opposition, and foretold what has since literally come to pass in consequence of it. When the statute was made, imposing duties upon glass, paper, India teas, etc. imported into the colonies, it was said, that this was another instance of taxation, for some of the dutied commodities were necessaries, we had them not without our- selves, were prohibited from importing them from any place except Great-Britain, and consequently, were obliged to pay the duties. Accordingly news-paper publications, pamphlets, resolves, non-importation agreements, and the whole system of American opposition was again put in motion. We obtained a partial repeal of this statute, which took off the duties from all the articles except teas. This was the lucky moment when to have closed the dispute. We might have made a safe and honor- able retreat. We had gained much, perhaps more than we ex- pected. If the parliament had passed an act declaratory of their right to tax us, our assemblies had resolved, ten times, that they had no such right. We could not complain of the three-penny duty on tea as burdensome, for a shilling which had been laid upon it, for the purpose of regulating trade, and therefore was allowed to be constitutional, was taken off; so that we were in fact gainers nine-pence in a pound by the new regulation. If the appropriation of the revenue, arising from this statute was disrelished, it was only our striking off one article of luxury from our manner of living, an article too, which if we may believe the resolves of most of the towns in this province, or rely on its collected wisdom in a resolve of the house of representatives, was to the last degree ruinous to health. It was futile to urge its being a precedent, as a reason for keeping up the ball of conten- tion; for, allowing the supreme legislature even to want a prece- dent, they had many for laying duties on commodities imported into the colonies. And beside we had great reason to believe that the remaining part of the statute would be repealed, as soon as the parliament should suppose it could be done with honor to themselves, as the incidental revenue arising from the former regulation, was four fold to the revenue arising from the latter. A claim of the right, could work no injury, so long as there was no grievous exercise of it, especially as we had protested against it, through the whole, and could not be said to have departed from our claims in the least. We might now upon good terms have dropped the dispute, and been happy in the affections of our mother-country; but that is yet to come. Party is inseperable from a free state. The several distributions of power, as they are limited by, so they create perpetual dissentions between each other, about their respective boundaries; but the greatest source is the competition of individuals for preferment in the state. Popularity is the ladder by which the partizans usually climb. Accordingly the struggle is, who shall have the greatest share of it. Each party professes disinterested patriotism, though some cynical writers have ventured to assert, that self-love is the ruling passion of the whole. There were two parties in this province of pretty long standing, known by the name of whig and tory, which at this time were not a little imbittered against each other. Men of abilities and acknowledged probity were on both sides. If the tories were suspected of pursuing their private interest through the medium of court favour, there was equal reason to suspect the whigs of pursuing their private interest by the means of popularity. Indeed some of them owed all their importance to it, and must in a little time have sunk into obscurity, had these turbulent commotions then subsided.

The tories and whigs took different routs, as usual. The tories were for closing the controversy with Great-Britain, the whigs for continuing it; the tories were for restoring government in the province, which had become greatly relaxed by these convulsions, to its former tone; the whigs were averse to it; they even refused to revive a temporary riot act, which expired about this time. Perhaps they thought that mobs were a necessary ingredient in their system of opposition: However, the whigs had great advantages in the unequal combat, their scheme flattered the people with the idea of independance; the tories plan supposed a degree of subordination, which is rather an humiliating idea; besides there is a propensity in men to believe themselves injured and oppressed whenever they are told so. The ferment raised in their minds in the time of the stamp-act was not yet allayed, and the leaders of the whigs had gained the confidence of the people by their successes in their former struggles, so that they had nothing to do but to keep up the spirit among the people, and they were sure of commanding in this province. It required some pains to prevent their minds settling into that calm which is ordinarily the effect of a mild government; the whigs were sensible that there was no oppression that could be either seen or felt; if any thing was in reality amiss in government, it was its being too lax. So far was it from the innocent being in danger of suffering, that the most atrocious offenders escaped with impunity. They accordingly applied themselves to work upon the imagination, and to inflame the passion. . . .

The tories have been censured for remissness in not having exerted themselves sufficiently at this period: the truth of the case is this, they saw and shuddered at the gathering storm, but durst not attempt to dispel it, lest it should burst on their own heads. Printers were threatened with the loss of their bread, for publishing freely on the tory side. One, Mr. Mein was forced to fly the country for persisting in it.

All our dissenting ministers were not inactive on this occasion. When the clergy engage in a political warfare, religion becomes a most powerful engine, either to support or overthrow the state. . . .

I shall next trace the effects of this spirit which the whigs had thus infused into the body of the people, through the courts of common law, and the general assembly, and mark the ways and means whereby they availed themselves of it to the subversion of our charter constitution, antecedent to the late act of parliament.

December 19, 1774   Massachusettensis

LETTER III

. . . The bulk of the people are generally but little versed in matters of state. Want of inclination or opportunity to figure in public life, makes them content to rest the affairs of government in the hands where accident or merit has placed them. . . . There is a latent spark however in their breasts capable of being kindled into a flame; to do this has always been the employment of the disaffected. They begin by reminding the people of the elevated rank they hold in the universe, as men; that all men by nature are equal; that Kings are but the ministers of the people; that their authority is delegated to them by the people for their good, and they have a right to resume it, and place it in other hands, or keep it themselves, whenever it is made use of to oppress them. . . . No government, however perfect in theory, is administered in perfection; the frailty of man does not admit of it. A small mistake, in point of policy, often furnishes a pretence to libel government, and persuade the people that their rulers are tyrants, and the whole government a system of oppression. Thus the seeds of sedition are usually sown, and the people are led to sacrifice real liberty to licentiousness, which gradually ripens into rebellion and civil war. And what is still more to be lamented, the generality of the people, who are thus made the dupes of artifice, and the mere stilts of ambition, are sure to be losers in the end. . . . My present business is, to trace the spirit of opposition to Great-Britain through the general court, and the courts of common law. In moderate times, a representative that votes for an unpopular measure, or opposes a popular one, is in danger of losing his election the next year; when party runs high, he is sure to do it. It was the policy of the whigs to have their questions, upon high matters, determined by yea and nay votes, which were published with the representatives names in the next gazette. This was commonly followed by severe strictures and the most illiberal invectives upon the dissentients, sometimes they were held up as objects of resentment, of contempt at others; the abuse was in proportion to the extravagance of the measure they opposed. . . . The scurrility made its way into the dissentient's town, it furnished his competitor with means to supplant him, and he took care to shun the rock his predecessor had split upon. In this temper of the times, it was enough to know who voted with Cassius and who with Lucius, to determine who was a friend and who an enemy to the country, without once adverting to the question before the house. The loss of a seat in the house was not of so much consequence, but when once he became stigmatized as an enemy to his country, he was exposed to insult, and if his profession or business was such, that his livelihood depended much on the good graces of his fellow citizens, he was in danger of losing his bread, and involving his whole family in ruin.

One particular set of members, in committee, always prepared the resolves and other spirited measures: At first they were canvassed freely, at length would slide through the house without meeting an obstacle. The lips of the dissentients were sealed up; they sat in silence, and beheld with infinite regret the measure they durst not oppose. Many were borne down against their wills by the violence of the current; upon no other principle can we reconcile their ostensible conduct in the house to their declarations in private circles. The apparent unanimity in the house encouraged the opposition out of doors, and that in its turn strengthened the party in the house. Thus they went on mutually supporting and up-lifting each other. Assemblies and towns resolved alternately; some of them only omitted resolving to snatch the sceptre out of the hands of our Sovereign, and to strike the imperial crown from his sacred head.

A master stroke in politics respecting the agent ought not to be neglected. Each colony has usually an agent residing at the court of Great-Britain: These agents are appointed by the three branches of their several assemblies, and indeed there cannot be a provincial agent without such appointment. The whigs soon found that they could not have such services rendered them from a provincial agent as would answer their purposes. The house therefore refused to join with the other two branches of the general court in the appointment. The house chose an agent for themselves, and the council appointed another. Thus we had two agents for private purposes, and the expence of agency doubled; and with equal reason a third might have been added, as agent for the Governor, and the charges been trebled.

The additional expence was of little consideration, compared with another inconvenience that attended this new mode of agency. The person appointed by the house was the ostensible agent of the province, though in fact he was only the agent of a few individuals that had got the art of managing the house at their pleasure. He knew his continuing in office depended upon them. An office that yielded several hundred pounds sterling annually; the business of which consisted in little more than attending the levees of the great, and writing letters to America, was worth preserving. Thus he was under a strong temptation to sacrifice the province to a party; and echoed back the sentiments of his patrons.

The advices continually received from one of the persons that was thus appointed agent, had great influence upon the members of the house of more moderate principles. He had pushed his researches deep into nature, and made important discoveries; they thought he had done the same in politics, and did not admire him less as a politician than as a philosopher. His intelligence as to the disposition of his Majesty, the ministry, the parliament and the nation in general, was deemed the most authentic. He advised us to keep up our opposition, to resolve and re-resolve, to cherish a military spirit, uniformly holding up this idea, that if we continued firm, we had nothing to fear from the government in England. He even proposed some modes of opposition himself. . . .

The councellors depended upon the general assembly for their political existance; the whigs reminded the council of their mortality. If a councellor opposed the violent measures of the whigs with any spirit, he lost his election the next May. The council consisted of twenty-eight. From this principle near half that number, mostly men of the first families, note and abilities, with every possible attachment to their native country, and as far from temptation as wealth and independance could remove them, were tumbled from their seats in disgrace. Thus the board which was intended to moderate between the extremes of prerogative and privilege, lost its weight in the scale, and the political balance of the province was destroyed.

Had the chair been able to retain its own constitutional influence, the loss of the board would have been less felt; but no longer supported by the board, that fell likewise. The Governor by the charter could do little or nothing without council. If he called upon a military officer to raise the militia, he was answered, they were there already. If he called upon his council for their assistance, they must first enquire into the cause. If he wrote to government at home to strengthen his hands, some officious person procured and sent back his letters.

It was not the person of a Bernard or Hutchinson that made them obnoxious, any other governors would have met with the same fate, had they discharged their duty with equal fidelity; that is, had they strenuously opposed the principles and practices of the whigs; and when they found that the government here could not support itself, wrote home for aid sufficient to do it. And let me tell you, had the intimations in those letters, which you are taught to execrate, been timely attended to, we had now been as happy a people as good government could make us. Governor Bernard came here recommended by the affections of the province over which he had presided. His abilities are acknowledged. True British honesty and punctuality are traits in his character too strongly marked to escape the eye of prejudice itself. . . .

Thus, disaffection to Great-Britain being infused into the body of the people, the subtle poison stole through all the veins and arteries, contaminated the blood, and destroyed the very stamina of the constitution. Had not the courts of justice been tainted in the early stages, our government might have expelled the virus, purged off the peccant humors and recovered its former vigour by its own strength. The judges of the superior court were dependant upon the annual grants of the general court for their support. Their salaries were small in proportion to the salaries of other officers in the government of less importance.

They had often petitioned the assembly to enlarge them, without success. They were at this time reminded of their dependance. However, it is but justice to say, that the judges remained unshaken, amid the raging tempests, which is to be attributed rather to their firmness than situation. But the spirit of the times was very apparent in the juries. The grand jurors were elective, and in such places where libels, riots and insurrections were the most frequent, the high whigs took care to get themselves chosen. The judges pointed out to them the seditious libels on governors, magistrates and the whole government, to no effect. They were enjoined to present riots and insurrections, of which there was ample evidence, with as little success.

It is difficult to account for so many of the first rate whigs being returned to serve on the petit jury at the term next after extraordinary insurrections, without supposing some legerdemain in drawing their names out of the box. It is certain that notwithstanding swarms of the most virulent libels infested the province, and there were so many riots and insurrections, scarce one offender was indicted, and I think not one convicted and punished. . . . The mere circumstance of the whigs gaining the ascendency over the tories is trifling. Had the whigs divided the province between them, as they once flattered themselves they should be able to do, it would have been of little consequence to the community, had they not cut a-sunder the very sinews of government, and broke in pieces the ligaments of social life in the attempt. I will mention two instances which I have selected out of many, of the weakness of our government, as they are recent and unconnected with acts of parliament. One Malcom, a loyal subject, and as such, intitled to protection, the evening before the last winter sessions of the general-court, was dragged out of his house, stript, tarred and feathered, and carted several hours in the severest frost of that winter, to the utmost hazard of his life. He was carried to the gallows with an halter about his neck, and in his passage to and from the gallows, was beaten with as cruel stripes as ever were administered by the hands of a savage. The whipping, however, kept up the circulation of his blood, and saved the poor man's life. When they had satiated their malice, they dispersed in good order. This was transacted in the presence of thousands of spectators, some of whom were members of the general-court. Malcom's life was despaired of several days, but he survived and presented a memorial to the general-assembly, praying their interposition. The petition was read, and all he obtained was leave to withdraw it. So that he was destitute of protection every hour until he left the country, as were thousands beside, until the arrival of the King's troops. This originated from a small fracas in the street, wherein Malcom struck or threatened to strike a person that insulted him, with a cutlass, and had no connection with the quarrel of the times, unless his sustaining a small post in the customs made it.

The other instance is much stronger than this, as it was totally detached from politics. It had been suspected that infection had communicated from an hospital, lately erected at Marblehead, for the purpose of innoculating the small-pox, to the town's people. This caused a great insurrection, the insurgents burnt the hospital; not content with that, threatened the proprietors and many others, some of the first fortunes and characters in the town, with burning their houses over their heads, and continued parading the streets, to the utmost terror of the inhabitants several days. A massacre and general devastation was apprehended. The persons threatened, armed themselves, and petitioned the general-assembly, which was then sitting, for assistance, as there was little or no civil authority in the place. A committee was ordered to repair to Marblehead, report the facts, and enquire into the cause: The committee reported the facts nearly as stated in the petition; the report was accepted, and nothing farther done by the assembly. Such demonstrations of the weakness of government, induced many persons to join the whigs, to seek from them that protection which the constitutional authority of the province was unable to afford.

Government at home, early in the day made an effort to check us in our career, and to enable us to recover from anarchy without her being driven to the necessity of altering our provincial constitution, knowing the predilection that people always have for an ancient form of government. The judges of the superior court had not been staggered, though their feet stood in slippery places, they depended upon the leading whigs for their support. To keep them steady, they were made independant of the grants of the general-assembly: But it was not a remedy any way adequate to the disease: The whigs now turned their artillery against them, and it played briskly. The chief justice, for accepting the crown grant, was accused of receiving a royal bribe.

Thus, my friends, those very persons that had made you believe that every attempt to strengthen government and save our charter, was an infringement of your privileges, little by little, destroyed your liberty, subverted your charter constitution, abridged the freedom of the house, annihilated the freedom of the board, and rendered the governor a mere doge of Venice. . . . The absolute necessity of the interposition of parliament is apparent. The good policy of the act for regulating the government in this province, will be the subject of some future paper.

December 26, 1774   Massachusettensis

LETTER IV

... An apprehension of injustice in the conduct of Great-Britain towards us, I have already told you was one source of our misery. Last week I endeavoured to convince you of the necessity of her regulating, or rather establishing some government amongst us. I am now to point out the principles and motives upon which the blockade act was made. The violent attack upon the property of the East-India company, in the destruction of their tea was the cause of it. In order to form a right judgment of that transaction, it is necessary to go back and view the cause of its being sent here. As the government of England is mixt, so the spirit or genius of the nation is at once monarchial, aristocratical, democratical, martial and commercial. It is difficult to determine which is the most predominant principle, but it is worthy of remark, that, to injure the British nation upon either of these points, is like injuring a Frenchman in the point of honor. Commerce is the great source of national wealth, for this reason it is cherished by all orders of men from the palace to the cottage. In some countries, a merchant is held in contempt by the nobles, in England they respect him. He rises to high honors in the state, often contracts alliances with the first families in the kingdom, and noble blood flows in the veins of his posterity. Trade is founded upon persons or countries mutually supplying each other with their redundances. Thus none are impoverished, all enriched, the asperities of human life worne away, and mankind made happier by it. Husbandry, manufacture and merchandize are its triple support, deprived of either of these, it would cease.

Agriculture is the natural livelihood of a country but thinly inhabited, as arts and manufactures are of a populous one. The high price of labour prevents manufactures being carried on to advantage in the first, scarcity of soil obliges the inhabitants to pursue them in the latter. Upon these, and considerations arising from the fertility and produce of different climates, and such like principles, the grand system of the British trade is founded. The collected wisdom of the nation has always been attentive to this great point of policy, that the national trade might be so ballanced and poised, as that each part of her extended dominions, might be benefited, and the whole concentre to the good of the empire. This evinces the necessity of acts for regulating trade.

To prevent one part of the empire being enriched at the expence and to the impoverishing of another, checks, restrictions and sometimes absolute prohibitions are necessary. These are imposed or taken off as circumstances vary. To carry the acts of trade into execution many officers are necessary. Thus, we see a number of custom-house officers so constituted as to be checks and controuls upon each other, and prevent their swerving from their duty, should they be tempted, and a board of commissioners appointed to superintend the whole, like the commissioners of the customs in England. Hence also arises the necessity of courts of admiralty.

The laws and regulations of trade are esteemed in England as sacred. An estate made by smuggling or pursuing an illicit trade is there looked upon as filthy lucre, as monies amassed by gaming, and upon the same principle, because it is obtained at the expence and often ruin of others. The smuggler not only injures the public, but often ruins the fair trader.

The great extent of sea-coast, many harbours, the variety of islands, the numerous creeks and navigable rivers, afford the greatest opportunity to drive an illicit trade in these colonies without detection. This advantage has not been overlooked by the avaricious, and many persons seem to have set the laws of trade at defiance: This accounts for so many new regulations being made, new officers appointed, and ships of war from time to time stationed along the continent. The way to Holland and back again is well known, and by much the greatest part of the tea that has been drank in America for several years, has been imported from then[ce] and other places, in direct violation of law. By this the smugglers have amassed great estates, to the prejudice of the fair trader. It was sensibly felt by the East-India company; they were prohibited from exporting their teas to America, and were obliged to sell it at auction in London; the London merchant purchased it, and put a profit upon it when he shipt it for America; the American merchant, in his turn, put a profit upon it, and after him the shopkeeper; so that it came to the consumer's hands, at a very advanced price. Such quantities of tea were annually smuggled that it was scarcely worth while for the American merchant to import tea from England at all. Some of the principal trading towns in America were wholly supplied with this commodity by smuggling; Boston however continued to import it, until advice was received that the parliament had it in contemplation to permit the East-India company to send their teas directly to America: The Boston merchants then sent their orders conditionally to their correspondents in England, to have tea shipt for them in case the East-India company's tea did not come out; one merchant, a great whig, had such an order lying in England for sixty chests, on his own account, when the company's tea was sent. An act of parliament was made to enable the East-India company to send their tea directly to America, and sell it at auction there, not with a view of raising a revenue from the three-penny duty, but to put it out of the power of the smugglers to injure them by their infamous trade. We have it from good authority, that the revenue was not the consideration before parliament, and it is reasonable to suppose it, for had that been the point in view, it was only to restore the former regulation, which was then allowed to be constitutional, and the revenue would have been respectable. Had this new regulation taken effect, the people in

America would have been great gainers. The wholesale merchant might have been deprived of some of his gains; but the retailer would have supplied himself with this article, directly from the auction, and the consumer reap the benefit, as tea would have been sold under the price that had been usual, by near one half. Thus the country in general would have been great gainers, the East-India company secured in supplying the American market with this article, which they are entitled to by the laws of trade, and smuggling suppressed, at least as to tea. A smuggler and a whig are cousin Germans, the offspring of two sisters, avarice and ambition. They had been playing into each others hands a long time. The smuggler received protection from the whig, and he in his turn received support from the smuggler. The illicit trader now demanded protection from his kinsman, and it would have been unnatural in him to have refused it, and beside, an opportunity presented of strengthening his own interest. The consignees were connected with the tories, and that was a further stimulus. Accordingly the press was again set to work, and the story repeated with additions about monopolies, and many infatuated persons once more wrought up to a proper pitch to carry into execution any violent measures that their leaders should propose. A bold stroke was resolved upon. The whigs, though they had got the art of managing the people, had too much sense to be ignorant that it was all a meer finesse, not only without, but directly repugnant to law, constitution and government, and could not last always. They determined to put all at hazard, and to be *aut Ca[e]sar aut nullus.* The approaching storm was foreseen, and the first ship that arrived with the tea detained below Castle-William. A body meeting was assembled at the old-south meeting-house, which has great advantage over a town-meeting, as no law has as yet ascertained the qualification of the voters; each person present, of whatever age, estate or country, may take the liberty to speak or vote at such an assembly; and that might serve as a skreen to the town where it originated, in case of any disastrous consequence. The body meeting consisting of several thousands, being thus assembled, with the leading whigs at its head, it [in] the first place sent for the owner of the tea ship, and required him to bring her to the wharf, upon pain of their displeasure; the ship was accordingly brought up, and the master was obliged to enter at the custom-house: He reported the tea, after which twenty days are allowed for landing it and paying the duty.

The next step was to resolve. They resolved that the tea should not be landed nor the duty paid, that it should go home in the same bottom that it came in, &c. &c. This was the same as resolving to destroy it, for as the ship had been compelled to come to the wharf, and was entered at the custom-house, it could not, by law, be cleared out, without the duties being first paid, nor could the Governor grant a permit for the vessel to pass Castle-William, without a certificate from the custom-house of such clearance, consistent with his duty. The body accordingly, ordered a military guard to watch the ship every night until further orders. The consignees had been applied to, by the selectmen, to send the tea to England, they answered that they could not for if they did, it would be forfeited by the acts of trade, and they should be liable to make good the loss to the East-India company. Some of the consignees were mobbed, and all were obliged to fly to the castle, and there immure themselves. They petitioned the Governor and Council to take the property of the East-India company under their protection. The council declined being concerned in it. The consignees then offered the body to store the tea under the care of the selectmen or a committee of the town of Boston, and to have no further concern in the matter until they could send to England, and receive further instructions from their principals. This was refused with disdain. The military guard was regularly kept in rotation till the eve of the twentieth day, when the duties must have been paid, the tea landed, or be liable to seizure; then the military guard was withdrawn, or rather omitted being posted, and a number of persons in disguise, forceably entered the ships (three being by this time arrived) split open the chests, and emptied all the tea, being of ten thousand pounds sterling value, into the dock, and perfumed the town with its fragrance. Another circumstance ought not to be omitted, the afternoon before the destruction of the tea, the body sent the owner of one of the ships to the Governor, to demand a pass, he answered, that he would as soon give a pass for that as any other vessel, if he had the proper certificate from the custom-house, without which he could not give a pass for any, consistent with his duty. It was known that this would be the answer when the message was sent, and it was with the utmost difficulty that the body were kept together till the messenger returned. When the report was made, a shout was set up in the galleries and at the door, and the meeting immediately dispersed. The Governor had previous to this, sent a proclamation by the sheriff, commanding the body to disperse, they permitted it to be read and answered it with a general hiss. These are the facts as truly and fairly stated, as I am able to state them. The ostensible reason for this conduct, was the teas being subject to the three-penny duty. Let us take the advocates for this transaction upon their own principle, and admit the duty to be unconstitutional, and see how the argument stands. Here is a cargo of tea subject upon its being entered and landed, to a duty of three-pence per pound, which is paid by the East-India company or by their factors, which amounts to the same thing. Unless we purchase the tea, we shall never pay the duty, if we purchase it, we pay the three-pence included in the price; therefore, lest we should purchase it, we have a right to destroy it. A flimsy pretext . . . and either supposes the people destitute of virtue, or that their purchasing the tea was a matter of no importance to the community; but even this gauze covering is stript off, when we consider that the Boston merchants, and some who were active at the body meeting, were every day importing from England, large quantities often subject to the same duty and vending it un-molested; and at this time had orders lying in their correspondent's hands, to send them considerable quantities of tea, in case the East-India company should not send it themselves.

When the news of this transaction arrived in England, and it was considered in what manner almost every other regulation of trade had been evaded by artifice, and when artifice could no longer serve, recourse was had to violence, the British lion was roused. The crown lawyers were called upon for the law, they answered high treason. Had a Cromwell, whom some amongst us deify and imitate in all his imitable perfections, had the guidance of the national ire, unless compensation had been made to the sufferers immediately upon its being demanded, your proud capital had been levelled with the dust, not content with that, rivers of blood would have been shed to make atonement for the injured honor of the nation. It was debated whether to attaint the principals of treason. We have a gracious King upon the throne, he felt the resentment of a man, softened by the relentings of a parent. The bowels of our mother country yearned towards her refractory, obstinate child.

It was determined to consider the offence in a milder light, and to compel an indemnification for the sufferers and prevent the like for the future, by such means as would be mild, compared with the insult to the nation, or severe as our future conduct should be; that was to depend upon us. Accordingly the blockade act was passed, and had an act of justice been done in indemnifying the sufferers, and an act of loyalty in putting a stop to seditious practices, our port had long since been opened. This act has been called unjust, because it involves the innocent in the same predicament with the guilty, but it ought to be considered, that our newspapers had announced to the world, that several thousands attended those body meetings, and it did not appear that there was one dissentient, or any protest entered. I do not know how a person could expect distinction, in such a case, if he neglected to distinguish himself. When the noble Lord proposed it in the house of commons, he called upon all the members present, to mention a better method of obtaining justice in this case, scarce one denied the necessity of doing something, but none could mention a more eligible way. Even ministerial opposition was abashed. If any parts of the act strike us, like the severity of a master, let us cooly advert to the aggravated insult, and perhaps we shall wonder at the lenity of a parent. After this transaction all parties seem to have laid upon their oars, waiting to see what parliament would do. When the blockade act arrived, many were desirous of paying for the tea immediately, and some who were guiltless of the crime, offered to contribute to the compensation; but our leading whigs must still rule the roast and that inauspicious influence that brought us hitherto, plunged us still deeper in misery. The whigs saw their ruin connected with a compliance with the terms of opening the port, as it would furnish a convincing proof of the wretchedness of their policy in the destruction of the tea, and they might justly have been expected to pay the money demanded themselves, and set themselves industriously to work to prevent it, and engage the other colonies to espouse their cause.

This was a crisis too important and alarming to the province to be neglected by its friends. A number of as respectable persons as any in this province, belonging to Boston, Cambridge, Salem and Marblehead, now came forward, publicly to disavow the proceedings of the whigs, to do justice to the much injured character of Mr. Hutchinson, and to strengthen his influence at the court of Great-Britain, where he was going to receive the well deserved plaudit of his Sovereign, that he might be able to obtain a repeal or some mitigation of that act, the terms of which they foresaw, the perverseness of the whigs would prevent a compliance with. This was done by several addresses, which were subscribed by upwards of two hundred persons, and would have been by many more, had not the sudden embarkation of Mr. Hutchinson prevented it. The justices of the

courts of common pleas and general sessions of the peace for
the county of Plymouth, sent their address to him in England.
There were some of almost all orders of men among these
addressers, but they consisted principally of men of property,
large family connections, and several were independant in
their circumstances, and lived wholly upon the income of their
estates. . . .

Their motives were truly patriotic. Let us now attend to the
. . . means by which the whigs prevented these exertions producing such effects. Previous to this, a new and till lately, un-
heard of, mode of opposition had been devised, said to be the
invention of the fertile brain of one of our party agents, called
a committee of correspondence. This is the foulest, subtlest and
most venomous serpent that ever issued from the eggs of sedition. These committees generally consist of the highest whigs,
or at least there is some high whigs upon them, that is the ruling
spirit of the whole. They are commonly appointed at thin town-
meetings, or if the meetings happen to be full, the moderate
men seldom speak or act at all when this sort of business comes
on: They have been by much too modest. Thus the meeting is
often prefaced with "At a full town-meeting," and the several
resolves headed with nem. con. with strict truth, when in fact,
but a small proportion of the town have had a hand in the
matter. It is said that the committee for the town of Boston was
appointed for a special purpose, and that their commission long
since expired. However that may be, these committees when
once established think themselves amenable to none, they assume a dictatorial stile and have an opportunity under the apparent sanction of their several towns, of clandestinely wreak-
ing private revenge on individuals, by traducing their
characters, and holding them up as enemies to their country
wherever they go, as also of misrepresenting facts and propagating sedition through the country. . . . they frequently erect
themselves into a tribunal, where the same persons are at once
legislator, accusers, witnesses, judges and jurors, and the mob

the executioners. The accused has no day in court, and the execution of the sentence is the first notice he receives. This is the channel through which liberty matters have been chiefly conducted the summer and fall past. . . . Let us waive the consideration of right and liberty, and see if this conduct can be reconciled to good policy. Do you expect to make converts by it? Persecution has the same effect in politics that it had in religion, it confirms the sectary. Do you wish to silence them that the inhabitants of the province may appear unanimous? The mal-treatment they receive for differing from you is undeniable evidence that we are not unanimous. It may not be amiss to consider, that this is a changeable world, and the time's rolling wheel may ere long bring them uppermost; in that case I am sure you would not wish to have them fraught with resentment. . . . But, to return from my digression, the committee of correspondence represented the destruction of the tea in their own way: They represented those that addressed Governor Hutchinson, as persons of no note or property, as mean, base wretches, and seekers that had been sacrificing their country in adulation of him. . . . By this means the humane and benevolent in various parts of the continent, were induced to advise us not to comply with the terms for opening our port, and engage to relieve us with their charities, from the distress that must otherwise fall upon the poor. . . . I do not address myself to whigs or tories, but to the whole people. I know you well. You are loyal at heart, friends to good order, and do violence to yourselves in harbouring one moment, disrespectful sentiments towards Great-Britain, the land of our forefathers nativity, and sacred repository of their bones; but you have been most insidiously induced to believe that Great-Britain is rapacious, cruel and vindictive, and envies us the inheritance purchased by the sweat and blood of our ancestors.

January 2, 1775   Massachusettensis

LETTER V

. . . Sedition has already been marked through its zigzag path to the present times. When the statute for regulating the government arrived, a match was put to the train, and the mine that had been long forming, sprung, and threw the whole province into confusion and anarchy. The occurrences of the summer and autumn past are so recent and notorious, that a particular detail of them is unnecessary. Suffice it to say, that every barrier that civil government had erected for the security of property, liberty and life was broken down, and law, constitution and government trampled under foot by the rudest invaders. . . .

Perhaps the whole story of empire does not furnish another instance of a forcible opposition to government with so much apparent and little real cause, with such apparent probability without any possibility of success. The stamp-act gave the alarm. The instability of the public councils from the Greenvillian administration to the appointment of the Earl of Hillsborough to the American department, afforded as great a prospect of success, as the heavy duties imposed by the stamp-act, did a colour for the opposition. . . . I suspect many of our politicians are wrong in their first principle, in denying that the constitutional authority of parliament extends to the colonies, if so, it must not be wondered at, that their whole fabric is so ruinous. . . .

The security of the people from internal rapacity and violence, and from foreign invasion is the end and design of government. The simple forms of government are monarchy, aristocracy and democracy, that is, where the authority of the state is vested in one, a few, or the many. Each of these species of government has advantages peculiar to itself, and would answer the ends of government, were the persons intrusted with the authority of the state always guided themselves by unerring wisdom and public virtue; but rulers are not always exempt from the weakness and depravity which make government necessary to society. Thus monarchy is apt to rush headlong into tyranny, aristocracy to beget faction and multiplied usurpation, and democracy, to degenerate into tumult, violence and anarchy. A government formed upon these three principles in due proportion, is the best calculated to answer the ends of government, and to endure. Such a government is the British constitution, consisting of King, Lords and Commons, which at once includes the principal excellencies, and excludes the principal defects of the other kinds of government. It is allowed, both by Englishmen and foreigners, to be the most perfect system that the wisdom of ages has produced. The distributions of power are so just, and the proportions so exact, as at once to support and controul each other. An Englishman glories in being subject to and protected by such a government. The colonies are a part of the British empire. The best writers upon the law of nations, tell us, that when a nation takes possession of a distant country, and settles there, that country though seperated from the principal establishment or mother-country, naturally becomes a part of the state, equal with its ancient possessions. Two supreme or independant authorities cannot exist in the same state. It would be what is called *imperium in imperio*, the heighth of political absurdity. The analogy between the political and human body is great. Two independant authorities in a state would be like two distinct principles of volition and action in the human body, dissenting, opposing and destroying each other. If then we are a part of the British empire, we must be subject to the supreme power of the state, which is vested in the estates of parliament, notwithstanding each of the colonies have legislative and executive powers of their own, delegated or granted to them for the purposes of regulating their own internal policy, which are subordinate to, and must necessarily be subject to the checks, controul and regulation of the supreme authority.

This doctrine is not new, but the denial of it is. It is beyond a doubt that it was the sense both of the parent country and our ancestors that they were to remain subject to parliament; it is evident from the charter itself, and this authority has been exercised by parliament, from time to time, almost ever since the first settlement of the country, and has been expressly acknowledged by our provincial legislatures. It is not less our interest than our duty to continue subject to the authority of parliament, which will be more fully considered hereafter. The principal argument against the authority of parliament, is this, the Americans are intitled to all the privileges of an Englishman, it is the privilege of an Englishman to be exempt from all laws that he does not consent to in person, or by representative; the Americans are not represented in parliament, and therefore are exempt from acts of parliament, or in other words, not subject to its authority. This appears specious; but leads to such absurdities as demonstrate its fallacy. If the colonies are not subject to the authority of parliament, Great-Britain and the colonies must be distinct states, as compleatly so as England and Scotland were before the union, or as Great-Britain and Hanover are now: The colonies in that case will owe no allegiance to the imperial crown, and perhaps not to the person of the King, as the title to the crown, is derived from an act of parliament, made since the settlement of this province, which act respects the imperial crown only. Let us waive this difficulty, and suppose allegiance due from the colonies to the person of the King of Great-Britain; he then appears in a new capacity, of King of America, or rather in several new capacities, of King of Massachusetts, King of Rhode-Island, King of Connecticut, &c. &c.

For if our connexion with Great-Britain by the parliament be dissolved, we shall have none among ourselves, but each colony become as distinct from the others as England was from Scotland before the union. Some have supposed that each state having one and the same person for its King is a sufficient connexion; were he an absolute Monarch it might be, but in a mixed government, it is no union at all: For as the King must govern each state by its parliament, those several parliaments would pursue the particular interest of its own state, and however well disposed the King might be to pursue a line of interest that was common to all, the checks and controul that he would meet with, would render it impossible. If the King of Great-Britain has really these new capacities, they ought to be added to his titles; and another difficulty will arise, the prerogatives of these new crowns have never been defined or limited. Is the monarchical part of the several provincial constitutions to be nearer or more remote from absolute monarchy, in an inverted ratio to each one's approaching to, or receding from a republic? But let us suppose the same prerogatives inherent in the several American crowns, as are in the imperial crown of Great-Britain, where shall we find the British constitution that we all agree we are entitled to. We shall seek for it in vain in our provincial assemblies. They are but faint sketches of the estates of parliament. The houses of representatives or Burgesses have not all the powers of the house of commons, in the charter governments they have not more than what is expressly granted by their several charters. The first charters granted to this province did not impower the assembly to tax the people at all. Our council-boards are as destitute of the constitutional authority of the house of lords, as their several members are of the noble independance and splendid appendages of peerage. The house of peers is the bulwark of the British constitution, and through successive ages, has withstood the shocks of monarchy, and the sappings of democracy, and the constitution gained strength by the conflict. Thus the supposition of our being independant states, or exempt from the authority of parliament, destroys the very idea of our having a British constitution. The provincial constitutions, considered as subordinate, are generally well adapted to those purposes of government, for which they were intended, that is, to regulate the internal police of the several colonies; but have no principle of stability within themselves, they may support themselves in moderate times, but would be merged by the violence of turbulent ones, and the several colonies become wholly monarchial or wholly republican, were it not for the checks, controuls, regulations and supports of the supreme authority of the empire. Thus the argument that is drawn from their first principle of our being intitled to English liberties, destroys the principle itself, it deprives us of the bill of rights, and all the benefits resulting from the revolution, of English laws and of the British constitution.

Our patriots have been so intent upon building up American rights, that they have overlooked the rights of Great-Britain, and our own interest. Instead of proving that we were entitled to privileges that our fathers knew our situation would not admit us to enjoy, they have been arguing away our most essential rights. If there be any grievance it does not consist in our being subject to the authority of parliament, but in our not having an actual representation in it. Were it possible for the colonies to have an equal representation to parliament, and it were refused upon proper application, I confess I should think it a grievance; but at present it seems to be allowed, by all parties, to be impracticable, considering the colonies are distant from Great-Britain a thousand transmarine leagues. If that be the case, the right or privilege that we complain of being deprived of, is not withheld by Britain, but the first principles of government and the immutable laws of nature, render it impossible for us to enjoy it. This is apparently the meaning of that celebrated passage in Governor Hutchinson's letter, that rang through the continent, viz. There must be an abridgment of what is called English liberties. He subjoins, that he had never yet seen the projection, whereby a colony three thousand miles distant from the parent state, might enjoy all the privileges of the parent state and remain subject to it, or in words to that effect. The obnoxious sentence, taken detached from the letter, appears very unfriendly to the colonies; but considered in connection with the other parts of the letter, is but a necessary result from our situation. Allegiance and protection are reciprocal. It is our highest interest to continue a part of the British empire, and equally our duty to remain subject to the authority of parliament. Our own internal police may generally be regulated by our provincial legislatures, but in national concerns, or where our own assemblies do not answer the ends of government with respect to ourselves, the ordinances or interposition of the great council of the nation is necessary. In this case the major must rule the minor. After many more centuries shall have rolled away, long after we who are now bustling upon the stage of life, shall have been received to the bosom of mother earth, and our names are forgotten, the colonies may be so far increased as to have the balance of wealth, numbers and power in their favour, the good of the empire make it necessary to fix the seat of government here; and some future GEORGE, equally the friend of mankind with him that now sways the British sceptre, may cross the Atlantic, and rule Great-Britain by an American parliament.

January 9, 1775   Massachusettensis

LETTER VI

Had a person, some fifteen years ago, undertaken to prove that the colonies were a part of the British empire or dominion, and as such subject to the authority of the British parliament, he would have acted as ridiculous a part, as to have undertaken to prove a self-evident proposition: Had any person denied it, he would have been called a fool or madman. At this wise period, individuals and bodies of men deny it, notwithstanding in doing it they subvert the fundamentals of government, deprive us of British liberties, and build up absolute monarchy in the colonies; for our charters suppose regal authority in the grantor; if the authority be derived from the British crown, it presupposes this territory to have been a part of the British dominion, and as such subject to the imperial Sovereign; if that authority was vested in the person of the King, in a different capacity, the British constitution and laws are out of the question, and the King must be absolute as to us, as his prerogatives have never been circumscribed. Such must have been the sovereign authority of the several Kings who have granted American charters previous to the several grants; there is nothing to detract from it at this time in those colonies that are destitute of charters, and the charter governments must severally revert to absolute monarchy as their charters may happen to be forfeited by the grantees not fulfilling the conditions of them, as every charter contains an express or implied condition.

It is curious indeed to trace the denial and oppugnation to the supreme authority of the state. When the stamp-act was made, the authority of parliament to impose internal taxes was denied, but their right to impose external ones; or in other words, to lay duties upon goods and merchandise was admitted. When the act was made imposing duties upon tea, &c. a new distinction was set up, that the parliament had a right to lay duties upon merchandise for the purpose of raising a revenue: That is, the parliament had good right and lawful authority to lay the former duty of a shilling on the pound, but had none to lay the present duty of three pence. Having got thus far safe, it was only taking one step more to extricate ourselves entirely from their fangs, and become independant states; that our patriots most heroically resolved upon, and flatly denied that parliament had a right to make any laws whatever, that should be binding upon the colonies. There is no possible medium between absolute independance and subjection to the authority of parliament. He must be blind indeed that cannot see our dearest interest in the latter, notwithstanding many pant after the former; misguided men! could they once overtake their wish, they would be convinced of the madness of the pursuit.

My dear countrymen, it is of the last importance that we settle this point clearly in our minds; it will serve as a sure test, certain criterion and invariable standard to distinguish the friends from the enemies of our country, patriotism from sedition, loyalty from rebellion. To deny the supreme authority of the state is a high misdemeanor, to say no worse of it; to oppose it by force is an overt act of treason, punishable by confiscation of estate and most ignominious death. The realm of England is an appropriate term for the ancient realm of England, in contradistinction to Wales and other territories that have been annexed to it. These as they have been severally annexed to the crown, whether by conquest or otherwise, became a part of the empire, and subject to the authority of parliament, whether they send members to parliament or not, and whether they have legislative powers of their own or not.

Thus Ireland, who has perhaps the greatest possible subordinate legislature, and sends no members to the British parliament, is bound by its acts, when expressly named. Guernsey and Jersey are no part of the realm of England, nor are they represented in parliament, but are subject to its authority: And, in the same predicament are the American colonies, and all the other dispersions of the empire. Permit me to request your attention to this subject a little longer; I assure you it is as interesting and important as it is dry and unentertaining.

Let us now recur to the first charter of this province, and we shall find irresistable evidence, that our being part of the empire, subject to the supreme authority of the state, bound by its laws and entitled to its protection, were the very terms and conditions by which our ancestors held their lands and settled the province. Our charter, like all other American charters, are under the great seal of England; the grants are made by the King, for his heirs and *successors*, the several tenures to be of the King, his heirs and *successors*, in like manner are the reservations. It is apparent the King acted in his royal capacity, as King of England, which necessarily supposes the territory granted, to be a part of the English dominions, holden of the crown of England.

The charter, after reciting several grants of the territory to Sir Henry Roswell and others, proceeds to incorporation in these words: "... *the company and society hereafter mentioned,* shall from time to time and at all times, forever hereafter, be by virtue of these presents, *one body corporate, politic in fact and name by the name of the Governor and company of the Massachusetts-Bay, in New-England;* and them by the name of the Governor and company of the Massachusetts-Bay, is New England, one body politic and corporate in deed, fact and name. .... *to implead and to be impleaded, and to prosecute, demand and answer and be answered unto all and singular suits, causes, quarrels and actions of what kind or nature soever; and also to have, take, possess, acquire and purchase, any lands, tenements and hereditaments, or any goods or chattles, the same to lease, grant, demise, aliene, bargain, sell and dispose of as our liege people of this our realm of England, or any other corporation or body politic of the same may do."* I would beg leave to ask one simple question, whether this looks like a distinct state or independent empire? Provision is then made for electing a governor, deputy governor and eighteen assistants. . . . "assistants or freemen of the said company as shall be present, or the greater number of them so assembled, whereof the governor or the deputy-governor and six of the assistants, at the least to be seven, shall have full power and authority . . . to make *laws and ordinances for the good and welfare of the said company,* and for the government and ordering of the said lands and plantations and the people inhabiting and to inhabit the same, as to them from time to time shall be thought meet: *So as such laws and ordinances be not contrary or repugnant to the laws and statutes of this our realm of England."*

Another clause is this, "And for their further encouragement, of our especial grace and favour, we do by these presents, for us, our heirs, and successors, yield and grant to the said governor and company and their successors, and every of them, their factors and assigns, that they and every of them shall be free and quit from all taxes, subsidies and customs in New-England for the space of seven years, and from all taxes and impositions for the space of twenty-one years, upon all goods and merchandise, at any time or times hereafter. . . ."

The exemption from taxes for seven years in one case, and twenty-one years in the other, plainly indicates that after their expiration, this province would be liable to taxation. Now I would ask by what authority those taxes were to be imposed. It could not be by the governor and company, for no such power was delegated or granted to them; and besides it would have been absurd and nugatory to exempt them from their own taxation, supposing them to have had the power, for they might have exempted themselves. It must therefore be by the King or parliament; it could not be by the King alone, for as King of

England, the political capacity in which he granted the charter, he had no such power, exclusive of the lords and commons, consequently it must have been by the parliament. This clause in the charter is as evident a recognition of the authority of the parliament over this province, as if the words, "acts of parliament," had been inserted, as they were in the Pennsylvania charter. There was no session of parliament after the grant of our charter until the year 1640. In 1642 the house of commons passed a resolve, "that for the better advancement of the plantations in New-England, and the encouragement of the planters to proceed in their undertaking, their exports and imports should be freed and discharged from all customs, subsidies, taxations and duties until the further order of the house." Which was gratefully received and recorded in the archives of our predecessors. This transaction shews very clearly in what sense our connection with England was then understood. It is true that in some arbitrary reigns, attempts were made by the servants of the crown to exclude the two houses of parliament, from any share of the authority over the colonies, they also attempted to render the King absolute in England, but the parliament always rescued the colonies, as well as England from such attempts.

I shall recite but one more clause of this charter, which is this, "And further our will and pleasure is, and we do hereby for us, our heirs and successors, ordain, declare and grant to the said governor and company, and their successors, that all and every of the subjects of us, our heirs and successors which shall go to inhabit within the said land and premises . . . shall have and enjoy *all liberties and immunities of free and natural subjects, within any of the dominions of us,* our heirs or successors, to all intents, constructions and purposes whatsoever, as if they and every of them were born within the realm of England." It is upon this, or a similar clause in the charter of William and Mary that our patriots have built up the stupendous fabric of American independance. They argue from it a total exemption from parliamentary authority, because we are not represented in parliament.

I have already shewn that the supposition of our being exempt from the authority of parliament, is pregnant with the grossest absurdities. Let us now consider this clause in connection with the other parts of the charter. It is a rule of law, founded in reason and common sense, to construe each part of an instrument, so as the whole may hang together, and be consistent with itself. If we suppose this clause to exempt us from the authority of parliament, we must throw away all the rest of the charter, for every other part indicates the contrary, as plainly as words can do it; and what is still worse, this clause becomes *felo de se*, and destroys itself, for if we are not annexed to the crown we are aliens, and no charter, grant or other act of the crown can naturalize us or entitle us to the liberties and immunities of Englishmen. It can be done only by act of parliament. An alien is one born in a strange country out of the allegiance of the King, and is under many disabilities though residing in the realm; as Wales, Jersey, Guernsey, Ireland, the foreign plantations, &c. were severally annexed to the crown, they became parts of one and the same empire, the natives of which are equally free as though they had been born in that territory which was the ancient realm. As our patriots depend upon this clause, detached from the charter, let us view it in that light. If a person born in England removes to Ireland and settles there, he is then no longer represented in the British parliament, but he and his posterity are and will ever be subject to the authority of the British parliament: If he removes to Jersey, Guernsey, or any other parts of the British dominions that send no members to parliament, he will still be in the same predicament. So that the inhabitants of the American colonies do in fact enjoy all the liberties and immunities of natural-born subjects. We are entitled to no greater privileges than those that are born within the realm, and they can enjoy no other than we do, when they reside out of it. Thus, it is evident that the clause amounts to no more than the royal assurance, that we are a part of the British empire are not aliens but natural-born subjects; and as such bound to obey the supreme power of the state, and entitled to protection from it. To avoid prolixity I shall not remark particularly upon other parts of this charter, but observe in general, that whoever reads it with attention will meet with irresistable evidence in every part of it, that our being a part of the English dominions, subject to the English crown, and within the jurisdiction of parliament, were the terms upon which our ancestors settled this colony, and the very tenures by which they held their estates.

No lands within the British dominions are perfectly allodial; they are held mediately or immediately of the King, and upon forfeiture, revert to the crown. My dear countrymen, you have many of you, been most falsely and wickedly told, by our patriots, that Great-Britain was meditating a land tax, and seeking to deprive us of our inheritance; but had all the malice and subtilty of men and devils been united, a readier method to effect it could not have been devised, than the late denials of the authority of parliament, and forcible oppositions to its acts: Yet, this has been planned and executed chiefly by persons of desperate fortunes.

January 16, 1775   Massachusettensis

LETTER VII

If we carry our researches further back than the emigration of
our ancestors, we shall find many things that reflect light upon
the object we are in quest of. It is immaterial when America was
first discovered or taken possession of by the English. In 1602
one Gosnold landed upon one of the islands, called Elizabeth-
islands, which were so named in honor of Queen Elizabeth,
built a fort and projected a settlement, his men were discouraged, and the project failed. In 1606 King James granted
all the continent from 34 to 45 degrees, which he divided into
two colonies, viz. the southern or Virginia, to certain merchants
at London, the northern or New-England to certain merchants
at Plymouth in England. In 1607 some of the patentees of the
northern colony began a settlement at Sogadahoc, but the emigrants were disheartened after the trial of one winter, and that
attempt failed of success. Thus this territory had not only been
granted by the crown for purposes of colonization, which are to
enlarge the empire or dominion of the parent state, and to open
new sources of national wealth, but actual possession had been
taken by the grantees, previous to the emigration of our ancestors, or any grant to them. In 1620 a patent was granted to the
adventurers for the northern colony, incorporating them by the
name of *the council for the affairs of New-Plymouth*. From this
company of merchants in England, our ancestors derived their
title to this territory. The tract of land called Massachusetts was
purchased of this company, by Sir Henry Roswell and associ-
ates, their deed bears date, March 19th, 1627. In 1628 they

obtained a charter of incorporation which I have already remarked upon. The liberties, privileges and franchises, granted by this charter, do not perhaps exceed those granted to the city of London and other corporations within the realm. The legislative power was very confined; it did not even extend to levying taxes of any kind, that power was however assumed under this charter, which by law worked a forfeiture, and for this among other things, in the reign of Charles the Second, the charter was adjudged forfeited and the franchises seized into the King's hands. This judgment did not affect our ancestors title to their lands that were not derived originally from the charter, though confirmed by it, but by purchase from the council at Plymouth, who held immediately under the crown. Besides our ancestors had now reduced what before was a naked right to possession and by persevering through unequalled toils, hardships and dangers, at the approach of which other emigrants had fainted, rendered New-England a very valuable acquisition both to the crown and nation. This was highly meritorious, and ought not to be overlooked in adjusting the present unhappy dispute, but our patriots would deprive us of all the merit, both to the crown and nation, by severing us from both. After the revolution, our ancestors petitioned the parliament to restore the charter. A bill for that purpose passed the house of commons, but went no further. In consequence of another petition, King William and Queen Mary granted our present charter, for uniting and incorporating the Massachusetts, New-Plymouth, and several other territories into one province. More extensive powers of legislation than those contained in the first charter were become necessary, and were granted. And the form of the legislature made to approach nearer to the form of the supreme legislature. The powers of legislation are confined to local or provincial purposes and further restricted by these words, viz. *So as the same be not repugnant or contrary to the laws of this our realm of England.* Our patriots have made many nice distinctions and curious refinements, to evade the force of these words, but after all, it is impossible to reconcile them to the idea of an independant state as it is to reconcile disability to omnipotence. The provincial power of taxation is also restricted to provincial purposes, and allowed to be exercised over such only as are inhabitants or proprietors within the province. I would observe here, that the granting subordinate powers of legislation, does not abridge or diminish the powers of the higher legislatures; thus we see corporations in England and the several towns in this province vested with greater or lesser powers of legislation, without the parliament, in one case, or the general court in the other, being restrained, from enacting those very laws, that fall within the jurisdiction of the several corporations. Had our present charter been conceived in such equivocal terms as that it might be construed as restraining the authority of parliament, the uniform usage ever since it passed the seal, would satisfy us that its intent was different. The parliament in the reign when it was granted, long before and in every reign since, has been making statutes to extend to the colonies, and those statutes have been as uniformly submitted to as authoritative, by the colonies, till within ten or a dozen years. Sometimes acts of parliament have been made, and sometimes have been repealed in consequence of petitions from the colonies. The provincial assemblies often refer to acts of parliament in their own, and have sometimes made acts to aid their execution. It is evident that it was the intention of their Majesties, to grant subordinate powers of legislation, without impairing or diminishing the authority of the supreme legislature. Had there been any words in the charter, that precluded that construction, or did the whole taken together contradict it, lawyers would tell us, that the King was deceived in his grant, and the patentees took no estate by it, because the crown can neither alienate a part of the British dominions, nor impair the supreme power of the empire. . . .

We find many unsuspecting persons prevailed on openly to oppose the execution of acts of parliament with force and arms.

My friends! some of the persons that beguiled you, could have turned to the chapter, page and section, where such insurrections are pronounced rebellion, by the law of the land; and had not their hearts been dead to a sense of justice, and steeled against every feeling of humanity, they would have timely warned you of your danger. Our patriots have sent us in pursuit of a mere *ignis fatuus,* a fascinating glare devoid of substance . . . They tell us, we are a match for Great-Britain. The twentieth part of the strength that Great-Britain could exert, were it necessary, is more than sufficient to crush this defenceless province to atoms, notwithstanding all the vapouring of the disaffected here and elsewhere. They tell us the army is disaffected to the service: What pains have our wretched politicians not taken to attach them to it? The officers conceive no very favourable opinion of the cause of the whigs, from the obloquy with which their General hath been treated, in return for his humanity, nor from the infamous attempts to seduce the soldiers from his Majesty's service. The policy of some of our patriots has been as weak and contemptible as their motives are sordid and malevolent, for when they found their success, in corrupting the soldiery, did not answer their expectations, they took pains to attach them firmer to the cause they adhered to, by preventing the erecting of barracks for their winter quarters, by which means many contracted diseases, and some lives were lost, from the unwholesome buildings they were obliged to occupy; and, as though some stimulus was still wanting, some provocation to prevent human nature revolting in the hour of battle, they deprived the soldiers of a gratification never denied to the brute creation, straw to lie on. . . . Those are matters of small moment compared to another, which is the cause they are engaged in. It is no longer a struggle between whigs and tories, whether these or those shall occupy posts of honor, or enjoy the emoluments of office, nor is it now whether this or the other act of parliament shall be repealed. The army is sent here to decide a question, intimately connected with the honor and interest of the nation, no less than whether the colonies shall continue a part of, or be for ever dismembered from the British empire. It is a cause in which no honest American, can wish our politicians success, though it is devoutly to be wished, that their discomfiture may be effected without recourse being had to the *ultima ratio,* the sword. This our wretched situation is but the natural consequence of denying the authority of parliament and forcibly opposing its acts.

Sometimes we are amused with intimations that Holland, France or Spain will make a diversion in our favour. These, equally with the others, are suggestions of despair. These powers have colonies of their own, and might not choose to set a bad example, by encouraging the colonies of any other state to revolt. The Dutch have too much money in the English funds, and are too much attached to their money to espouse our quarrel. The French and Spaniards have not yet forgot the drubbing they received from Great-Britain [in the] last war; and all three fear to offend that power which our politicians would persuade us to despise.

Lastly, they tell us that the people in England will take our part, and prevent matters from coming to extremity. This is their fort, where when driven from every other post, they fly for refuge.

Alas! my friends, our congresses have stopped up every avenue that leads to that sanctuary. We hear, by every arrival from England, that it is no longer a ministerial (if it ever was) but a national cause. My dear countrymen, I deal plainly with you; I never should forgive myself if I did not. Are there not eleven regiments in Boston? A respectable fleet in the harbour? Men of war stationed at every considerable port along the continent? Are there not three ships of the line sent here, notwithstanding the danger of the winter coast, with more than the usual complement of marines? Have not our congresses, county, provincial and continental, instead of making advances for an accomodation, bid defiance to Great-Britain: *He that runs may read.*

. . . I have many things to add, but must now take my leave, for this week, by submitting to your judgment whether there be not an absolute necessity of immediately protesting against all traiterous resolves, leagues and associations, of bodies of men that appear to have acted in a representative capacity. Had our congresses been accidental or spontaneous meetings, the whole blame might have rested upon the individuals that composed them, but as they appear in the character of the peoples delegates, is there not the utmost danger of the innocent being confounded with the guilty, unless they take care timely to distinguish themselves?

January 23, 1775   Massachusettensis

LETTER VIII

As the oppugnation to the King in parliament tends manifestly to independance, and the colonies would soon arrive at that point, did not Great-Britain check them in their career; let us indulge the idea, however extravagant and romantic, and suppose ourselves for ever seperated from the parent state. Let us suppose Great-Britain sinking under the violence of the shock, and overwhelmed by her ancient hereditary enemies; or what is more probable, opening new sources of national wealth, to supply the deficiency of that which used to flow to her through American channels, and perhaps planting more loyal colonies in the new discovered regions of the south, still retaining her pre-eminence among nations, though regardless of America.

Let us now advert to our own situation: Destitute of British protection, that impervious barrier, behind which, in perfect security, we have increased to a degree almost exceeding the bounds of probability, what other Britain could we look to when in distress? What succedaneum does the world afford to make good the loss? Would not our trade, navigation and fishery, which no nation dares violate or invade, when distinguished by British colours, become the sport and prey of the maritime powers of Europe? Would not our maritime towns be exposed to the pillaging of every piratical enterprize? Are the colonies able to maintain a fleet, sufficient to afford one idea of security to such an extensive sea-coast? Before they can defend themselves against foreign invasions, they must unite into one empire, otherwise the jarring interests and opposite propensities,

would render the many headed monster in politics unwieldy
and inactive. Neither the form or seat of government would be
readily agreed upon; more difficult still would it be to fix upon
the person or persons, to be invested with the imperial authority. There is perhaps as great a diversity between the tempers
and habits of the inhabitants of this province, and the tempers
and habits of the Carolinians, as there subsist between some
different nations; nor need we travel so far, the Rhode-Islanders
are as diverse from the people of Connecticut, as those mentioned before. Most of the colonies are rivals to each other in
trade. Between others there subsist deep animosities, respecting their boundaries, which have heretofore produced violent
altercations, and the sword of civil war has been more than once
unsheathed, without bringing these disputes to a decision. It is
apparent that so many discordant heterogeneus particles could
not suddenly unite and consolidate into one body: It is most
probable, that if they were ever united, the union would be
effected by some aspiring genius, putting himself at the head of
the colonists' army (for we must suppose a very respectable one
indeed before we are severed from Britain) and taking advantage of the enfeebled, bleeding and distracted state of the colonies, subjugate the whole to the yoke of despotism. Human
nature is every where the same, and this has often been the
issue of those rebellions that the rightful Prince was unable to
subdue. We need not travel through the states of ancient
Greece and Rome, or the modern ones in Europe, to pick up
the instances, with which the way is strewed; we have a notable
one in our own. So odious and arbitrary was the protectorate of
Cromwell, that when death had delivered them from the dread
of the tyrant, all parties conspired to restore monarchy, and
each one strove to be the foremost in inviting home and placing
upon the imperial throne, their exiled Prince, the son of the
same Charles, who, not many years before, had been murdered
on a scaffold: The republicans themselves now rushed to the
opposite extreme, and had Charles the second been as ambi-

tious, as some of his predecessors were, he might have established in England a power more arbitrary than the first Charles ever had in contemplation.

Let us now suppose the colonies united and moulded into some form of government. Think one moment of the revenue necessary to support this government, and to provide for even the appearance of defence. Conceive yourselves in a manner exhausted by the conflict with Great-Britain, now staggering and sinking under the load of your own taxes, and the weight of your own government. Consider further, that to render government operative and salutary, subordination is necessary. This our patriots need not be told of, and when once they had mounted the steed, and found themselves so well seated as to run no risk of being thrown from the saddle, the severity of their discipline to restore subordination, would be in proportion to their former treachery in destroying it. We have already seen specimens of their tyranny, in their inhuman treatment of persons guilty of no crime, except that of differing in sentiment from the whigs. What then must we expect from such scourges of mankind, when supported by imperial power?

To elude the difficulty resulting from our defenceless situation, we are told that the colonies would open a free trade with all the world, and all nations would join in protecting their common mart. A very little reflection will convince us that this is chimerical. American trade however beneficial to Great-Britain, while she can command it, would be but as a drop of the bucket or the light dust of the balance, to all the commercial states of Europe: Besides, were British fleets and armies no longer destined to our protection, in a very short time France and Spain would recover possession of those territories, that were torn, reluctant and bleeding from them, in the last war, by the superior strength of Britain. Our enemies would again extend their line of fortification, from the northern to the southern shore, and by means of our late settlements stretching themselves to the confines of Canada, and the communication opened from one country to the other, we should be exposed to perpetual incursions from Canadians and savages; but our distress would not end here, for when once these incursions should be supported by the formidable armaments of France and Spain, the whole continent would become their easy prey, and would be parcelled out, Poland like. Recollect the consternation we were thrown into last war, when Fort-William Henry was taken by the French: It was apprehended that all New England would be over-run by their conquering arms: It was even proposed, for our own people to burn and lay waste all the country west of Connecticut river, to impede the enemies march and prevent their ravaging the country east of it. This proposal came from no inconsiderable man. Consider what must *really* have been our fate, unaided by Britain in the last war.

Great-Britain aside, what earthly power could stretch out the compassionate arm to shield us from those powers, that have long beheld us with the sharp, piercing eyes of avidity, and have heretofore bled freely and expended their millions to obtain us? Do you suppose their lust of empire is satiated? Or do you suppose they would scorn to obtain so glorious a prize by an easy conquest? Or can any be so visionary or impious as to believe that the Father of the universe will work miracles in favour of rebellion? And after having, by some unseen arm and mighty power destroyed Great-Britain for us, will in the same mysterious way defend us against other European powers? Sometimes we are told, that the colonies may put themselves under the protection of some one foreign state, but it ought to be considered that to do that, we must throw ourselves into their power. We can make them no return for protection but by trade, and of that they can have no assurance, unless we become subject to their laws; this is evident by our contention with Britain.

Which state would you prefer being annexed to, France, Spain or Holland? I suppose the latter, as it is a republic; but are

you sure that the other powers of Europe would be idle spectators, content to suffer the Dutch to ingross the American Colonies or their trade? And what figure would the Dutch probably
make in an unequal contest? Their sword has been long since
sheathed in commerce. Those of you that have visited Surinam
and seen a Dutch governor dispensing at discretion his own
opinions for law, would not suddenly exchange the English for
Dutch government.

January 30, 1775   Massachusettensis

LETTER IX

When we reflect upon the constitutional connection between Great-Britain and the colonies, view the reciprocation of interest, consider that the welfare of Britain in some measure, and the prosperity of America wholly depends upon that connection, it is astonishing, indeed almost incredible, that one person should be found on either side of the Atlantic, so base and destitute of every sentiment of justice, as to attempt to destroy or weaken it. If there are none such, in the name of Almighty God, let me ask, wherefore is rebellion, that implacable fiend to society, suffered to rear its ghastly front among us, blasting with haggard look, each social joy, and embittering every hour?

Rebellion is the most atrocious offence that can be perpetrated by man, save those which are committed more immediately against the supreme Governor of the universe, who is the avenger of his own cause. It dissolves the social band, annihilates the security resulting from law and government; introduces fraud, violence, rapine, murder, sacrilege, and the long train of evils that riot uncontrouled in a state of nature. Allegiance, and protection are reciprocal. The subject is bound by the compact to yield obedience to government, and in return is entitled to protection from it; thus the poor are protected against the rich, the weak against the strong, the individual against the many, and this protection is guaranteed to each member, by the whole community; but when government is laid prostrate, a state of war of all against all commences; might overcomes right; innocence itself has no security, unless the individual sequesters himself from his fellowmen, inhabits his own cave, and seeks his own prey. This is what is called a state of nature. I once thought it chimerical.

The punishment inflicted upon rebels and traitors in all states, bears some proportion to the aggravated crime. By our law the punishment is, "That the offender be drawn to the gallows, and not be carried or walk; that he be hanged by the neck, and then cut down alive, that his entrails be taken out and burned while he is yet alive, that his head be cut off, that his body be divided into four parts, that his head and quarters be at the King's disposal." The consequences of attainder are forfeiture and corruption of blood. . . .

It is remarkable however, that this offence, notwithstanding it is of a crimson colour, and the deepest dye, and its just punishment is not confined to the person of the offender, but beggars all his family, is sometimes committed by persons who are not conscious of guilt: Sometimes they are ignorant of the law, and do not forsee the evils they bring upon society; at others, they are induced to think that their cause is founded in the eternal principles of justice and truth, that they are only making an appeal to heaven, and may justly expect its decree in their favour. Doubtless many of the rebels in the year 1745 were buoyed up with such sentiments, nevertheless they were cut down like grass before the scythe of the mower; the gibbet and scaffold received those that the sword, wearied with destroying, had spared; and what loyalist shed one pitying tear over their graves? They were incorrigible rebels, and deserved their fate. The community is in less danger when the disaffected attempt to excite a rebellion against the person of the Prince, than when government itself is the object, because in the former case the questions are few, simple, and their solutions obvious, the fatal consequences more apparent, and the loyal people more alert to suppress it in embryo; whereas, in the latter, a hundred rights of the people, inconsistent with government, and as many grievances, destitute of foundation, the mere creatures of distempered brains, are portrayed in the liveliest colours, and serve as bugbears to affright from their duty, or as decoys to allure the ignorant, the credulous and the unwary to their destruction. Their suspicions are drowned in the perpetual roar for liberty and country; and even the professions of allegiance to the person of the King, are improved as means to subvert his government.

In mentioning high-treason in the course of these papers, I may not always have expressed myself with the precision of a lawyer; they have a language peculiar to themselves: I have examined their books, and beg leave to lay before you some further extracts which deserve your attention: "To levy war against the King," was high-treason by the common law, 3 Inst. 9. This is also declared to be high-treason by the stat. of 25 Ed. 3. c. 2. and by the law of this province, 8 W. 3. c. 5. Assembling in warlike array, against a statute, is levying war against the King, 1 Hale 133. So to destroy any trade generally, 146. Riding with banners displayed, or forming into companies—or being furnished with military officers—or armed with military weapons, as swords, guns &c. any of these circumstances carries the *speciem belli*, and will support an indictment for high-treason in levying war, 150. . . . Every assembling of a number of men in a warlike manner, with a design to redress any *public grievance*, is likewise an overt act of this species of treason, because this being an attempt to do that by *private authority*, which only ought to be done by the King's authority, is an invasion of the prerogative, 5 Bac. 117. cites 3 Inst. 9. Ha. p. c. 14. Kel. 71. Sid. 358. 1. Hawk. 37. Every assembling of a number of men in a *warlike* manner, with an intention to reform the government, or the law, is an overt act of this species of treason, 5 Bac. 117. cites 3 Inst. 9, 10. Poph. 122 Kel. 76. 7. 1 Hawk. 37. *Levying war* may be by taking arms, not only to dethrone the King, but under pretence to reform religion, or the *laws*, or to remove evil councellors, or other grievances, whether *real* or *pretended*, 4 Black. 81. Foster 211. . . .

The *painful* task of applying the above rules of law to the several transactions that we have been eye witnesses to, will never be mine. Let me however intreat you, to make the application in your own minds; and those of you that have continued hitherto faithful among the faithless, Abdiel like, to persevere in your integrity, and those of you that have been already ensnared by the accursed wiles of designing men, to cast yourselves immediately upon that mercy, so conspicuous through the British constitution, and which is the brightest jewel in the imperial diadem.

February 6, 1775   Massachusettensis

LETTER X

... Let us now take a view of American grievances, and try, by the sure touchstone of reason and the constitution, whether there be any act or acts, on the part of the King or parliament, that will justify the whigs even in *soro conscientuae,* in thus forcibly opposing their government. Will the alteration of the mode of appointing one branch of our provincial legislature furnish so much as an excuse for it, considering that our politicians, by their intrigues and machinations, had rendered the assembly incapable of answering the purpose of government, which is protection, and our charter was become as inefficacious as an old ballad; or can a plea of justification be founded on the parliament's giving us an exact transcript of English laws for returning jurors, when our own were insufficient to afford compensation to the injured, to suppress seditions, or even to restrain rebellion? It has been heretofore observed, that each member of the community is entitled to protection; for this he pays taxes, for this he relinquishes his natural right of revenging injuries and redressing wrongs, and for this the sword of justice is placed in the hands of the magistrate. It is notorious that the whigs had usurped the power of the province in a great measure, and exercised it by revenging themselves on their opponents, or in compelling them to inlist under their banners. Recollect the frequency of mobs and riots, the invasions and demolitions of dwelling-houses and other property, the personal abuse, and frequent necessity of persons abandoning their habitations, the taking sanctuary on board men of war, or at the castle, previous to the regulating bill. Consider that these sufferers were loyal subjects, violators of no law, that many of them were crown officers, and were thus persecuted for no other offence than that of executing the King's law. Consider, further, that if any of the sufferers sought redress in a court of law, he had the whole whig interest to combat, they gathered like a cloud and hovered like harpies round the seat of justice, until the suitor was either condemned to pay cost to his antagonist, or recovered so small damages, as that they were swallowed up in his own. Consider further, that these riots were not the accidental or spontaneous risings of the populace, but the result of the deliberations and mature councils of the whigs, and were sometimes headed and led to action by their principals. Consider further, that the general assembly lent no aid to the executive power. Weigh these things, my friend, and doubt if you can, whether the act for regulating our government did not flow from the parental tenderness of the British councils, to enable us to recover from anarchy, without Britain being driven to the necessity of inflicting punishment, which is her strange work. Having taken this cursory view of the convulsed state of the province, let us advert to our charter form of government, and we shall find its distributions of power to have been so preposterous as to render it next to impossible for the province to recover by its own strength. The council was elective annually by the house, liable to the negative of the chair, and the chair restrained from acting even in the executive department, without the concurrence of the board. The political struggle is often between the governor and the house, and it is a maxim with politicians, that he that is not for us is against us. Accordingly when party ran high, if a counsellor adhered to the governor, the house refused to elect him the next year; if he adhered to the house the governor negatived him; if he trimmed his bark so as to steer a middle course between Scylla and Charybdis, he was in danger of suffering more by the neglect of both parties, than of being wrecked but on one.

In moderate times this province has been happy under our charter form of government, but when the political storm arose, its original defect became apparent: We have sometimes seen half a dozen sail of tory navigation unable, on an election day, to pass the bar formed by the flux and reflux of the tides at the entrance of the harbour, and as many whiggish ones stranded the next morning on Governor's Island. The whigs took the lead in this game, and therefore I think the blame ought to rest upon them, though the tables were turned upon them in the sequel. A slender acquaintance with human nature will inform, experience has evinced, that a body of men thus constituted, are not to be depended upon to act that vigorous, intrepid and decisive part, which the emergency of the late times required, and which might have proved the salvation of the province. In short, the board which was intended to moderate between the governor and the house, or perhaps rather to support the former, was incapable of doing either by its original constitution. By the regulating act the members of the board are appointed by the King in the council, and are not liable even to the suspension of the governor; their commissions are *durante bene placito,* and they are therefore far from independance. The infant state of the colonies does not admit of a peerage, nor perhaps of any third branch of legislature wholly independant. In most of the colonies the council is appointed by mandamus, and the members are moreover liable to be suspended by the governor, by which means they are more dependant than those appointed according to the regulating act, but no inconvenience arises from that mode of appointment. Long experience has evinced its utility. By this statute extraordinary powers are devolved upon the chair, to enable the governor to maintain his authority, and to oppose with vigour the daring spirit of independance, so manifest in the whigs. Town-meetings are restrained to prevent their passing traiterous resolves. Had these and many other innovations contained in this act, been made in moderate times, when due reverence was yielded to the magistrate, and obedience to the law, they might have been called grievances; but we have no reason to think, that had the situation of the province been such that this statute would ever have had an existence nor have we any reason to doubt, but that it will be repealed, in whole or part, should our present form of government be found by experience to be productive of rapine or oppression. It is impossible that the King, lords or commons could have any sinister views in regulating the government of this province. Sometimes we are told that charters are sacred: However sacred, they are forfeited through negligence or *abuse* of their franchises, in which cases the law judges that the body politic has broken the condition upon which it was incorporated.

There are many instances of the negligence and abuse that work the forfeiture of charters delineated in law books. They also tell us that all charters may be vacated by act of parliament. Had the form of our provincial legislature been established by act of parliament, that act might have been constitutionally and equitably repealed, when it was found to be incapable of answering the end of its institution. Stronger still is the present case, where the form of government was established by one branch of the legislature only, viz. the King, and all three join in the revocation. This act was however a fatal stroke to the ambitious views of our republican patriots. The monarchial part of the constitution was so guarded by it as to be no longer vulnerable by their shafts, and all their fancied greatness vanished like the baseless fabric of a vision. Many that had been long striving to attain a Seat at the board, with their faces thitherward, beheld, with infinite regret, their competitors advanced to the honors they aspired to themselves. These disappointed, ambitious and envious men instill the poison of disaffection into the minds of the lower classes, and as soon as they are properly impregnated, exclaim, *the people* never will submit to it. They now would urge them into certain ruin, to prevent the execution of an act of parliament, designed and calculated to restore peace and harmony to the province, and to recall that happy state, when year rolled round on year, in a continual increase of our felicity.

The Quebec bill is another capital grievance, because the Canadians are tolerated in the enjoyment of their religion, which they were entitled to, by an article of capitulation, when they submitted to the British arms. This toleration is not an exclusion of the protestant religion, which is established in every part of the empire, as firmly as civil polity can establish it. It is a strange kind of reasoning to argue, from the French inhabitants of the conquered province of Quebec, being tolerated in the enjoyment of the Roman Catholic religion in which they were educated, and in which alone they repose their hope of eternal salvation that therefore government intends to deprive us of the enjoyment of the protestant religion in which alone we believe, especially as the political interests of Britain depend upon protestant connexions and the King's being a protestant himself is an indispensable condition of his wearing the crown. This circumstance however served admirably for a fresh stimulus, and was eagerly grasped by the disaffected of all orders. It added pathos to pulpit oratory. We often see resolves and seditious letters interspersed with *popery* here and there in Italics. If any of the clergy have endeavoured, from this circumstance, to alarm their too credulous audiences, with an apprehension that their religious privileges were in danger, thereby to excite them to take up arms, we must lament the depravity of the best of men; but human nature stands apalled when we reflect upon the aggravated guilt of prostituting our holy religion to the accursed purposes of treason and rebellion. . . .

February 13, 1775   Massachusettensis

LETTER XI

. . . Upon this point, whether the colonies are distinct states or not, our partiots have rashly tendered Great-Britain an issue, against every principle of law and constitution, against reason and common prudence. There is no arbiter between us but the sword, and that the decision of that tribunal will be against us, reason foresees, as plainly as it can discover any event that lies in the womb of futurity. No person, unless actuated by ambition, pride, malice, envy, or a malignant combination of the whole that verges towards madness, and harries the man away from himself, would wage war upon such unequal terms. . . . I have observed that the press was heretofore open to but one side of the question, which has given the offence to a writer in Edes and Gill's paper, under the signature of Novanglus, to whom I have many things to say. I would at present ask him, if the convention of committees for the county of Worcester in recommending to the inhabitants of that county not to take news papers published by two of the printers in this town, and two at New-York, have not affected to be licensers of the press? And whether, by proscribing these printers, and endeavouring to deprive them of a livelihood, they have not manifested an illiberal, bigoted, arbitrary, malevolent disposition? And whether, by thus attempting to destroy the liberty of the press, they have not betrayed a consciousness of the badness of their cause?

Our warriors tell us, that the parliament shall be permitted to legislate for the purposes of regulating trade, but the parliament hath most unrighteously asserted, that it "had, hath, and of right ought to have, full power and authority to make laws and statutes of sufficient force and validity to bind the colonies in all cases whatever," that this claim is without any qualification or restriction, is an innovation, and inconsistent with liberty. Let us candidly enquire into these three observations, upon the statute declaratory of the authority of parliament. As to its universality, it is true there are no exceptions expressed, but there is no general rule without exceptions, expressed or implied.

The implied ones in this case are obvious. It is evident that the intent and meaning of this act, was to assert the supremacy of parliament in the colonies, that is, that its constitutional authority to make laws and statutes binding upon the colonies, is, and ever had been as ample, as it is to make laws binding upon the realm. No one that reads the declaratory statute, not even prejudice itself, can suppose that the parliament meant to assert thereby a right or power to deprive the colonists of their lives, to enslave them, or to make any law respecting the colonies, that would not be constitutional, were it made respecting Great-Britain. By an act of parliament passed in the year 1650, it was declared concerning the colonies and plantations in America, that they had "ever since the planting thereof been and ought to be subject to such laws, orders and regulations, as are or shall be made by the parliament of England." This declaration though differing in expression, is the same in substance with the other. Our House of representatives, in their dispute with Governor Hutchinson, concerning the supremacy of parliament, say, "It is difficult, if possible, to draw a line of distinction between the universal authority of parliament over the colonies and no authority at all."

The declaratory statute was intended more especially to assert the right of parliament, to make laws and statutes for raising a revenue in America, lest the repeal of the stamp act might be urged as a disclaimer of the right. Let us now enquire whether a power to raise a revenue be not the inherent, unalienable right of the supreme legislative of every well-regulated state, where the hereditary revenue of the crown, or established revenues of the state are insufficient of themselves; and whether that power be not necessarily coextensive with the power of legislation, or rather necessarily implied in it.

The end or design of government, as has been already observed, is the security of the people from internal violence and rapacity, and from foreign invasion. The supreme power of a state must necessarily be so extensive and ample as to answer those purposes, otherwise it is constituted in vain, and degenerates into empty parade and mere ostentatious pageantry. These purposes cannot be answered without a power to raise a revenue, for without it neither the laws can be executed nor the state defended. This revenue ought in national concerns to be apportioned throughout the whole empire according to the abilities of the several parts, as the claim of each to protection, is equal; a refusal to yield the former is as unjust as the withholding of the latter. Were any part of an empire exempt from contributing their proportionable part of the revenue necessary for the whole, such exemption would be manifest injustice to the rest of the empire, as it must of course bear more than its proportion of the public burden, and it would amount to an additional tax. If the proportion of each part was to be determined only by itself in a separate legislature, it would not only involve in it the absurdity of *imperium in imperio,* but the perpetual contention arising from the predominant principle of self-interest in each, without having any common arbiter between them, would render the disjointed, discordant, torn and dismembered state incapable of collecting or conducting its force and energy for the preservation of the whole, as emergencies might require. A government thus constituted would contain the seeds of dissolution in its first principles, and must soon destroy itself.

I have already shewn that by your first charter, this province was to be subject to taxation after the lapse of twenty-one years, and that the authority of parliament to impose such taxes was claimed so early as the year 1642.

These are stubborn facts, they are incapable of being winked out of existence, how much soever we may be disposed to shut our eyes upon them. They prove that the claim of a right to raise a revenue in the colonies, exclusive of the grants of their own assemblies, is coeval with the colonies themselves. I shall next shew that there has been an actual, uninterrupted exercise of that right by the parliament time immemorial.

February 20, 1775   Massachusettensis

LETTER XII

By an act of parliament made in the twenty-fifth year of the reign of Charles the second, duties are laid upon goods and merchandise of various kinds exported from the colonies to foreign countries, or carried from one colony to another, payable on exportation. . . .

It is apparent from the reasoning of this statute that these duties were imposed for the sole purpose of revenue. There has lately been a most ingenious play upon the words and expressions, *tax, revenue, purpose of raising a revenue, sole purpose of raising a revenue, express purpose of raising a revenue,* as though their being inserted in, or left out of a statute, would make any essential difference in the statute. This is mere playing with words; for if, from the whole tenor of the act, it is evident that the intent of the legislature was to tax, rather than to regulate the trade, by imposing duties on goods and merchandise, it is to all intents and purposes an instance of taxation, be the form of words, in which the statute is conceived, what it will. That such was the intent of the legislature, in this instance, any one that will take the pains to read it will be convinced. There have been divers alterations made in this by subsequent statutes, but some of the above taxes remain, and are collected and paid in the colonies to this day. By an act of the 7th and 8th of William and Mary it is enacted, 'that every seaman whatsoever that shall serve his Majesty, or any other person whatever in any of his Majesty's ships or vessels whatsoever, belonging or to belong to any subjects of England, or any other his Majesty's dominions, shall allow, and there shall be paid out of the wages of every such seaman, to grow due for such his service, six pence per annum for the better support of the said hospital, and to augment the *revenue* thereof.' This tax was imposed in the reign of King William the third, of blessed memory, and is still levied in the colonies. It would require a volume to recite or minutely remark upon all the revenue acts that relate to America. We find them in many reigns, imposing new duties, taking of[f], or reducing, old ones, and making provision for their collection, or new appropriations of them. By an act of the 7th and 8th of William and Mary, entitled 'an act for preventing frauds and regulating abuses in the plantations,' all former acts respecting the plantations are renewed, and all ships and vessels coming into any port here, are liable to the same regulations and restrictions as ships in the ports in England are liable to. . . .

The act of the 9th of Queen Ann, for establishing a post-office, gives this reason for its establishment, and for laying taxes thereby imposed on the carriage of letters in Great-Britain and Ireland, the colonies and plantations in North-America and the West-Indies, and all other his Majesty's dominions and territories, 'that the business may be done in such manner as may be most beneficial to the people of these kingdoms, and her Majesty may be supplied, and the revenue arising by the said office, better improved, settled and secured to her Majesty, her heirs and successors.' The celebrated patriot, Dr. Franklin, was till lately one of the principal collectors of it. The merit in putting the post-office in America upon such a footing as to yield a large revenue to the crown, is principally ascribed to him by the whigs. I would not wish to detract from the real merit of that gentleman, but had a tory been half so assiduous in increasing the American revenue, Novanglus would have wrote parricide at the end of his name. By an act of the sixth of George the second, a duty is laid on all foreign rum, melasses, syrups, sugars and paneles, to be *raised, levied, collected and paid unto and for the use of his Majesty, his heirs and successors.* The preamble of an act of the fourth of his present Majesty declares, that *'it is just and necessary that a revenue in America for defraying the expences of defending, protecting and securing the same, &c.'* by which act duties are laid upon foreign sugars, coffee, Madeira wine; upon Portugal, Spanish and all other wine (except French wine) imported from Great-Britain; upon silks, bengals, stuffs, calico, linen cloth, cambrick and lawn imported from particular places.

Thus, my friends, it is evident, that the parliament has been in the actual, uninterrupted use and exercise of the right claimed by them, to raise a revenue in America from a period more remote than the grant of the present charter, to this day. These revenue acts have never been called unconstitutional till very lately. Both whigs and tories acknowledged them to be constitutional. In 1764 Governor Bernard wrote and transmitted to his friends, his polity alluded to, and in part recited by Novanglus, wherein he asserts the right or authority of the parliament to tax the colonies. Mr. Otis, whose patriotism, sound policy, profound learning, integrity and honor, is mentioned in strong terms by Novanglus in the self-same year, in a pamphlet which he published to the whole world, asserts the right or authority of parliament to tax the colonies as roundly as ever Governor Bernard did, which I shall have occasion to take an extract from hereafter. Mr. Otis was at that time the most popular man in the province, and continued his popularity many years afterwards.

Is it not a most astonishing instance of caprice, or infatuation, that a province, torn from its foundations, should be precipitating itself into a war with Great-Britain because the British parliament asserts its right of raising a revenue in America, inasmuch as the claim of that right is as ancient as the colonies themselves, and there is at present no grievous exercise of it? The parliament's refusing to repeal the tea act is the ostensible foundation of our quarrel. If we ask the whigs whether the pitiful three penny duty upon a luxurious unwholesome, foreign commodity gives just occasion for the opposition, they tell us it is the precedent they are contending about, insinuating that it is an innovation. But this ground is not tenable, for a total repeal of the tea-act would not serve us upon the score of precedents. They are numerous without this. The whigs have been extremely partial respecting tea. Poor tea has been made the shibboleth of party, while melasses, wine, coffee, indigo, &c. &c. have been unmolested. A person that drinks New-England rum distilled from melasses subject to a like duty, is equally deserving of a coat of tar and feathers with him that drinks tea. A coffee drinker is as culpable as either, viewed in a political light. But say our patriots, if the British parliament may take a penny from us without our consent they may a pound, and so on, till they have filched away all our property. This incessant incantation operates like a spell or charm, and checks the efforts of loyalty in many an honest breast. Let us give it its full weight. Do they mean that if the parliament has a right to raise a revenue of one penny on the colonies, that they must therefore have a *right* to wrest from us all our property? If this be their meaning, I deny their deduction; for the supreme legislature can have no right to tax any part of the empire to a greater amount than its just and equitable proportion of the necessary, national expence. This is a line drawn by the constitution itself. Do they mean, that if we admit that the parliament may constitutionally raise one penny upon us for the purposes of revenue, they will probably proceed from light to heavy taxes, till their impositions become grievous and intolerable? This amounts to no more than a denial of the right lest it should be abused. But an argument drawn from the actual abuse of a power, will not conclude to the illegality of such power, much less will an argument drawn from a capability of its being abused. If it would, we might readily argue away all power that man is intrusted with. I will admit that a power of taxation is more liable to abuse than legislation separately considered; and it would give me pleasure to see some other line drawn, some other barrier erected than what the constitution has already done, if it be possible, whereby the constitutional authority of the supreme legislature might be preserved intire, and America be guaranteed in every right and exemption, consistent with her subordination and dependance. But this can only be done by parliament. I repeat I am no advocate for a land-tax, or any other kind of internal tax, nor do I think we were in any danger of them; I have not been able to discover one symptom of any such intention in the parliament since the repeal of the stamp-act. Indeed the principal speakers of the majority that repealed the stamp-act drew the line for us, between internal and external taxation, and I think we ought, in honor, justice and good policy to have acquiesced therein, at least until there was some burdensome exercise of taxation. For there is but little danger from the latter, that is from duties laid upon trade, as any grievous restriction or imposition on American trade would be sensibly felt by the British; and I think with Dr. Franklin, that 'they (the British nation) have a natural and equitable right to some toll or duty upon merchandises carried through that part of their dominions, viz. the American seas, towards defraying the expence they are at in ships to maintain the safety of that carriage.' These were his words in his examination at the bar of the house, in 1765. *Sed tempora mutantur et nos mutamur in illis.* Before we appeal to heaven for the justice of our cause, we ought to determine with ourselves, some other questions, whether America is not obliged in equity to contribute something toward the national defence. Whether that the present American revenue, amounts to our proportion. . . .

February 27, 1775   Massachusettensis

LETTER XIII

Novanglus and all others have an indisputable right to publish their sentiments and opinions to the world, provided they conform to truth, decency and the municipal laws of the society of which they are members. He has wrote with a professed design of exposing the errors and sophistry which he supposes are frequent in my publications: His design is so far laudable, and I intend to correct them where ever he convinces me there is an instance of either. I have no objection to the minutest disquisition; contradiction and disputation, like the collision of flint and steel, often strike out new light. . . . He accuses the late Governor Shirley, Governor Hutchinson, the late Lieut. Governor Oliver, the late Judge Russell and Mr. Paxton, of a conspiracy to enslave their country. . . . That the charge is groundless respecting Governor Bernard, Governor Hutchinson, and the late Lieutenant Governor, I dare assert, because they have been acquitted of it in such a manner as every good citizen must acquiesce in. Our house of representatives acting as the grand inquest of the province, presented them before the King in Council, and after a full hearing they were acquitted with honor, and the several impeachments dismissed, as groundless, vexatious and scandalous. . . . This calumniator nevertheless has the effrontery to renew the charge in a public newspaper, although thereby he arraigns our most gracious Sovereign and Lords of the Privy Council, as well as the gentlemen he has named: Not content with wounding the honor of Judges, Counsellors and Governors, with missile weapons, darted from an obscure corner, he now aims a blow at Majesty itself. . . . The crimes are these, the persons named by him conspired together to enslave their country, in consequence of a plan, the outlines of which have been drawn by Sir Edmond Andross and others, and handed down by tradition to the present times. He tells us that Governor Shirley in 1754, communicated the profound secret, the great design of taxing the colonies by act of Parliament, to the sagacious gentleman, eminent philosopher, and distinguished patriot, Dr. Franklin. The profound secret is this, after the commencement of hostilities between the English and French colonies in the last war, a convention of committees from several provinces were called by the King, to agree upon some general plan of defence: The principal difficulty they met with was in devising means whereby each colony might be obliged to contribute its proportionable part. General Shirley proposed *that application should be made to parliament to impower the committees of the several colonies to tax the whole according to their several proportions.* This plan was adopted by the convention and approved of by the Assembly in New-York, who passed a resolve in these words: "That the scheme proposed by Governor Shirley for the defence of the British colonies in North America, is well concerted, and that this colony joins therein." This however did not succeed, and he proposed another, viz for the parliament to assess each ones proportion, and in case of failure to raise it on their part, that it should be done by parliament. This is the profound secret. . . . This attempt of Governor Shirley for a parliamentary taxation, is however a circumstance strongly militating with this writer's hypothesis, for the approbation shewn to the Governor's proposal by the convention, which consisted of persons from the several colonies, not inferior in point of discernment, integrity, knowledge or patriotism to the members of our late grand Congress, and the vote of the New-York Assembly furnishes pretty strong evidence that the authority of parliament, even in point of taxation, was not doubted in that day: Even Dr. Franklin, in the letter alluded to, does not deny the right. His opinions go to the inexpediency of the measure. He supposes it would create uneasiness in the minds of the colonists should they be thus taxed, unless they were previously allowed to send representatives to parliament. If Dr. Franklin really supposes that the parliament has no constitutional right to raise a revenue in America, I must confess myself at a loss to reconcile his conduct in accepting the office of postmaster, and his assiduity in increasing the revenue in that department, to the patriotism predicated of him by Novanglus, especially as this unfortunately happens to be an internal tax. This writer then tells us, that the plan was interrupted by the war and afterwards by Governor Pownal's administration. That Messieurs Hutchinson and Oliver, stung with envy at Governor Pownal's favourites, propagated slanders respecting him to render him uneasy in his seat. My answer is this, that he publishes such falsehoods as these in a public newspaper, with an air of seriousness, insults the understanding of the public, more than he injures the individuals he defames. In the next place, we are told that Governor Bernard was the proper man for this purpose, and he was employed by the junto to suggest to the ministry the project of taxing the colonies by act of parliament. . . . After making these assertions with equal gravity and assurance, he tells us, he does not advance this without evidence. I had been looking out for evidence a long time, and was all attention when it was promised, but my disappointment was equal to the expectation he had raised when I found the evidence amounted to nothing more than Governor Bernard's letters and principles of law and polity, wherein he asserts the supremacy of Parliament over the colonies both as to legislation and taxation. Where this writer got his logic, I do not know. Reduced to a syllogism, his argument stands thus, Governor Bernard in 1764 wrote and transmitted to England certain letters and principles of law and polity, wherein he asserts the right of parliament to tax the colonies. Messieurs Hutchinson and Oliver were in unison with him in all his measures, therefore Messieurs Hutchinson and Oliver employed Governor Bernard to suggest to the ministry the project of taxing the colonies by act of Parliament. The letters and principles are the whole of the evidence, and this is all the appearance of argument contained in his publication. Let us examine the premisses. That Governor Bernard asserted the right of Parliament to tax the colonies in 1764 is true. So did Mr. Otis, in a pamphlet he published the self same year, from which I have already taken an extract. In a pamphlet published in 1765, Mr. Otis tells us "it is certain that the Parliament of Great Britain hath a just, clear, equitable and constitutional right, power and authority to bind the colonies by all acts wherein they are named. Every lawyer, nay every Tyro, knows this; no less certain is it that the parliament of Great Britain has a just and equitable right, power and authority to impose taxes on the colonies internal and external, on lands as well as on trade." But does it follow from Governor Bernard's transmitting his principles of polity to four persons in England or from Mr. Otis's publishing to the whole world similar principles, that either the one or the other suggested to the ministry the project of taxing the colonies by act of parliament? Hardly, supposing the transmission and publication had been prior to the resolution of parliament to that purpose, but very unfortunately for our reasoner they were both subsequent to it, and were the effect and not the cause.

The history of the stamp-act is this: At the close of the last war, which was a native of America, and increased the national debt upwards of sixty millions, it was thought by parliament to be but equitable, that an additional revenue should be raised in America, towards defraying the necessary charges of keeping it in a state of defence: A resolve of this nature was passed, and the colonies made acquainted with it through their agents, in 1764, that their assemblies might make the necessary provision if they would. The assemblies neglected doing anything, and the parliament passed the stamp-act. There is not so much as a colourable pretence that any American had a hand in the matter: Had Governor Bernard, Governor Hutchinson, or the late Lieutenant Governor been any way instrumental in obtaining the stamp-act? It is very strange that not a glimpse of evidence should ever have appeared, especially when we consider that their private correspondence has been published, letters which were written in the full confidence of unsuspecting friendship. The evidence, as Novanglus calls it, is wretchedly deficient as to fixing the charge upon Governor Bernard: But, even admitting that Governor Bernard suggested to the ministry the design of taxing, there is no kind of evidence to prove that the junto, as this elegant writer calls the others, approved of it, much less that they employed him to do it. But, says he, no one can doubt but that Messieurs Hutchinson and Oliver were in unison with Governor Bernard, in all his measures: This is not a fact, Mr. Hutchinson dissented from him respecting the alteration of our charter, and wrote to his friends in England to prevent it. Whether Governor Bernard wrote in favour of the stamp-act being repealed or not I cannot say, but I know that Governor Hutchinson did, and have reason to think his letters had great weight in turning the scale, which hung doubtful a long time, in favour of the repeal. These facts are known to many in the province, whigs as well as tories, yet such was the infatuation that prevailed, that the mob destroyed his house upon supposition that he was the patron of the stamp-act; even in the letters wrote to the late Mr. Whately, we find him advising to a total repeal of the tea act. It cannot be fairly inferred from peoples intimacy or mutual confidence, that they always approve of each others plans. Messieurs Otis, Cushing, Hancock and Adams were as confidential friends, and made common cause equally with other gentlemen. May we thence infer, that the three latter held that the parliament has a just and equitable right to impose taxes on the colonies? Or, that "the time may come when the real interest of the whole may require an act of parliament to annihilate all their charters," for these also are

Mr. Otis's words: Or may we lay it down as a principle to reason from, that these gentlemen never disagree respecting measures? We know they do often very materially. This writer is unlucky both in his principles and inferences. But where is the evidence respecting Brigadier Ruggles, Mr. Paxton and the late Judge Russell? He does not produce even a shadow of a shade. He does not even pretend that they were in unison with Governor Bernard in all his measures. In matters of small moment a man may be allowed to amuse with ingenious fiction, but in personal accusation, in matters so interesting both to the individual and to the public, reason and candour require something more than assertion without proof, declamation without argument and censure without dignity or moderation. . . .

These gentlemen were all of them, and the survivors still continue to be friends of the English constitution, equally tenacious of the privileges of the people and of the prerogative of the crown, zealous advocates for the colonies continuing their constitutional dependence upon Great-Britain, as they think it no less the interest than the duty of the colonists, averse to tyranny and oppression in all their forms. . . . This republican party is of long standing, they lay however, in a great measure, dormant for several years. The distrust, jealousy and ferment raised by the stamp-act, afforded scope for action. At first they wore the garb of hypocrisy, they professed to be friends to the British constitution in general, but claimed some exemptions from their local circumstances; at length threw off their disguise, and now stand confessed to the world in their true characters, American republicans. These republicans knew, that it would be impossible for them to succeed in their daring projects, without first destroying the influence of these adherents to the constitution. Their only method to accomplish it, was by publications charged with falsehood and scurrility. . . . The gentlemen named by Novanglus, have nevertheless persevered with unshaken constancy and firmness, in their patriotic principles and conduct, through a variety of fortune; and have at present, the mournful consolation of reflecting, that had their admonitions and councils been timely attended to, their country would never have been involved in its present calamity.

March 6, 1775   Massachusettensis

LETTER XIV

Our patriotic writers, as they call each other, estimate the services rendered by, and the advantages resulting from the colonies to Britain, at a high rate, but allow but little, if any, merit in her towards the colonies. Novanglus would persuade us that exclusive of her assistance in the last war, we have had but little of her protection, unless it was such that her name alone afforded. Dr. Franklin when before the House of Commons in 1765, denied that the late war was entered into for the defence, of the people in America. The Pennsylvania Farmer tells us in his letters that the war was undertaken solely for the benefit of Great Britain, and that however advantageous the subduing or keeping any of these countries, viz. Canada, Nova-Scotia and the Floridas may be to Great Britain, the acquisition is greatly injurious to these colonies. And that the colonies as constantly as streams tend to the ocean, have been pouring the fruits of all their labours into their mother's lap. Thus they would induce us to believe, that we derive little or no advantage from Great Britain, and thence they infer the injustice, rapacity and cruelty of her conduct towards us. I fully agree with them, that the services rendered by the colonies are great and meritorious. The plantations are additions to the empire of inestimable value. The American market for British manufactures, the great nursery for seamen formed by our shipping, the cultivation of deserts and our rapid population, are increasing and inexhaustible sources of national wealth and strength. . . . The principal difficulties that the adventurers met with after the struggle of a few of the first years were over, were the incursions of the French and savages conjointly, or of the latter instigated and supported by the former. Upon a representation of this to England, in the time of the interregnum, Acadia, which was then the principal source of our disqui[e]tude, was reduced by an English armament. At the request of this colony, in Queen Ann's reign, a fleet of fifteen men-of-war, besides transports, troops, &c. were sent to assist us in an expedition against Canada; the fleet suffered shipwreck, and the attempt proved abortive. It ought not to be forgot that the siege of Louisbourg, in 1745, by our own forces, was covered by a British fleet of ten ships, four of 60 guns, one of fifty and five of 40 guns, besides the Vigilant of sixty-four, which was taken during the siege, as she was attempting to throw supplies into the garrison. It is not probable that the expedition would have been undertaken without an expectation of some naval assistance, or that the reduction could have been effected without it. In January, 1754, our assembly, in a message to Governor Shirley, prayed him to represent to the King, 'that the French had made such extraordinary encroachments, and taken such measures, since the conclusion of the preceding war, as threatened great danger, and perhaps, in time, even the intire destruction of this province, without the interposition of his Majesty, notwithstanding any provision we could make to prevent it'. . . .

The commissioners who met at Albany the same year, represented, 'that it was the evident design of the French to surround the British colonies. . . . That it seemed absolutely necessary that speedy and effectual measures should be taken to secure the colonies from the slavery they were threatened with.'

We did not pray in vain; Great-Britain, ever attentive to the *real grievances* of her colonies, hastened to our relief with maternal speed. She covered our seas with her ships, and sent forth the bravest of her sons to fight our battles. They fought, they bled and conquered with us. Canada, Nova-Scotia, the Floridas, and all our American foes were laid at our feet. It was a dear bought victory; the wilds of America were enriched with the blood of the noble and the brave.

The war, which at our request, was thus kindled in America spread through the four quarters of the globe, and obliged Great-Britain to exert her whole force and energy to stop the rapid progress of its devouring flames.

To these instances of actual exertions for our immediate protection and defence, ought to be added, the fleets stationed on our coast and the convoys and security afforded to our trade and fishery, in times of war; and her maintaining in times of peace such a navy and army, as to be always in readiness to give protection as exigencies may require; and her ambassadors residing at foreign courts to watch and give the earliest intelligence of their motions. By such precautions every part of her wide extended empire enjoys as ample security as human power and policy can afford. Those necessary precautions are supported at an immence expence, and the colonies reap the benefit of them equally with the rest of the empire. To these considerations it should likewise be added, that whenever the colonies have exerted themselves in war, though in their own defence, to a greater degree than their proportion with the rest of the empire, they have been reimbursed by parliamentary grants. This was the case in the last war with this province.

From this view, which I think is an impartial one, it is evident that Great-Britain is not less attentive to our interest than her own. . . .

March 13, 1775   Massachusettensis

LETTER XV

The outlines of British commerce have been heretofore sketched; and the interest of each part in particular, and of the whole empire conjointly have been shewn to be the principles by which the grant system is poized and balanced. Whoever will take upon himself the trouble of reading and comparing the several acts of trade which respect the colonies, will be convinced, that the cherishing their trade and promoting their interest have been the objects of parliamentary attention equally with those of Britain. He will see that the great council of the empire has ever esteemed our prosperity as inseperable from the British; and if in some instances the colonies have been restricted to the emolument of other parts of the empire, they in their turn, not excepting England itself, have been also restricted sufficiently to restore the balance, if not to cause a preponderation in our favor. . . .

A calculation has lately been made both of the amount of the revenue arising from the duties with which our trade is at present charged, and of the bounties and encouragement paid out of the British revenue upon articles of American produce imported into England, and the latter is found to exceed the former more than four fold. This does not look like a partiality to our disadvantage. However there is no surer method of determining whether the colonies have been oppressed by the laws of trade and revenue, than by observing their effects.

From what source has the wealth of the colonies flowed? When is it derived? Not from agriculture only. Exclusive of commerce the colonists would this day have been a poorer people, possessed of little more than the necessaries for supporting life; of course their members would be few; for population always keeps pace with the ability of maintaining a family; there would have been but little or no resort of strangers here; the arts and sciences would have made but small progress; the inhabitants would rather have degenerated into a state of ignorance and barbarity. Or had Great-Britain laid such restrictions upon our trade, as our patriots would induce us to believe, that is, had we been pouring the fruits of all our labour into the lap of our parent and been enriching her by the sweat of our brow, without receiving an equivalent, the patrimony derived from our ancestors must have dwindled from little to less, until their posterity should have suffered a general bankruptcy.

But how different are the effects of our connection with and subordination to Britain? They are too strongly marked to escape the most careless observer. Our merchants are opulent, and our yeomanry in easier circumstances than the noblesse of some states. Population is so rapid as to double the number of inhabitants in the short period of twenty-five years. Cities are springing up in the depths of the wilderness. Schools, colleges and even universities are interspersed through the continent. Our country abounds with foreign refinements, and flows with exotic luxuries. These are infallible marks not only of opulence but of freedom. . . .

Where are the traces of the slavery that our patriots would terrify us with? The effects of slavery are as glaring and obvious in those countries that are cursed with its abode, as the effects of war, pestilence or famine. Our land is not disgraced by the wooden shoes of France, or the uncombed hair of Poland. We have neither racks nor inquisitions, tortures or assassinations. The mildness of our criminal jurisprudence is proverbial, 'a man must have many friends to get hanged in New England.' Who has been arbitrarily imprisoned, disseized of his freehold, or despoiled of his goods? Each peasant that is industrious may acquire an estate, enjoy it his life time, and at his death transmit a fair inheritance to his posterity. The protestant religion is established as far as human laws can establish it. . . .

[March 20, 1775]   Massachusettensis

LETTER XVI

Our patriots exclaim, 'That humble and reasonable petitions from the representatives of the people have been frequently treated with contempt.' This is as virulent a libel upon his Majesty's government, as falsehood and ingenuity combined could fabricate. Our humble and reasonable petitions have not only been graciously received, when the established mode of exhibiting them has been observed, but generally granted. Applications of a different kind, have been treated with neglect, though not always with the contempt they deserved. These either originated in illegal assemblies, and could not be received without implicitly countenancing such enormities, or contained such matter, and were conceived in such terms, as to be at once an insult to his Majesty and a libel on his government. Instead of being decent remonstrances against real grievances, or prayers for their removal, they were insidious attempts to wrest from the crown or the supreme legislature, their inherent, unalienable prerogatives or rights.

We have a recent instance of this kind of petition, in the application of the continental congress to the King, which starts with these words: 'A standing army has been kept in these colonies ever since the conclusion of the late war, *without the consent of our assemblies.'* This is a denial of the King's authority to station his military forces in such parts of the empire as his Majesty may judge expedient for the common safety. They might with equal propriety have advanced one step further and denied its being a prerogative of the crown to declare war, or conclude a peace by which the colonies should be affected, without the consent of our assemblies. Such petitions carry the marks of death in their faces, as they cannot be granted but by surrendering some constitutional right at the same time; and therefore afford grounds for suspicion at least, that they were never intended to be granted, but to irritate and provoke the power petitioned to. It is one thing to remonstrate the inexpediency or inconveniency of a particular act of the prerogative, and another to deny the existence of the prerogative. It is one thing to complain of the inutility or hardship of a particular act of parliament, and quite another to deny the authority of parliament to make any act. Had our patriots confined themselves to the former, they would have acted a part conformable to the character they assumed, and merited the encomiums they arrogate.

There is not one act of parliament that respects us, but would have been repealed upon the legislators being convinced that it was oppressive; and scarcely one, but would have shared the same fate, upon a representation of its being generally disgustful to America. But, by adhering to the latter, our politicians have ignorantly or wilfully betrayed their country. Even when Great-Britain has relaxed in her measures, or appeared to recede from her claims, instead of manifestations of gratitude, our politicians have risen in their demands, and sometimes to such a degree of insolence, as to lay the British government under a necessity of persevering in its measures to preserve its honor. . . .

A congress or convention of committees from the several colonies constitutionally appointed by the supreme authority of the state, or by the several provincial legislatures, amenable to or controlable by the power that convened them, would be salutary in many supposeable cases: such was the convention of 1754; but a congress otherwise appointed, must be an unlawful assembly, wholly incompatible with the constitution, and dangerous in the extreme, more especially as such assemblies will ever chiefly consist of the most violent partizans. The Prince or Sovereign, as some writers call the supreme authority of a state, is sufficiently ample and extensive to provide a remedy for every wrong in all possible emergencies and contingencies; consequently a power that is not derived from such authority, springing up in a state, must incroach upon it, and in proportion as the usurpation inlarges itself, the rightful Prince must be diminished; indeed they cannot long subsist together, but must continually militate till one or the other be destroyed. Had the continental congress consisted of committees from the several houses of assemblies, although destitute of the consent of the several governors, they would have had some appearance of authority; but many of them were appointed by other committees, as illegally constituted by themselves. However, at so critical and delicate a juncture, Great-Britain being alarmed with an apprehension that the colonies were aiming at independance on the one hand, and the colonies apprehensive of grievous impositions and exactions from Great-Britain, on the other, many real patriots imagined that a congress might be eminently serviceable, as they might prevail on the Bostonians to make restitution to the East-India company, might still the commotions in this province, remove any ill-founded apprehensions respecting the colonies, and propose some plan for a cordial and permanent reconciliation, which might be adopted by the several assemblies, and make its way through them to the supreme legislature. Placed in this point of light, many good men viewed it with an indulgent eye, and tories as well as whigs, bade the delegates Godspeed.

The path of duty was too plain to be overlooked, but unfortunately some of the most influential of the members were the very persons that had been the *wilful* cause of the evils they were expected to remedy. . . .

Some of the members, of the first rate abilities, and characters endeavoured to confine the deliberations and resolves of the congress to the design of its institution, which was 'to restore peace, harmony and mutual confidence,' but were obliged to succumb to the intemperate zeal of some, and at length were so circumvented and wrought upon by the artifice and duplicity of others, as to lend the sanction of their names to such measures as they condemned in their hearts. Vide a pamphlet published by one of the delegates intitled, A candid examination, &c.

The Congress could not be ignorant of what everybody else knew, that their appointment was repugnant to, and inconsistant with, every idea of government, and therefore wisely determined to destroy it. Their first essay that transpired, and which was matter of no less grief to the friends of our country than of triumph to its enemies, was the ever memorable resolve approbating and adopting the Suffolk resolves, thereby undertaking to give a continental sanction to a forcible opposition to acts of parliament, shutting up the courts of justice, and thereby abrogating all human laws, seizing the King's provincial revenue, raising forces in opposition to the King's, and all the tumultuary violence with which this unhappy province had been rent asunder.

This fixed the complexion and marked the character of the congress. We were therefore but little surprized when it was announced, that as far as was in their power, they had dismembered the colonies from the parent country. This they did by resolving that 'the colonists are entitled to an exclusive power of legislation in their several provincial legislatures.' This stands in its full force, and is an absolute denial of the authority of parliament respecting the colonies.

Their subjoining that '*from necessity* they consent to the *operation* (not the authority) of such acts of the *British* parliament as *are* (not shall be) *bona fide* restrained to external commerce,' is so far from weakening their first principle that it strengthens it, and is an adoption of the acts of trade. This resolve is a manifest revolt from the British empire. Consistent with it, is their overlooking the supreme legislature, and addressing the inhabitants of Great-Britain, in the stile of a manifesto in which they flatter, complain, coax, and threaten alternately: Their prohibiting all commercial intercourse between the two countries; with equal propriety and justice the congress might have declared war against Great-Britain, and they intimate that they might justly do it, and actually shall, if the measures already taken prove ineffectual. . . .

This is treating Great-Britain as an alien enemy, and if Great-Britain be such, it is justifiable by the law of nations. But their attempt to alienate the affections of the inhabitants of the new conquered province of Quebec from his Majesty's government, is altogether unjustifiable, even upon that principle. In the truly jesuitical address to the Canadians, the congress endeavour to seduce them from their allegiance, and prevail on them to join the confederacy. . . . The treachery of the congress in this address is the more flagrant, by the Quebec bill's having been adapted to the genius and manners of the Canadians, formed upon their own petition, and received with every testimonial of gratitude. . . . Instead of confining themselves to those acts, which occasioned the misunderstanding, they demand a repeal of fourteen, and bind the colonies by a law not to trade with Great-Britain until that shall be done. Then and not before, the colonists are to treat Great-Britain as an alien friend, and in no other light is the parent country ever after to be viewed; for the parliament is to surcease enacting laws to respect us for ever. These demands are such as cannot be complied with, consistent with either the honor or interest of the empire, and are therefore insuperable obstacles to a union via congress.

The delegates erecting themselves into the States-General or supreme legislature of all the colonies, from *Nova-Scotia* to *Georgia*, does not leave a doubt respecting their aiming, in good earnest, at independency. This they did by enacting laws. Although they recognize the authority of the several provincial legislatures, yet they consider their own authority as paramount or supreme, otherwise they would not have acted decisively, but submitted their plans to the final determination of the assemblies. Sometimes indeed they use the terms request and recommend, at others they speak in the stile of authority. Such is the resolve of the 27th of September: 'Resolved from and after the first day of December next there be no importation into British America from Great-Britain or Ireland of any goods, wares or merchandize whatsoever, or from any other place of any such goods, wares or merchandize as shall have been exported from Great-Britain or Ireland, and that no such goods, wares or merchandize imported after the said first day of December next, be used or purchased. . . .' Here we find the congress enacting laws, that is, establishing, as the representatives of the people, certain rules of conduct to be observed and kept by all the inhabitants of these colonies, under certain pains and penalties, such as masters of vessels being dismissed from their employment; goods to be seized and sold at auction, and the first cost only returned to the proprietor, a different appropriation made of the overplus; persons being stigmatized in the gazette, as enemies to their country, and excluded the benefits of society, &c. . . .

By their assuming the powers of legislation, the congress have not only superseded our provincial legislatures, but have excluded every idea of monarchy; and not content with the havock already made in our constitution, in the plenitude of their power, have appointed another congress to be held in May.

Those that have attempted to establish new systems have generally taken care to be consistent with themselves. Let us compare the several parts of the continental proceedings with each other.

The delegates call themselves and constituents 'his Majesty's most loyal subjects,' his Majesty's most faithful subjects affirm, that the colonists are entitled 'to all the immunities and priviledges granted and confirmed to them by royal charters,' declare that they 'wish not a diminution of the prerogative, nor solicit the grant of any new right or favour,' and they 'shall always carefully and zealously endeavour to support his royal authority and our connection with Great-Britain;' yet deny the King's prerogative to station troops in the colonies, disown him in the capacity in which he granted the provincial charters; disclaim the authority of the King in parliament; and undertake to enact and execute laws without any authority derived from the crown. This is dissolving all connection between the colonies and the crown, and giving us a new King, altogether incomprehensible, not indeed from the infinity of his attributes, but from a privation of every royal prerogative, and not leaving even a semblance of a connection with Great-Britain.

They declare, that the colonists 'are entitled to all the rights liberties and immunities of free and natural born subjects within the realm of England,' and 'all the benefits secured to the subject by the English constitution,' but disclaim all obedience to British government; in other words, they claim the protection, and disclaim the allegiance. They remonstrate as a grievance that 'both houses of parliament have resolved that the colonists may be tried in England for offences alledged to have been committed in America by virtue of a statute passed in the thirty-fifth year of Henry the eighth'; and yet resolve that they are entitled to the benefit of such English statutes as existed at the time of their colonization, and are applicable to their several local and other circumstances. They resolve that the colonists are entitled to a free and *exclusive* power of legislation in their several provincial assemblies; yet undertake to legislate in congress.

The immutable laws of nature, the principles of the English constitution, and our several charters, are the basis upon which they pretend to found themselves, and complain more especially of being deprived of trials by juries; but establish ordinances incompatible with either the laws of nature, the English constitution, or our charter; and appoint committees to punish the violaters of them, not only without a jury, but even without a form of trial.

They repeatedly complain of the Roman Catholic religion being established in Canada, and in their address to the Canadians, ask 'if liberty of conscience be offered them *in their religion* by the Quebec bill,' and answer, 'no; God gave it to you and the temporal powers which you have been and are connected, firmly stipulated for your enjoyment of it. If laws *divine* and *human* could secure it against the despotic caprices of wicked men, it was secured before.'

They say, to the people of Great-Britain, 'place us in the same situation that we were in at the close of the last war, and our harmony will be restored.' Yet some of the principal grievances which are to be redressed existed long before that aera, viz. The King's keeping a standing army in the colonies; judges of admiralty receiving their fees, &c. from the effects condemned by themselves; counsellors holding commissions during pleasure, exercising legislative authority; and the capital grievance of all, the parliament claiming and exercising over the colonies a right both of legislation and taxation. However, the wisdom of the grand continental congress may reconcile these seeming inconsistancies.

Had the delegates been appointed to devise means to irritate and enrage the inhabitants of the two countries, against each other, beyond a possibility of reconciliation. . . . more promising means to effect the whole could not have been devised than those the congress adopted. Any deviation from their plan, would have been treachery to their constituents, and an abuse of the trust and confidence reposed in them. Some idolaters have attributed to the congress the collected wisdom of the continent. It is as near the truth to say, that every particle of disaffection, petulance, ingratitude and disloyalty that for ten years past have been scattered through the continent, were united and consolidated in them. Are these thy Gods, O Israel!

[March 27, 1775]   Massachusettensis

LETTER XVII

The advocates for the opposition to parliament often remind us of the rights of the people, repeat the Latin adage *vox populi vox dei,* and tell us that government in the dernier resort is in the people; they chime away melodiously, and to render their music more ravishing tell us, that these are *revolution* principles. I hold the rights of the people as sacred, and revere the principles that have established the succession to the imperial crown of Great-Britain in the line of the illustrious house of Brunswick; but that the difficulty lies in applying them to the causes of the whigs, *hic labor hoc opus est;* for admitting that the collective body of the people, that are subject to the British empire, have an inherent right to change their form of government, or race of Kings, it does not follow, that the inhabitants of a single province or of a number of provinces, or any given part under a majority of the whole empire, have such a right. By admitting that the less may rule or sequester themselves from the greater, we unhinge all government. Novanglus has accused me of traducing the people of this province. I deny the charge. . . . Fully convinced that our calamities were chiefly created by the leading whigs, and that a persevering in the same measures that gave rise to our troubles, would compleat our ruin, I have written freely. . . . The terms whig and tory have been adopted according to the arbitrary use of them in this province, but they rather ought to be reversed; an American tory is a supporter of our excellent constitution, and an American whig a subverter of it.

Novanglus abuses me, for saying that the whigs aim at independance. The writer from Hampshire county is my advocate. He frankly asserts the independency of the colonies without any reserve, and is the only consistent writer I have met with on that side of the question; for by separating us from the King as well as the parliament, he is under no necessity of contradicting himself. Novanglus strives to hide the inconsistencies of his hypothesis, under a huge pile of learning. Surely he is not to learn that arguments drawn from obsolete maxims, raked out of the ruins of the feudal system, or from principles of absolute monarchy, will not conclude to the present constitution of government. When he has finished his essays, he may expect some particular remarks upon them. . . .

Many appear to consider themselves as *procul a Jove a fulmine procul*, and because we never have experienced any severity from Great-Britain, think it impossible that we should. The English nation will bear much from its friends, but whoever has read its history must know that there is a line that cannot be passed with impunity. It is not the fault of our patriots if that line be not already passed. They have demanded of Great-Britain more than she can grant consistent with honor, her interest, or our own, and are now brandishing the sword of defiance.

Do you expect to conquer in war? War is no longer a simple but an intricate science, not to be learned from books or two or three campaigns, but from long experience. You need not be told that his Majesty's Generals, Gage and Haldimand, are possessed of every talent requisite to great commanders, matured by long experience in many parts of the world, and stand high in military fame. That many of the officers have been bred to arms from their infancy, and a large proportion of the army *now* here, have already reaped immortal honors in the iron harvest of the field. Alas! My friends, you have nothing to oppose to this force, but a militia unused to service, impatient of command, and destitute of resources. Can your officers depend upon the privates, or the privates upon the officers? Your war can be but little more than mere tumultuary rage. . . . This province does not produce its necessary provision, when the husbandman cannot pursue his calling without molestation. What then must be your condition, when the demand shall be increased and the resource in the manner cut off? Figure to yourselves what must be your distress should your wives and children be driven from such places as the King's troops shall occupy, into the interior parts of the province, and they as well as you, be destitute of support. I take no pleasure in painting these scenes of distress. The whigs affect to divert you from them by ridicule; but should war commence, you can expect nothing but its severities. Might I hazard an opinion, but few of your leaders ever intended to engage in hostilities, but they may have rendered inevitable what they intended for intimidation. Those that unsheath the sword of rebellion may throw away the scabbard, they cannot be treated with while in arms; and if they lay them down, they are in no other predicament than conquered rebels. The conquered in other wars do not forfeit the rights of men, nor all the rights of citizens, even their bravery is rewarded by a generous victor; far different is the case of a routed rebel host. My dear countrymen, you have before you, at your election, peace or war, happiness or misery. May the God of our forefathers direct you in the way that leads to peace and happiness, before your feet stumble on the dark mountains, before the evil days come wherein you shall say, we have no pleasure in them.

[April 3, 1775]   Massachusettensis

To the Inhabitants of the Colony of Massachusetts Bay

Novanglus
[John Adams]

I

My friends,

A writer, under the signature of *Massachusettensis*, has addressed you, in a series of papers, on the great national subject of the present quarrel between the British administration and the Colonies. As I have not in my possession, more than one of his essays, and that is in the Gazette of December 26, I will take the liberty, in the spirit of candor and decency, to bespeak your attention upon the same subject.

There may be occasion, to say very severe things, before I shall have finished what I propose, in opposition to this writer, but there ought to be no reviling. *Rem ipsam dic, mitte male loqui,* which may be justly translated, speak out the whole truth boldly, but use no bad language. . . .

He tells you, "that the temporal salvation of this province depends upon an entire and speedy change of measures, which must depend upon a change of sentiments respecting our own conduct and the justice of the British nation."

. . . It is true, as this writer observes, "that the bulk of the people are generally but little versed in the affairs of state, that they rest the affairs of government where accident has placed them." If this had not been true, the designs of the tories had been many years ago, entirely defeated. It was clearly seen, by a few, more than ten years since, that they were planning and pursuing the very measures we now see executing. The people were informed of it, and warned of their danger. But they had been accustomed to confide in certain persons, and could never be persuaded to believe, until prophecy became history. Now, they see and feel that the horrible calamities are come upon them, which were foretold so many years ago, and they now sufficiently execrate the men who have brought these things upon them. Now, alas! when perhaps it is too late. If they had withdrawn their confidence from them in season, they would have wholly disarmed them.

. . . "There is a latent spark in the breasts of the people, capable of being kindled into a flame, and to do this has always been the employment of the disaffected." What is this "latent spark?" The love of Liberty. *A Deo, hominis est indita naturae.* Human nature itself is evermore an advocate for liberty. There is also in human nature a resentment of injury and indignation against wrong; a love of truth, and a veneration for virtue.

These amiable passions are the "latent spark" to which those whom this writer calls the "disaffected" apply. If the people are capable of understanding, seeing, and feeling the difference between true and false, right and wrong, virtue and vice, to what better principle can the friends of mankind apply, than to the sense of this difference?

Is it better to apply, as this writer and his friends do, to the basest passions in the human breast—to their fear, their vanity, their avarice, ambition, and every kind of corruption? I appeal to all experience, and to universal history, if it has ever been in the power of popular leaders, uninvested with other authority than what is conferred by the popular suffrage, to persuade a large people, for any length of time together, to think them-selves wronged, injured, and oppressed, unless they really were, and saw and felt it to be so.

"They," the popular leaders, "begin by reminding the people of the elevated rank they hold in the universe as men; that all men by nature are equal; that kings are but the ministers of the people; that their authority is delegated to them by the people for their good, and they have a right to resume it, and place it in other hands, or keep it themselves, whenever it is made use of to oppress them. Doubtless there have been instances when these principles have been inculcated to obtain a redress of real grievances; but they have been much oftener perverted to the worst of purposes."

These are what are called revolution principles. They are the principles of Aristotle and Plato, of Livy and Cicero, of Sidney, Harrington, and Locke. The principles of nature and eternal reason. The principles on which the whole government over us now stands. It is therefore astonishing, if any thing can be so, that writers, who call themselves friends of government, should in this age and country be so inconsistent with themselves, so indiscreet, so immodest, as to insinuate a doubt concerning them. . . .

Massachusettensis is more discreet than either of the others. Sensible that these principles would be very troublesome to him, yet conscious of their truth, he has neither admitted nor denied them. But we have a right to his opinion of them, before we dispute with him. He finds fault with the application of them. They have been invariably applied, in support of the revolution and the present establishment, against the Stuarts, the Charles's, and James's, in support of the reformation and the protestant religion, against the worst tyranny, that the genius of toryism, has ever yet invented; I mean the Romish superstition. Does this writer rank the revolution and present establishment, the reformation and protestant religion, among his worst of purposes? What "worse purpose" is there than established tyranny? Were these principles ever inculcated in favour of such tyranny? Have they not always been used against such tyrannies, when the people have had knowledge enough to be apprized of them, and courage to assert them? Do not those who aim at depriving the people of their liberties, always inculcate opposite principles, or discredit these?

"A small mistake in point of policy," says he, "often furnishes a pretence to libel government, and persuade the people that their rulers are tyrants, and the whole government a system of oppression." This is not only untrue, but inconsistent with what he said before. The people are in their nature so gentle, that there never was a government yet, in which thousands of mistakes were not overlooked. The most sensible and jealous people are so little attentive to government, that there are no instances of resistance, until repeated, multiplied oppressions have placed it beyond a doubt, that their rulers had formed settled plans to deprive them of their liberties; not to oppress an individual or a few, but to break down the fences of a free constitution, and deprive the people at large of all share in the government and all the checks by which it is limited. Even Machiavel himself allows, that not ingratitude to their rulers, but much love is the constant fault of the people.

This writer is equally mistaken, when he says, the people are sure to be loosers in the end. They can hardly be loosers, if unsuccessful; because if they live, they can but be slaves, after an unfortunate effort, and slaves they would have been, if they had not resisted. So that nothing is lost. If they die, they cannot be said to lose, for death is better than slavery. If they succeed, their gains are immense. They preserve their liberties. The instances in antiquity which this writer alludes to, are not mentioned and therefore cannot be answered, but that in the country from whence we are derived, is the most unfortunate for his purpose, that could have been chosen. The resistance to Charles the first and the case of Cromwell, no doubt he means. But the people of England, and the cause of liberty, truth, virtue, and humanity, gained infinite advantages by that resistance. In all human probability, liberty, civil and religious, not only in England, but in all Europe, would have been lost. Charles would undoubtedly have established the Romish religion, and a despotism as wild as any in the world. And as England has been a principal bulwark from that period to this, of civil liberty and the protestant religion in all Europe, if Charles's schemes had succeeded, there is great reason to apprehend that the light of science would have been extinguished, and mankind drawn back to a state of darkness and misery, like that which prevailed from the fourth to the fourteenth century. It is true and to be lamented that Cromwell did not establish a government as free, as he might and ought; but his government was infinitely more glorious and happy to the people than Charles's. Did not the people gain by the resistance to James the second? Did not the Romans gain by the resistance to Tarquin? Without that resistance, and the liberty that was restored by it, would the great Roman orators, poets, and historians, the great teachers of humanity and politeness, the pride of human nature, and the delight and glory of mankind for seventeen hundred years, ever have existed?. . . .

[January 23, 1775]   Novanglus

II

My Friends,

I have heretofore intimated my intention, of pursuing the Tories, through all their dark intrigues and wicked machinations, and to show the rise and progress of their schemes for enslaving this country. The honour of inventing and contriving these measures is not their due. They have been but servile copyers of the designs of Andross, Randolph, Dudley, and other champions of their cause towards the close of the last century. These latter worthies accomplished but little; and their plans had been buried with them, for a long course of years, untill in the administration of the late Governor Shirley, they were revived by the persons who are now principally concern'd in carrying them into execution. Shirley was a crafty, busy, ambitious, intrigueing, enterprizing man; and, having mounted, no matter by what means, to the chair of this province, he saw, in a young, growing country, vast prospects of ambition opening before his eyes, and he conceived great designs of aggrandizing himself, his family, and his friends. Mr. Hutchinson and Mr. Oliver, the two famous letter-writers, were his principal ministers of state; Russell, Paxton, Ruggles, and a few others, were *subordinate* instruments. Among other schemes of this junto, one was to have a Revenue in America, by authority of parliament.

In order to effect their purpose, it was necessary to concert measures with the other colonies. Dr. Franklin, who was known to be an active and very able man, and to have great influence in the province of Pennsylvania, was in Boston in the year 1754, and Mr. Shirley communicated to him the profound secret, the great design of taxing the colonies by act of parliament. This sagacious gentleman, this eminent philosopher and distinguished patriot, to his lasting honour, sent the Governor an answer in writing, with the following remarks upon his scheme. Remarks which would have discouraged any honest man from the pursuit. The remarks are these:—

"That the people always bear the burden best, when they have, or think they have, some *share* in the direction.

"That when public measures are generally distasteful to the people, the wheels of government must move more heavily.

"That excluding the people of America from all share in the choice of a grand council for their own defence, and taxing them in parliament, where they have no representative, would probably give extreme dissatisfaction.

"That there was no reason to doubt the willingness of the colonists to contribute for their own defence.

"That the people themselves, whose all was at stake, could better judge of the force necessary for their defence, and of the means for raising money for the purpose, than a British parliament at so great distance. . . .

"That compelling the colonies to pay money for their own defence, without their consent, would show a suspicion of their loyalty, or of their regard for their country, or of their common sense, and would be treating them as conquered enemies, and not as free Britons, who hold it for their undoubted right, not to be taxed but by their own consent, given through their representatives.

"That parliamentary taxes, once laid on, are often continued, after the necessity for laying them on ceases; but that if the colonists were trusted to tax themselves, they would remove the burden from the people as soon as it should become unnecessary for them to bear it any longer.

"That if parliament is to tax the colonies, their assemblies of representatives may be dismissed as useless. . . .

"That the colonists have always been indirectly taxed by the mother country, (besides paying the taxes necessarily laid on by their own assemblies); inasmuch as they are obliged to purchase the manufactures of Britain, charged with innumerable heavy taxes, some of which manufactures they could make, and others could purchase cheaper at other markets.

"That the colonists are besides taxed by the mother country, by being obliged to carry great part of their produce to Britain, and accept a lower price than they might have at other markets. The difference is a tax paid to Britain.

"That the whole wealth of the colonists centers at last in the mother country, which enables her to pay her taxes.

"That the colonies have, at the hazard of their lives and fortunes, extended the dominions and increased the commerce and riches of the mother country; that therefore the colonists do not deserve to be deprived of the native right of Britons, the right of being taxed only by representatives chosen by themselves.

"That an adequate representation in parliament would probably be acceptable to the colonists, and would best unite the views and interests of the whole empire."

The last of these propositions seems not to have been well considered, because an adequate representation in parliament is totally impracticable; but the others have exhausted the subject. If any one should ask what authority or evidence I have of this anecdote, I refer him to the second volume of Political Disquisitions, pages 276, 7, 8, 9. A book which ought to be in the hands of every American who has learned to read.

Whether the ministry at home, or the junto here, were discouraged by these masterly remarks, or by any other cause, the project of taxing the colonies was laid aside; Mr. Shirley was removed from this government, and Mr. Pownal was placed in his stead.

Mr. Pownal seems to have been a friend to liberty and to our constitution, and to have had an aversion to all plots against either, and consequently to have given his confidence to other persons than Hutchinson and Oliver, who, stung with envy against Mr. Pratt and others, who had the lead in affairs, set themselves, by propagating slanders against the Governor, among the people, and especially among the clergy, to raise discontents, and make him uneasy in his seat. Pownal, averse to wrangling, and fond of the delights of England, solicited to be recalled, and after some time Mr. Bernard was removed from New Jersey to the chair of this province.

Bernard was the man for the purpose of the junto. Educated in the highest principles of monarchy, naturally daring and courageous, skilled enough in law and policy to do mischief, and avaricious to a most infamous degree; needy at the same time, and having a numerous family to provide for, he was an instrument suitable in every respect, excepting one, for this junto to employ. The exception I mean, was blunt frankness, very opposite to that cautious cunning, that deep dissimulation, to which they had by long practice disciplined themselves. However, they did not despair of teaching him this necessary artful quality by degrees, and the event showed that they were not wholly unsuccessful, in their endeavours to do it.

While the war lasted, these simple provinces were of too much importance in the conduct of it, to be disgusted by any open attempt against their liberties. The junto, therefore, contented themselves with preparing their ground, by extending their connections and correspondencies in England, and by conciliating the friendship of the crown-officers occasionally here, and insinuating their designs as necessary to be undertaken in some future favourable opportunity, for the good of the empire, as well as of the colonies.

The designs of providence are inscrutable. It affords to bad men, conjunctures favourable for their designs, as well as to good. The conclusion of the peace was the most critical opportunity for our junto that could have presented. A peace founded on the destruction of that system of policy, the most glorious for the nation, that ever was formed, and which was never equalled in the conduct of the English government, except in the interregnum, and perhaps in the reign of Elizabeth; which system, however, by its being abruptly broken off, and its chief conductor discarded before it was compleated, proved unfortunate to the nation by leaving it sinking in a bottomless gulph of debt, oppressed and borne down with taxes.

At this lucky time, when the British financier was driven out of his wits for ways and means to supply the demands upon him, Bernard is employed by the junto, to suggest to him the project of taxing the Colonies by act of parliament.

I don't advance this without evidence. I appeal to a publication made by Sir Francis Bernard himself, the last year, of his own select letters on the trade and government of America, and the principles of law and polity applied to the American colonies. I shall make much use of this pamphlet before I have done.

In the year 1764, Mr. Bernard transmitted home to different noblemen and gentlemen, four copies of his principles of law and polity, with a preface, which proves incontestibly, that the project of new-regulating the American colonies were not first suggested to him by the ministry, but by him to them. The words of this preface are these: "The present expectation, that a new regulation of the American governments will soon take place, probably arises more from the opinion the public has of the abilities of the present ministry, than from any thing that has transpired from the cabinet. It cannot be supposed that their penetration can overlook the necessity of such a regulation, nor their public spirit fail to carry it into execution. But it may be a question, whether the present is a proper time for this work; more urgent business may stand before it; some preparatory steps may be required to precede it; but these will only serve to postpone. As we may expect that this reformation, like all others, will be opposed by powerful prejudices, it may not be amiss to reason with them at leisure, and endeavor to take off their force before they become opposed to government."

These are the words of that arch-enemy of North America, written in 1764, and then transmitted to four persons, with a desire that they might be communicated to others.

Upon these words, it is impossible not to observe: First, that the ministry had never signified to him any intention of new-regulating the colonies, and therefore, that it was he who most officiously and impertinently put them upon the pursuit of this *will-with-a-whisp,* which has led him and them into so much mire. 2. The artful flattery with which he insinuates these projects into the minds of the ministry, as matters of absolute necessity, which their great penetration could not fail to discover, nor their great regard to the public, omit. 3. The importunity with which he urges a speedy accomplishment of his pretended reformation of the governments, and 4. his consciousness that these schemes would be opposed, altho he affects to expect from powerful prejudices only, that opposition, which all Americans say, has been dictated by sound reason, true policy, and eternal justice. The last thing I shall take notice of is, the artful, yet most false and wicked insinuation, that such new regulations were then generally expected. This is so absolutely false, that excepting Bernard himself, and his junto, scarcely any body on this side the water, had any suspicion of it, insomuch that, if Bernard had made public, at that time, his preface and principles, as he sent them to the ministry, it is much to be doubted whether he could have lived in this country; certain it is, he would have had no friends in this province out of the junto.

The intention of the junto was, to procure a revenue to be raised in America by act of parliament. Nothing was further from their designs and wishes, than the drawing or sending this revenue into the exchequer in England, to be spent there in discharging the national debt, and lessening the burdens of the poor people there. They were more selfish. They chose to have the fingering of the money themselves. Their design was, that

the money should be applied, first in a large salary to the governor. This would gratify Bernard's avarice, and then it would
render him and all other governors, not only independent of
the people, but still more absolutely a slave to the will of the
minister. They intended likewise a salary for the lieut. governor. This would appease in some degree the gnawings of Hutchinson's avidity, in which he was not a whit behind Bernard
himself. In the next place, they intended a salary to the judges
of the common law, as well as admiralty. And thus, the whole
government, executive and judicial, was to be rendered wholly
independent of the people, (and their representatives rendered
useless, insignificant, and even burthensome,) and absolutely
dependent upon, and under the direction of the will of the
minister of state. They intended, further, to new model the
whole continent of North America, make an entire new division
of it into distinct, though more extensive and less numerous
colonies, to sweep away all the charters upon the continent with
the destroying besom of an act of parliament; and reduce all the
governments to the plan of the royal governments, with a nobility in each colony, not hereditary indeed, at first, but for life.
They did indeed flatter the ministry and people in England,
with distant hopes of a revenue from America, at some future
period, to be appropriated to national uses there. But this was
not to happen in their minds for some time. The governments
must be new-modelled, new-regulated, reformed first, and then
the governments here would be able and willing to carry into
execution any acts of parliament, or measures of the ministry,
for fleecing the people here, to pay debts, or support pensioners
on the American establishment, or bribe electors or members
of parliament, or any other purpose that a virtuous ministry
could desire.

But, as ill luck would have it, the British financier was as
selfish as themselves, and instead of raising money for them,
chose to raise it for himself. He put the cart before the horse.
He chose to get the revenue into the exchequer, because he had

hungry cormorants enough about him in England, whose cooings were more troublesome to his ears than the croaking of the ravens in America. And he thought if America could afford any revenue at all, and he could get it by authority of parliament, he might have it himself, to give to his friends, as well as raise it for the junto here, to spend themselves, or give to theirs. This unfortunate, preposterous improvement, of Mr. Grenville, upon the plan of the junto, had wellnigh ruined the whole.

I will proceed no further without producing my evidence. Indeed to a man who was acquainted with this junto, and had any opportunity to watch their motions, observe their language, and remark their countenances, for these last twelve years, no other evidence is necessary; it was plain to such persons what this junto were about. But we have evidence enough now under their own hands of the whole of what was said of them by their opposers, through this whole period.

Governor Bernard, in his letter of July 11, 1764, says, "that a general reformation of the American governments would become not only a desirable but a necessary measure." What his idea was, of a general reformation of the American governments, is to be learned from his principles of law and polity, which he sent to the ministry in 1764. I shall select a few of them in his own words; but I wish the whole of them could be printed in the news-papers, that America might know more generally the principles and designs and exertions of our junto.

His 29th proposition is: "The rule that a British subject shall not be bound by laws, or liable to taxes, but what he has consented to by his representatives, must be confined to the Inhabitants of Great-Britain only; and is not strictly true even there.

"30. The Parliament of Great-Britain, as well from its rights of sovereignty, as from occasional exigences, has a right to make laws for, and impose taxes upon its subjects in its external dominions, although they are not represented in such parliament. But,

"31. Taxes imposed upon the external dominions ought to be

applied to the use of the people from whom they are raised.

"32. The parliament of Great-Britain has a right and duty to take care to provide for the defence of the American colonies; especially as such colonies are unable to defend themselves.

"33. The parliament of Great-Britain has a right and a duty to take care that provision be made for a sufficient support of the American governments." Because,

"34. The support of the government is one of the principal conditions upon which a colony is allowed the power of legislation." Also, because,

"35. Some of the American colonies have shown themselves deficient in the support of their several governments, both as to sufficiency and independency."

His 75th proposition is: "Every American government is capable of having its constitution altered for the better.

"76. The grants of the powers of governments to American colonies by charters, cannot be understood to be intended for other than their infant or growing states.

"77. They cannot be intended for their mature state, that is, for perpetuity; because they are in many things unconstitutional, and contrary to the very nature of a British government. Therefore,

"78. They must be considered as designed only as temporary means, for settling and bringing forward the peopling the colonies; which being effected, the cause of the peculiarity of their constitution ceases.

"79. If the charters can be pleaded against the authority of parliament, they amount to an alienation of the dominions of Great Britain, and are, in effect, acts of dismembering the British empire, and will operate as such, if care is not taken to prevent it.

"83. The notion which has heretofore prevailed, that the dividing America into many governments, and different modes of government, will be the means to prevent their uniting to revolt, is ill-founded; since, if the governments were ever so much consolidated, it will be necessary to have so many distinct states, as to make a union to revolt impracticable." Whereas,

"84. The splitting America into many small governments, weakens the governing power and strengthens that of the people; and thereby makes revolting more probable and more practicable.

"85. To prevent revolts in future times, (for there is no room to fear them in the present,) the most effectual means would be, to make the governments large and respectable, and balance the powers of them.

"86. There is no government in America at present, whose powers are properly balanced; there not being in any of them a real and distinct third legislative power mediating between the king and the people, which is the peculiar excellence of the British constitution.

"87. The want of such a third legislative power adds weight to the popular, and lightens the royal scale, so as to destroy the balance between the royal and popular powers.

"88. Although America is not now, (and probably will not be for many years to come) ripe enough for a hereditary nobility, yet it is now capable of a nobility for life.

"89. A nobility appointed by the king for life, and made independent, would probably give strength and stability to the American governments as effectually as a hereditary nobility does to that of Great Britain.

"90. The reformation of the American governments should not be controlled by the present boundaries of the colonies, as they were mostly settled upon partial, occasional, and accidental considerations, without any regard to the whole.

"91. To settle the American governments to the greatest possible advantage, it will be necessary to reduce the number of them; in some places to unite and consolidate; in others to separate and transfer; and in general to divide by natural boundaries instead of imaginary lines.

"92. If there should be but one form of government established for all the North American provinces, it would greatly facilitate the reformation of them; since, if the mode of government was everywhere the same, people would be more indifferent under what division they were ranged.

"93. No objection ought to arise to the alteration of the boundaries of provinces from proprietors, on account of their property only; since there is no occasion that it should in the least affect the boundaries of properties.

"94. The present distinctions of one government being more free or more popular than another, tends to embarrass and to weaken the whole, and should not be allowed to subsist among people subject to one kind and one law, and all equally fit for one form of government.

"95. The American colonies, in general, are at this time arrived at that state, which qualifies them to receive the most perfect form of government which their situation and relation to Great-Britain make them capable of.

"96. The people of North America, at this time, expect a revisal and reformation of the American governments, and are better disposed to submit to it than ever they were, or perhaps ever will be again.

"97. This is, therefore, the proper and critical time to reform the American governments, upon a general, constitutional, firm, and durable plan; and if it is not done now, it will probably every day grow more difficult, till at last it becomes impracticable."

My friends, these are the words, the plans, principles and endeavours of Governor Bernard, in the year 1764. That Hutchinson and Oliver, notwithstanding all their disguises, which you well remember, were in unison with him in the whole of his measures, can be doubted by no man. It appeared sufficiently in the part they all along acted, notwithstanding their professions. And it appears incontestibly from their detected letters; of which more hereafter.

Now, let me ask you, if the parliament of Great-Britain had

all the natural foundations of authority, wisdom, goodness, justice, power, in as great perfection as they ever existed in any body of men since Adam's fall; and if the English nation was the most virtuous, pure, and free that ever was; would not such an unlimited subjection of three millions of people to that parliament, at three thousand miles distance be real slavery? There are but two sorts of men in the world, freemen and slaves. The very definition of a freeman is one who is bound by no law to which he has not consented. Americans would have no way of giving or withholding their consent to the acts of this parliament, therefore they would not be freemen. But when luxury, effeminacy, and venality are arrived at such a shocking pitch in England, when both electors and elected are become one mass of corruption, when the nation is oppressed to death with debts and taxes, owing to their own extravagance and want of wisdom, what would be your condition under such an absolute subjection to parliament? You would not only be slaves, but the most abject sort of slaves, to the worst sort of masters! at least this is my opinion. Judge you for yourselves between Massachusettensis and Novanglus.

[January 30, 1775]   Novanglus

III

My Friends,

This history of the Tories, begun in my last, will be interrupted for some time; but it shall be resumed, and minutely related in some future papers. Massachusettensis, who shall now be pursued in his own serpentine path, in his first paper complains that the press is not free; that a party, by playing off the resentment of the populace against printers and authors, has gained the ascendency so far as to become the licenser of it; that the press is become an engine of oppression and licentiousness, much devoted to the partisans of liberty, who have been indulged in publishing what they pleased, *fas vel nefas,* while little has been published on the part of government.

The art of this writer, which appears in all his productions, is very conspicuous in this. It is intended to excite a resentment against the friends of liberty, for tyrannically depriving their antagonists, of so important a branch of freedom, and a compassion towards the Tories, in the breasts of the people, in the other colonies and in Great Britain, in insinuating that they have not had equal terms. But nothing can be more injurious, nothing farther from the truth. Let us take a retrospective view of the period, since the last peace, and see, whether, they have not uniformly had the press at their service, without the least molestation to authors or printers. Indeed, I believe, that the Massachusetts Spy, if not the Boston Gazette, has been open to them as well as to others. The Evening Post, Massachusetts Gazette, and Boston Chronicle have certainly been always as free for their use as the air. Let us dismiss prejudice and passion, and examine impartially whether the Tories have not been chargeable with at least as many libels, as much licentiousness of the press, as the Whigs? Dr. Mayhew was a Whig of the first magnitude, a clergyman equalled by very few of any denomination in piety, virtue, genius, or learning, whose works will maintain his character as long as New-England shall be free, integrity esteemed, or wit, spirit, humour, reason, and knowledge admired. How was he treated from the press? Did not the Reverend Tories, who were pleased to write against him, the Missionaries of Defamation, as well as Bigotry and passive obedience, in their pamphlets and newspapers, bespatter him all over with their filth? With equal falsehood and malice charge him with every thing evil? Mr. Otis was in civil life, and a senator, whose parts, literature, eloquence, and integrity, proved him a character in the world equal to any of the time in which he flourished, of any party in the province. Now, be pleased to recollect the Evening Post. For a long course of years, that gentleman, his friends and connections, of whom the world has, and grateful posterity will have a better opinion than Massachusettensis will acknowledge, were pelted with the most infernally malicious, false, and atrocious Libels that ever issued from any press in Boston. I will mention no other names, lest I give too much offence to the modesty of some, and the envy and rancour of others.

There never was before, in any part of the world, a whole town insulted to their faces, as Boston was by the Boston Chronicle. Yet the printer was not molested for printing. It was his mad attack upon other printers with his clubs, and upon other gentlemen with his pistols, that was the cause, or rather the pretence, of his flight. The truth was, he became too polite to attend to his business; his shop was neglected; procreations* were coming for more than two thousand [pounds] sterling,

*Procurations—Ed.

which he had no inclination to pay.

Printers may have been less eager after the productions of the tories than of the whigs, and the reason has been, because the latter have been more consonant to the general taste and sense and consequently more in demand. Notwithstanding this, the former have ever found one press, at least, devoted to their service, and have used it as licentiously as they could wish. Whether the revenue-chest has kept it alive, and made it profitable against the general sense, or not, I wot not. Thus much is certain, that 200, 3[00], 4[00], 5[00], 600, 800, 1500 [pounds] sterling a year, has been the constant reward of every scribbler who has taken up the pen on the side of the ministry, with any reputation, and commissions have been given here for the most wretched productions of dulness itself. Whereas the writers on the side of liberty have been rewarded only with the consciousness of endeavoring to do good, with the approbation of the virtuous, and the malice of men in power.

But this is not the first time that writers have taken advantage of the times. Massachusettensis knows the critical situation of this province. The danger it is in, without government or law. The army in Boston. The people irritated and exasperated in such a manner as was never before borne by any people under heaven. Much depends upon their patience at this critical time, and such an example of patience and order this people have exhibited, in a state of nature, under such cruel insults, distresses, and provocations, as the history of mankind cannot parallel. In this state of things, protected by an army, the whole junto are now pouring forth the whole torrents of their billingsgate, propagating thousands of the most palpable falsehoods, when they know that the writers on the other side have been restrain'd by their prudence and caution from engaging in a controversy that must excite heats, lest it should have unhappy and tragical consequences.

There is nothing in this world so excellent that it may not be abused. The abuses of the press are notorious. It is much to be desired, that writers on all sides would be more careful of truth and decency; but, upon the most impartial estimate, the tories will be found to have been the least so of any party among us.

The honest Veteran, who ought not to be forgotten in this place, says, "If an inhabitant of Bern or Amsterdam could read the newspapers,&c., he would be at a loss how to reconcile oppression with such unbounded licence of the press, and would laugh at the charge, as something much more than a paradox, as a palpable contradiction." But with all his taste and manly spirit, the Veteran is little of a statesman. His ideas of liberty are quite inadequate; his notions of government very superficial. Licence of the press is no proof of liberty. When a people is corrupted, the press may be made an engine to compleat their ruin; and it is now notorious, that the ministry are daily employing it, to encrease and establish corruption, and to pluck up virtue by the roots. Liberty can no more exist without virtue and independence, than the body can live and move without a soul. When these are gone, and the popular branch of the constitution is become dependent on the minister, as it is in England, or cut off, as it is in America, all other forms of the constitution may remain; but if you look for liberty, you will grope in vain, and the freedom of the press, instead of promoting the cause of liberty, will but hasten its destruction, as the best cordials, taken by patients, in some distempers, become the most rancid and corrosive poisons. . . .

A stronger proof cannot be wish'd, of the scandalous license of the tory presses, than the swarms of pamphlets and speculations, in New York and Boston, since last October, "madness, folly, delusion, delirium, infatuation, frenzy, high treason, and rebellion," are charged in every page, upon three millions of as good and loyal, as sensible and virtuous people, as any in the empire; nay, upon that congress, which was as full and free a representative, as ever was constituted by any people, chosen universally without solicitation, or the least tincture of corruption; that congress which consisted of governors, counsellors, some of them by mandamus too, judges of supreme courts, speakers of assemblies, planters and merchants of the first fortune and character, and lawyers of the highest class, many of them educated at the temple, call'd to the bar in England, and of abilities and integrity equal to any there.

Massachusettensis, conscious that the people of this continent have the utmost abhorrence of treason and rebellion, labours to avail himself of the magic in these words. But his artifice is vain. The people are not to be intimidated by hard words, from a necessary defence of their liberties. Their attachment to their constitution, so dearly purchased by their own and their ancestors' blood and treasure; their aversion to the late innovations, their horror of arbitrary power and the Romish religion, are much deeper rooted than their dread of rude sounds and unmannerly language. They don't want the advice of an honest lawyer, if such an one could be found, nor will they be deceived by a dishonest one. They know what offence it is, to assemble, armed and, forcibly obstruct the course of justice. They have been many years considering and enquiring, they have been instructed by Massachusettensis and his friends, in the nature of treason, and the consequences of their own principles and actions. They know upon what hinge the whole dispute turns. That the *fundamentals* of the government over them are disputed, that the minister pretends, and had the influence to obtain the voice of the last parliament in his favour, that parliament is the only supream, sovereign, absolute, and uncontroulable legislative over all the colonies, that therefore the minister and all his advocates will call resistance to acts of parliament, by the names of treason and rebellion. But at the same time they know, that in their own opinions, and in the opinions of all the colonies, parliament has no authority over them, excepting to regulate their trade, and this not by any principle of common law, but merely by the consent of the colonies, founded on the obvious necessity of a case, which was never in contemplation of that law, nor provided for by it, that therefore they have as good a right to charge that minister, Massachusettensis, and the whole army to which he has fled for protection, with treason and rebellion. For if the parliament has not a legal authority to overturn their constitution, and subject them to such acts as are lately passed, every man, who accepts of any commission, and takes any steps to carry those acts into execution, is guilty of overt acts of treason and rebellion against his majesty, his royal crown and dignity, as much as if he should take arms against his troops, or attempt his sacred life. They know that the resistance against the Stamp Act, which was made through all America, was in the opinion of Massachusettensis and George Grenville, high treason, and that Brigadier Ruggles and good Mr. Ogden, pretended at the congress of New York, to be of the same mind, and have been held in utter contempt and derision by the whole continent, for the same reason, ever since; because, in their own opinion, that resistance was a noble stand against tyranny, and the only opposition to it, which could have been effectual. That if the American resistance to the act for destroying your charter, and to the Resolves for arresting persons here and sending them to England for tryal, is treason, the lords and commons, and the whole nation, were traitors at the revolution.

They know that all America is united in sentiment, and in the plan of opposition to the claims of administration and parliament. The junto in Boston, with their little flocks of adherents in the country, are not worth taking into the account; and the army and navy, tho' these are divided among themselves, are no part of America; in order to judge of this union, they begin at the commencement of the dispute, and run through the whole course of it. At the time of the Stamp Act, every colony expressed its sentiments by resolves of their assemblies, and every one agreed that parliament had no right to tax the colonies. The house of representatives of the Massachusetts Bay, then consisted of many persons, who have since figured as friends to government; yet every member of that house concurred most chearfully in the resolves then passed. The congress which met that year at New York, expressed the same opinion in their resolves. . . . The several assemblies expressed the same sentiments, and when your colony wrote the famous circular letter, notwithstanding all the mandates and threats, and cajolings of the minister and the several governors, and all the crown officers through the continent, the assemblies with one voice echoed their entire approbation of that letter, and their applause to your colony for sending it. In the year 1768, when a non-importation was suggested and planned by a few gentlemen at a private clubb in one of our large towns, as soon as it was proposed to the public, did it not spread thro' the whole continent? Was it not regarded, like the laws of the Medes and Persians, in almost all the colonies? When the paint and paper act was repealed, the southern colonies agreed to depart from the association in all things but the dutied articles, but they have kept strictly to their agreement against importing them, so that no tea worth the mentioning has been imported into any of them from Great Britain to this day. In the year 1770, when a number of persons were slaughtered in King Street, such was the brotherly sympathy of all the colonies, such their resentment against an hostile administration; that the innocent blood then spilt, has never been forgotten, nor the murderous minister and governors, who brought the troops here, forgiven, by any part of the continent, and never will be. When a certain masterly statesman, invented a committee of correspondence in Boston, which has provoked so much of the spleen of Massachusettensis, of which much more hereafter; did not every colony, nay, every county, city, hundred, and town upon the whole continent, adopt the measure. I had almost said, as if it had been a revelation from above, as the happiest means of cementing the union and acting in concert? What proofs of union have been given since the last March! Look over the resolves of the several colonies, and you will see that one understanding governs, one heart animates the whole body. Assemblies, conventions, congresses, towns, cities, and private clubs and circles, have been actuated by one great, wise, active and noble spirit, one masterly soul animating one vigorous body.

The congress at Philadelphia, have expressed the same sentiments with the people of New England, approved of the opposition to the late innovations, unanimously advised us to persevere in it, and assured us that if force is attempted to carry these measures against us, all America ought to support us. Maryland and the Lower Counties on Delaware, have already, to show to all the world their approbation of the measures of New England, and their determination to join in them, with a generosity, a wisdom, and magnanimity, which ought to make the Tories consider, taken the power of the militia into the hands of the people, without the governor or minister, and established it by their own authority, for the defence of Massachusetts, as well as of themselves. Other colonies are only waiting to see if the necessity of it will become more obvious. Virginia, and the Carolinas, are preparing for military defence, and have been for some time. When we consider the variety of climates, soils, religions, civil governments, commercial interests, &c. which were represented at the congress, and the various occupations, educations, and characters of the gentlemen who composed it, the harmony and unanimity which prevailed in it, can scarcely be parallelled in any assembly that ever met. When we consider, that at the revolution, such mighty questions, as whether the Throne was vacant or not, and whether the Prince of Orange should be king or not, were determined in the Convention Parliament by small majorities of two or three, and four or five only; the great majorities, the almost unanimity with which all great questions have been decided in your house of representatives, and other assemblies, and especially in the Continental Congress, cannot be considered in any other light than as the happiest omens indeed, as providential dispensations, in our favour, as well as the clearest demonstrations of the cordial, firm, radical, and indissoluble union of the colonies.

The grand aphorism of the policy of the whigs has been to unite the people of America, and divide those of Great Britain. The reverse of this has been the maxim of the tories, viz. to unite the people of Great Britain, and divide those of America. All the movements, marches, and countermarches of both parties, on both sides of the Atlantic, may be reduced to one or the other of these rules. I have shown, in opposition to Massachusetensis, that the people of America are united more perfectly than the most sanguine whig could ever have hoped, or than the most timid tory could have fear'd. Let us now examine whether the people of Great Britain are equally united against us. For if the contending countries were equally united, the prospect of success in the quarrel would depend upon the comparative wisdom, firmness, strength and other advantages of each. And if such a comparison was made, it would not appear to a demonstration that Great Britain could so easily subdue and conquer. It is not so easy a thing for the most powerful state to conquer a country a thousand leagues off. How many year's time, how many millions of money, did it take, with five and thirty-thousand men, to conquer the poor province of Canada? And after all the battles and victories, it never would have submitted, without a capitulation, which secured to them their religion and properties.

But we know that the people of Great Britain are not united against us. We distinguish between the Ministry, the House of Commons, the Officers of the Army, Navy, Excise, Customs, &c., who are dependent on the Ministry, and tempted if not obliged, to eccho their voices; and the body of the people. We are assured by thousands of letters from persons of good intelligence, by the general strain of publications in public papers, pamphlets, and magazines, and by some larger works written for posterity, that the body of the people are friends to America, and wish us success in our struggles against the claims of parliament and administration. We know that millions in England and Scotland will think it unrighteous, impolitic and ruinous, to make war upon us, and a minister, tho' he may have a marble heart, will proceed with a diffident, desponding spirit. We know that London and Bristol, the two greatest commerical cities in the empire, have declared themselves in the most decisive manner, in favour of our cause. So explicitly that the former has bound her members under their hands to assist us, and the latter has chosen two known friends of America, one attached to us by principle, birth, and the most ardent affection, the other an able advocate for us on several great occasions. We know that many of the most virtuous and independent of the nobility and gentry, are for us, and among them the best Bishop that adorns the bench, as great a Judge as the nation can boast, and the greatest statesman it ever saw. We know that the nation is loaded with debts and taxes, by the folly and iniquity of its ministers, and that, without the trade of America, it can neither long support its fleet and army, nor pay the interest of its debt.

But we are told that the nation is now united against us, that they hold, they have a right to tax us and legislate for us, as firmly as we deny it. That we are a part of the British Empire, that every state must have an uncontroulable power coextensive with the empire, that there is little probability of serving ourselves by ingenious distinctions between external and internal taxes. If we are not a part of the state, and subject to the supreme authority of parliament, Great-Britain will make us so; that if this opportunity of reclaiming the colonies is lost, they will be dismembered from the empire; and although they may continue their allegiance to the King, they will own none to the imperial crown.

To all this I answer, That the nation is not so united, that they do not so universally hold they have such a right, and my reasons I have given before. That the terms "British Empire" are not the language of the common law, but the language of newspapers and political pamphlets. That the dominions of the king of Great Britain has no uncontroulable power coextensive with them. I would ask by what law the parliament has authority over America? By the law of God in the Old and New Testament, it has none. By the law of nature and nations, it has none. By the common law of England it has none. For the common law, and the authority of parliament founded on it, never extended beyond the four seas. By statute law it has none, for no statute was made before the settlement of the colonies for this purpose; and the declaratory act made in 1766, was made without our consent, by a parliament which had no authority beyond the four seas. What religious, moral, or political obligation then are we under, to submit to parliament as a supreme legislative? None at all. When it is said, that if we are not subject to the supreme authority of parliament, Great Britain will make us so, all other laws and obligations are given up, and recourse is had to the *ratio ultima* of Louis the XIVth, and the *suprema lex* of the king of Sardinia, to the law of brickbats and cannon balls, which can be answer'd only by brickbats and balls.

This language, "the imperial crown of Great Britain," is not the style of the common law, but of court sycophants. It was introduced in allusion to the Roman empire, and intended to insinuate that the prerogative of the imperial crown of England, was like that of the Roman emperor, after the maxim was established, *quod principi placuit legis habet vigorem*, and so far from including the two houses of parliament in the idea of this imperial crown, it was intended to insinuate that the crown was absolute, and had no need of lords or commons to make or dispense with laws. Yet even these court sycophants, when driven to an explanation, never dared to put any other sense upon the words *imperial crown*, than this, that the crown of England was independent of France, Spain, and all other kings and states in the world.

When he says that the king's dominions must have an uncontroulable power, coextensive with them, I ask whether they have such power or not? and utterly deny that they have, by any law but that of Lewis the fourteenth and the king of Sardinia. If they have not, and it is necessary that they should have, it then follows that there is a defect in what he calls the British empire, and how shall this defect be supplied? It cannot be supplied consistently with reason, justice, policy, morality, or humanity, without the consent of the colonies, and some new plan of connection. But if Great Britain will set all these at defiance, and resort to the *ratio ultima,* all Europe will pronounce her a tyrant, and America never will submit to her, be the danger of disobedience as great as it will.

But there is no need of any other power than that of regulating trade, and this the colonies ever have been and will be ready and willing to concede to her. But she will never obtain from America any further concession while she exists.

We are then asked, "for what she protected and defended the colonies against the maritime power of Europe from their first settlement to this day?" I answer, for her own interest, because all the profits of our trade centered in her lap. But it ought to be remembered, that her name, not her purse, nor her fleets and armies, ever protected us, until the last war, and then the minister who conducted that war, informs us that the annual millions from America enabled her to do it.

We are then asked, for what she purchased New-York of the Dutch? I answer she never did. The Dutch never owned it, were never more than trespassers and intruders there, and were finally expelled by conquest. It was ceded it is true by the treaty of Breda, and it is said in some authors, that some other territory in India was ceded to the Dutch in lieu of it. But this was the transaction of the king, not of parliament, and therefore makes nothing to the argument. But admitting, for argument sake, (since the cautious Massachusettensis will urge us into the discussion of such questions,) what is not a supposeable case, that the nation should be so sunk in sloth, luxury and corruption, as to suffer their minister to persevere in his mad blunders, and send fire and sword against us, how shall we defend ourselves? The colonies south of Pennsylvania have no men to spare, we are told. But we know better, we know that all those colonies have a back country which is inhabited by a hardy, robust people, many of whom are emigrants from New England, and habituated, like multitudes of New Englandmen, to carry their fuzees or rifles upon one shoulder to defend themselves against the Indians, while they carry'd their axes, scythes, and hoes upon the other to till the ground. Did not those colonies furnish men the last war excepting Maryland. Did not Virginia furnish men, one regiment particularly equal to any regular regiment in the service. Does the soft Massachusettensis imagine that in the unnatural horrid war, he is now supposing their exertions would be less. If he does he is very ill informed of their principles, their present sentiments and temper. But "have you arms and ammunition?" I answer we have; but if we had not, we could make a sufficient quantity of both. What should hinder? We have many manufacturers of fire-arms now, whose arms are as good as any in the world. Powder has been made here, and may be again, and so may saltpetre. What should hinder? We have all the materials in great abundance, and the process is very simple. But if we neither had them nor could make them, we could import them. But "the British navy!" Ay, there's the rub. But let us consider, since the prudent Massachusettensis will have these questions debated. How many ships can Britain spare to carry on this humane and political war, the object of which is a pepper corn? let her send all the ships she has round her island. What if her ill-natured neighbours, France and Spain should strike a blow in their absence? in order to judge what they could all do when they arrived here, we should consider what they are all able to do round the island of Great Britain. We know that the utmost vigilance and exertions of them added to all the terms of sanguinary laws, are not sufficient to prevent continual smuggling, into their own island. Are there not 50 bays, harbours, creeks, and inlets upon the whole coast of North America, where there is one round the island of Great Britain. Is it to be supposed then, that the whole British navy could prevent the importation of arms and ammunition into America, if she should have occasion for them to defend herself against the hellish warfare, that is here supposed?

But what will you do for discipline and subordination? I answer we will have them in as great perfection as the regular troops. If the provincials were not brought in the last war to a proper discipline, what was the reason? Because regular generals would not let them fight, which they ardently wished, but employed them in cutting roads. If they had been allowed to fight they would have brought the war to a conclusion too soon. The provincials did submit to martial law, and to the mutiny and desertion act, the last war, and such an act may be made here by a legislature which they will obey with much more alacrity than an act of parliament.

The new-fangled militia, as the specious Massachusettensis calls it, is such a militia as he never saw. They are commanded through the province, not by men who procured their commissions from a governor as a reward for making themselves pimps to his tools, and by discovering a hatred of the people but by gentlemen whose estates, abilities, and benevolence, have rendered them the delight of the soldiers, and there is an esteem and respect for them visible through the province, which has not been used in the militia. Nor is there that unsteadiness that is charged upon them. In some places, where companies have been split into two or three, it has only served, by exciting an emulation between the companies, to encrease the martial spirit and skill.

The plausible Massachusettensis may write as he will, but in a land war, this continent might defend itself against all the world. We have men enough, and those men have as good natural understandings, and as much natural courage as any other men. If they were wholly ignorant now, they might learn the art of war. But at sea we are defenceless. A navy might burn our seaport towns. What then? If the insinuating Massachusettensis, has ever read any speculations concerning an Agrarian law, and I know he has, he will be satisfied that 350 thousand landholders, will not give up their rights and the constitution by which they hold them, to save fifty thousand inhabitants of maritime towns. Will the minister be nearer his mark, after he has burnt a beautiful town and murdered 30,000 innocent people? So far from it, that one such event would occasion the loss of all the colonies to Great Britain forever. It is not so clear that our trade, fishery, and navigation, could be taken from us. Some persons, who understand this subject better than Massachusetensis, with all his sprightly imaginations, are of a different opinion. They think that our trade would be increased. But I will not enlarge upon this subject, because I wish the trade of this continent, may be confined to Great Britain, at least as much of it, as it can do her any good to restrain.

The Canadians and savages are brought in to thicken the horrors of a picture with which the lively fancy of this writer has terrified him. But although we are sensible that the Quebec act has laid a foundation for a fabrick, which if not seasonably demolished, may be formidable, if not ruinous to the colonies, in future times, yet we know that these times are yet at a distance, at present we hold the power of the Canadians as nothing. But we know their dispositions are not unfriendly to us. The savages will be more likely to be our friends than enemies; but if they should not, we know well enough how to defend ourselves against them.

I ought to apologize for the immoderate length of this paper. But general assertions are only to be confuted by an examination of particulars, which necessarily fills up much space. I will trespass on the readers patience only while I make one observation more upon the art, I had almost said chicanery, of this writer.

He affirms that we are not united in this province, and that associations are forming in several parts of the province. The association he means has been laid before the public, and a very curious piece of ledgerdemain it is. Is there any article in it acknowledging the authority of parliament, the unlimited authority of parliament? Brigadier Ruggles himself, Massachusettensis himself, could not have signed it if there had, consistent with their known declared opinions. They associate to stand by the king's laws, and this every whig will subscribe. But after all, what a wretched fortune has this association made in the world, the numbers who have signed it would appear so inconsiderable, that I dare say the Brigadier will never publish to the world their numbers or names. But, "has not Great Britain been a nursing-mother to us?" Yes, and we have behaved as nurse-children commonly do, been very fond of her, and rewarded her all along tenfold for all her care and expense in our nurture.

But "is not all our distraction owing to parliament's taking off a shilling-duty on tea and imposing three pence, and is not this a more unaccountable frenzy, more disgraceful to the annals of America, than the witchcraft!"

Is the three pence upon tea our only grievance? Are we not in this province deprived of the priviledge of paying our governors, judges, &c.? Are not trials by jury taken from us?! Are we not to be sent to England for tryal! Is not a military government put over us? Is not our constitution demolished to the foundation? Have not the ministry shown by the Quebec bill, that we have no security against them for our religion any more than our property, if we once submit to the unlimited claims of parliament! This is so gross an attempt to impose on the most ignorant of the people, that it is a shame to answer it.

Obsta principiis, nip the shoots of arbitrary power in the bud, is the only maxim which can ever preserve the liberties of any people. When the people give way, their deceivers, betrayers and destroyers press upon them so fast that there is no resisting afterwards. The nature of the encroachment upon American constitution is such, as to grow every day more and more encroaching. Like a cancer, it eats faster and faster every hour. The revenue creates pensioners, and the pensioners urge for more revenue. The people grow less steady, spirited, and virtuous, the seekers more numerous and more corrupt and every day increases the circles of their dependents and expectants, untill virtue, integrity, public spirit, simplicity, frugality, become the objects of ridicule and scorn, and vanity, luxury, foppery, selfishness, meanness, and downright venality swallow up the whole society.

[February 6, 1775]   Novanglus

IV

Massachusettensis, whose pen can wheedle with the tongue of King Richard the third, in his first paper, threatens you with the vengeance of Great Britain, and assures you, that if she had no authority over you, yet she would support her claims by her fleets and armies, Canadians and Indians. In his next, he alters his tone, and soothes you with the generosity, justice, and humanity of the nation.

I shall leave him to show how a nation can claim an authority which they have not by right, and support it by fire and sword, and yet be generous and just. The nation, I believe, is not vindictive, but the minister has discovered himself to be so in a degree that would disgrace a warrior of a savage tribe.

The wily Massachusettensis thinks our present calamity is to be attributed to the bad policy of a popular party, whose measures, whatever their intentions were, have been opposite to their profession, the public good. The present calamity seems to be nothing more nor less than reviving the plans of Mr. Bernard and the junto, and Mr. Grenville and his friends, in 1764. Surely this party are, and have been, rather unpopular. The popular party did not write Bernard's letters, who so long ago pressed for the demolition of all the charters upon the continent, and a parliamentary taxation to support government and the administration of justice in America. The popular party did not write Oliver's letters, who enforces Bernard's plans; nor Hutchinson's, who pleads with all his eloquence and pathos for parliamentary penalties, ministerial vengeance, and an abridgment of English liberties.

There is not in human nature a more wonderful phenomenon, nor in the whole theory of it a more intricate speculation, than the *shiftings, turnings, windings,* and *evasions* of a guilty conscience. Such is our unalterable moral constitution, that an internal inclination to do wrong is criminal; and a wicked thought stains the mind with guilt, and makes it tingle with pain. Hence it comes to pass, that the guilty mind can never bear to think that its guilt is known to God or man, no, nor to itself.

> "Cur tamen hos tu
> Evasisse putes, quos diri conscia sacti
> Mens habet attonitos, et surdo verbere caedit
> Occultum quatiente animo tortore flagellum?
> Poena autem vehemens ac multo saevior illis,
> Quas et Caeditius gravis invenit aut Rhadamanthus,
> Nocte dieque suum gestare in pectore testem."*

*Juv.Sat.13. 192.

Massachusettensis and his friends the tories are startled at the calamities they have brought upon their country; and their conscious guilt, their smarting, wounded mind, will not suffer them to confess, even to themselves, what they have done. Their silly denials of their own share in it, before a people who, they know, have abundant evidence against them, never fail to remind me of an ancient *fugitive,* whose conscience could not bear the recollection of what he had done. "I know not; am I my brother's keeper?" he replies, with all the apparent simplicity of truth and innocence, to one from whom he was very sensible his guilt could not be hid. The still more absurd and ridiculous attempts of the tories, to throw off the blame of these calamities from themselves to the whigs, remind me of another story, which I have read in the Old Testament. When Joseph's brethren had sold him to the Ishmaelites for twenty pieces of silver, in order to conceal their own avarice, malice, and envy, they dip the coat of many colors in the blood of a kid, and say that an evil beast had rent him in pieces and devoured him. However, what the sons of Israel intended for ruin to Joseph, proved the salvation of the family; and I hope and believe that the whigs will have the magnanimity, like him, to suppress their resentment, and the felicity of saving their ungrateful brothers.

This writer has a faculty of insinuating errors into the mind almost imperceptibly, he dresses them so in the guise of truth. He says, that "the revenue to the crown from America amounted to but little more than the charges of collecting it," at the close of the last war. I believe it did not to so much. The truth is, there never was a pretence of raising a revenue in America before that time, and when the claim was first set up, it gave an alarm like a warlike expedition against us. True it is, that some duties had been laid before by parliament, under pretence of regulating our trade, and, by a collusion and combination between the West India planters and the North American governors, some years before, duties had been laid upon molasses, &c. under the same pretence; but, in reality, merely to advance the value of the estates of the planters in the West India Islands, and to put some plunder, under the name of thirds of seizures, into the pockets of the governors. But these duties, though more had been collected in this province than in any other, in proportion, were never regularly collected in any of the colonies. So that the idea of an American revenue, for one purpose or another, had never, at this time, been formed in American minds.

Our writer goes on: "She Great-Britain tho't it as reasonable that the colonies should bear a part of the national burthen, as that they should share in the national benefit."

Upon this subject Americans have a great deal to say. The national debt, before the last war, was near an hundred millions. Surely America had no share in running into that debt.

What is the reason, then, that she should pay it? But a small part of the sixty millions spent in the last war was for her benefit. Did she not bear her full share of the burden of the last war in America? Did not the province pay twelve shillings in the pound in taxes for the support of it; and send a sixth or seventh part of her sons into actual service? And, at the conclusion of the war, was she not left half a million sterling in debt? Did not all the rest of New England exert itself in proportion? What is the reason that the Massachusetts has paid its debt, and the British minister, in thirteen years of peace, has paid none of his? Much of it might have been paid in this time, had not such extravagance and peculation prevailed, as ought to be an eternal warning to America, never to trust such a minister with her money. What is the reason that the great and necessary virtues of simplicity, frugality, and economy cannot live in England, Scotland, and Ireland, as well as America?

We have much more to say still. Great Britain has confined all our trade to herself. We are willing she should, so far as it can be for the good of the empire. But we say, that we ought to be allowed as credit, in the account of public burdens and expenses, so much, paid in taxes, as we are obliged to sell our commodities to her cheaper than we could get for them at foreign markets. This difference is really a tax upon us, for the good of the empire. We are obliged to take from Great-Britain commodities that we could purchase cheaper elsewhere. This difference is a tax upon us for the good of the empire. We submit to this chearfully; but insist that we ought to have credit for it in the account of the expences of the empire, because it is really a tax upon us.

Another thing. I will venture a bold assertion. Let Massachusettensis or any other friend of the minister, confute me. The three million Americans, by the tax aforesaid upon what they are obliged to export to Great-Britain only, what they are obliged to import from Great-Britain only, and the quantities of British manufactures which in these climates they are obliged to consume more than the like number of people in any part of the three kingdoms, ultimately pay more of the taxes and duties that are apparently paid in Great-Britain, than any three million subjects in the three kingdoms. All this may be computed and reduced to stubborn figures, by the minister, if he pleases. We cannot do it. We have not the accounts, records, &c. Now let this account be fairly stated, and I will engage for America, upon any penalty, that she will pay the overplus, if any, in her own constitutional way, provided it is to be applied for national purposes, as paying off the national debt, maintaining the fleet, &c., not to the support of a standing army in time of peace, placemen, pensioners, &c.

Besides, every farthing of expence which has been incurred, on pretence of protecting, defending, and securing America, since the last war, has been worse than thrown away, it has been applied to do mischief. Keeping an army in America has been nothing but a public nuisance.

Furthermore, we see that all the public money that is raised here, and have reason to believe all that will or can be raised, will be applied, not for public purposes, national or provincial, but merely to corrupt the sons of America, and create a faction to destroy its interest and happiness.

There is scarcely three sentences together, in all the voluminous productions of this plausible writer, which do not convey some error in fact or principle, tinged with a colouring to make it pass for truth. He says "the idea, that the stamps were a tax, not only exceeding our proportion, but beyond our utmost ability to pay, united the colonies generally in opposing it." That we thought it beyond our proportion and ability is true, but it was not this thought which united the colonies in opposing it. When he says that at first we did not dream of denying the authority of parliament to tax us, much less to legislate for us, he discovers plainly either a total inattention to the sentiments of America at that time, or a disregard of what he affirms.

The truth is, the authority of parliament was never generally acknowledged in America. More than a century since, the Massachusetts and Virginia both protested against even the act of navigation, and refused obedience, for this very reason, because they were not represented in parliament and were therefore not bound; and afterwards confirmed it by their own provincial authority. And from that time to this, the general sense of the colonies has been, that the authority of parliament was confined to the regulation of trade, and did not extend to taxation or internal legislation.

In the year 1764, your house of representatives sent home a petition to the king against the plan of taxing them. Mr. Hutchinson, Oliver, and their relations and connections were then in the legislature, and had great influence there. It was by their influence that the two houses were induced to waive the word rights and an express denial of the right of parliament to tax us, to the great grief and distress of the friends of liberty in both houses. Mr. Otis and Mr. Thatcher laboured in the committee to obtain an express denial. Mr. Hutchinson expressly said, he agreed with them in opinion, that parliament had no right, but thought it ill policy to express this opinion in the petition. In truth, I will be bold to say, there was not any member of either house who thought that parliament had such a right at that time. The house of representatives, at that time, gave their approbation to Mr. Otis's Rights of the Colonies, in which it was shewn to be inconsistent with the right of British subjects to be taxed but by their own representatives.

In 1765, our house expressly resolved against the right of parliament to tax us. The Congress at New York resolved

"3. That it is inseparably essential to the freedom of a people, and the undoubted right of Englishmen, that no tax be imposed on them, but with their own consent, given personally, or by their representatives.

"4. That the people of the colonies are not, and from their local circumstances cannot, be represented in the house of Commons of Great-Britain.

"5. That the only representatives of the people of the colonies are the persons chosen therein by themselves; and that no taxes ever have been, or can be constitutionally imposed on them, but by their respective legislatures."

Is it not a striking disregard to truth, in the artful Massachusettensis, to say, that at first we did not dream of denying the right of parliament to tax us? It was the principle that united the colonies to oppose it, not the quantum of the tax. Did not Dr. Franklin deny the right in 1754, in his remarks upon Governor Shirley's scheme, and suppose that all America would deny it? We had considered ourselves as connected with Great-Britain, but we never thought parliament the supreme legislature over us. We never generally supposed it to have any authority over us, but from necessity, and that necessity we thought confined to the regulation of trade, and to such matters as concern'd all the colonies together. We never allowed them any authority in our internal concerns.

This writer says, acts of parliament for regulating our internal polity were familiar. This I deny. So far otherwise, that the hatter's act was never regarded; the act to destroy the Land Bank Scheme raised a greater ferment in this province than the Stamp-Act did, which was appeased only by passing province laws directly in opposition to it. The act against slitting-mills and tilt-hammers never was executed here. As to the postage, it was so useful a regulation, so few persons paid it, and they found such a benefit by it, that little opposition was made to it: yet every man who thought about it, call'd it an usurpation. Duties for regulating trade we paid, because we thought it just and necessary that they should regulate the trade which their power protected. As for duties for a revenue, none were ever laid by parliament for that purpose, until 1764, when, and ever since, its authority to do it has been constantly denied. Nor is this complaisant writer near the truth when he says, "We knew that in all those acts of government, the good of the whole had been consulted." On the contrary, we know that the private interest of provincial governors and West India planters had been consulted in the duties on foreign molasses, &c. and the private interest of a few Portugal merchants, in obliging us to touch at Falmouth with Fruit, &c., in opposition to the good of the whole, and in many other instances.

The resolves of the House of Burgesses of Virginia upon the stamp act did great honor to that province, and to the eminent patriot, Patrick Henry, who composed them. But these resolves made no alteration in the opinion of the colonies, concerning the right of parliament to make that act. They expressed the universal opinion of the continent at that time; and the alacrity with which every other colony, and the Congress at New York, adopted the same sentiment in similar resolves, proves the entire union of the colonies in it, and their universal determination to avow and support it. What follows here, that it became so popular, that his life was in danger who suggested the contrary? and that the Press was open to one side only, are direct misrepresentations and wicked calumnies.

Then we are told, by this sincere writer, that when we obtained a partial repeal of the statute imposing duties on glass, paper, and teas, this was the lucky moment when to have closed the dispute. What? with a Board of Commissioners remaining, the sole end of whose creation was to form and conduct a revenue? With an act of parliament remaining, the professed design of which, expressed in the preamble, was to raise a revenue, and appropriate it to the payment of governors and judges salaries; the duty remaining, too, upon an article which must raise a large sum, the consumption of which would constantly increase? Was this a time to retreat? Let me ask this sincere writer a simple question. Does he seriously believe that the designs of imposing other taxes, and of new-modling our governments, would have been laid aside, by the ministry or by the servants of the crown here? Does he think that Mr. Bernard, Mr. Hutchinson, the Commissioners, and others would have been content then to have desisted? If he really thinks so, he knows little of the human heart, and still less of those gentlemens hearts. It was at this very time that the salary was given to the governor, and an order soliciting for that to the judges.

Then we are entertained with a great deal of ingenious talk about Whigs and Tories, and at last are told, that some of the Whigs owed all their importance to popularity. And what then? Did not as many of the Tories owe their importance to popularity? And did not many more owe all their importance to unpopularity? If it had not been for their taking an active part on the side of the ministry, would not some of the most conspicuous and eminent of them have been unimportant enough? Indeed, through the two last administrations to despise and hate the people, and to be despised and hated by them, were the principal recommendations to the favours of government, and all the qualification that was required.

The Tories, says he, were for closing the controversy. That is, they were for contending no more, and it was equally true, that they never were for contending at all, but lying at mercy. It was the very end they had aimed at from the beginning. They had now got the Governor's salary out of the revenue, a number of pensions and places, and they knew they could at any time get the judges salaries from the same fountain, and they wanted to get the people reconcil'd and familiarised to this, before they went upon any new projects.

The Whigs were averse to restoring government, they even refused to revive a temporary riot act which expired about this time. Government had as much vigour then as ever, excepting only in those cases which affected this dispute. The riot act expired in 1770, immediately after the Massacre in King Street. It was not revived and never will be in this colony, nor will any one ever be made in any other, while a standing army is illegally posted here to butcher the people, whenever a governor or a magistrate, who may be a tool, shall order it. "Perhaps the Whigs tho't that mobs were a necessary ingredient in their system of opposition." Whether they did or no, it is certain that mobs have been thought a necessary ingredient by the Tories in their system of administration, mobs of the worst sort, with red coats, fusees, and bayonets, and the lives and limbs of the whigs have been in greater danger from these, than ever the tories were from others.

"The scheme of the whigs flattered the people with the idea of independence; the tories plan supposed a degree of subordination." This is artful enough, as usual, not to say jesuitical. The word independence is one of those, which this writer uses, as he does treason and rebellion, to impose upon the undistinguishing on both sides of the Atlantic. But let us take him to pieces. What does he mean by independence? Does he mean independent of the crown of Great-Britain, and an independent republic in America, or a confederation of independent republics? No doubt he intended the undistinguishing should understand him so. If he did, nothing can be more wicked, or a greater slander on the whigs, because he knows there is not a man in the province among the whigs, nor ever was, who harbours a wish of that sort. Does he mean that the people were flattered with the idea of total independence o[f] parliament? If he does, this is equally malicious and injurious, because he knows that the equity and necessity of parliament's regulating trade has always been acknowledged, our determination to consent and submit to such regulations constantly expressed, and all the acts of trade in fact to this very day, much more submitted to and strictly executed in this province, than any other in America.

There is equal ambiguity, in the words "degree of subordination." The whigs acknowledge a subordination to the king, in as strict and strong a sense as the tories. The whigs acknowledge a voluntary subordination to parliament, as far as the regulation of trade. What degree of subordination, then, do the tories acknowledge? An absolute dependence upon parliament as their supreme legislative, in all cases whatsoever, in their internal polity, as well as taxation? This would be too gross, and would loose him all his readers, for there is nobody here who will expose his understanding so much, as explicitly to adopt such a sentiment. Yet it is such an absolute independence and submission that these writers would persuade us to, or else there is no need of changing our sentiments and conduct. Why will not these gentlemen speak out, shew us plainly their opinion, that the new government they have fabricated for this province is better than the old, and that all the other measures we complain of are for our and the public good, and exhort us directly to submit to them? The reason is, because they know they should loose their readers.

"The whigs were sensible that there was no oppression that could be seen or felt." The tories have so often said and wrote this to one another, that I sometimes suspect they believe it to be true. But it is quite otherwise. The castle of the province was taken out of their hands and garrisoned by regular soldiers; this they could see, and they thought it indicated an hostile intention and disposition towards them. They continually paid their money to collectors of duties, this they could both see and feel. An host of placemen, whose whole business it was to collect a revenue, were continually rolling before them in their chariots. These they saw. Their governor was no longer paid by themselves, according to their charter, but out of the new revenue, in order to render their assemblies useless, and indeed contemptible. The judges salaries were threatened every day to be paid in the same unconstitutional manner. The dullest eye-sight could not but see to what all this tended, viz.—to prepare the way for greater innovations and oppressions. They knew a minister would never spend his money in this way, if he had not some end to answer by it. Another thing they both saw and felt. Every man, of every character, who, by voting, writing, speaking, or otherwise, had favoured the stamp act, the tea act, and every other measure of a minister or governor, who they knew was aiming at the destruction of their form of government, and introducing parliamentary taxation, was uniformly, in some department or other, promoted to some place of honour and profit for ten years together; and, on the other hand, every man who favoured the people in their opposition to those innovations, was depressed, degraded, and persecuted, as far as it was in the power of the government to do it.

This they considered as a systematical means of encouraging every man of abilities to espouse the cause of parliamentary taxation, and the plan of destroying their charter privileges, and to discourage all from exerting themselves in opposition to them. This they thought a plan to enslave them, for they uniformly think that the destruction of their charter, making the council and judges wholly dependent on the crown, and the people subject to the unlimited power of parliament as their supreme legislative, is slavery. They were certainly rightly told then that the ministry and their governors together had formed a design to enslave them, and that when once this was done, they had the highest reason to expect window-taxes, hearth-taxes, land-taxes, and all others; and that these were only paving the way for reducing the country to lordships. Were the people mistaken in these suspicions? Is it not now certain, that Governor Bernard, in 1769, had formed a design of this sort? Read his principles of polity—and that Lieutenant-Governor Oliver, as late as 1768 or 9 inforced the same plan? Read his letters.

Now, if Massachusettensis will be ingenuous, avow this design, shew the people its utility, and that it ought to be done by parliament, he will act the part of an honest man. But to insinuate that there was no such plan, when he knows there was, is acting the part of one of the junto.

It is true, that the people of this country in general, and of this province in special, have an hereditary apprehension of and aversion to lordships, temporal and spiritual. Their ancestors fled to this wilderness to avoid them. They suffer'd sufficiently under them in England. And there are few of the present generation who have not been warned of the danger of them by their fathers or grandfathers, and injoined to oppose them. And neither Bernard nor Oliver ever dared to avow before them, the designs which they had certainly formed to introduce them. Nor does Massachusettensis dare to avow his opinion in their favour. I don't mean that such avowal would expose their persons to danger, but their characters and writings to universal contempt.

When you were told that the people of England were depraved, the parliament venal, and the ministry corrupt, were you not told most melancholy truths? Will Massachusettensis deny any of them? Does not every man who comes from England, whig or tory, tell you the same thing? Do they make any secret of it, or use any delicacy about it? Do they not most of them avow that corruption is so established there, as to be incurable, and a necessary instrument of government? Is not the British constitution arrived nearly to that point, where the Roman republic was when Jugurtha left it, and pronounced it, a venal city, ripe for destruction, if it can only find a purchaser? If Massachusettensis can prove that it is not, he will remove from my mind, one of the heaviest loads which lies upon it.

Who has censured the tories for remissness, I know not. Whoever it was, he did them great injustice. Every one that I know of that character, has been thro' the whole tempestuous period, as indefatigable as human nature will admit, going about seeking whom he might devour, making use of art, flattery, terror, temptation, and allurement, in every shape in which human wit could dress it up, in public and private. But all to no purpose. The people have grown more and more weary of them every day, untill now the land mourns under them.

Massachusettensis is then seized with a violent fit of anger at the clergy. It is curious to observe the conduct of the Tories towards this sacred body. If a clergyman preaches against the principles of the revolution, and tells the people that upon pain of damnation they must submit to an established government of whatever character, the Tories cry him up as an excellent man, and a wonderful preacher, invite him to their tables, procure him missions from the society, and chaplainships to the navy and flatter him with the hopes of lawn sleeves. But if a clergyman preaches Christianity, and tells the magistrates that they were not distinguished from their brethren for their private emolument, but for the good of the people, that the people are bound in conscience to obey a good government, but are not bound to submit to one that aims at destroying all the ends of government—Oh Sedition! Treason!

The clergy in all ages and countries, and in this in particular, are disposed enough to be on the side of government, as long as it is tolerable. If they have not been generally in the late administrations on that side, it is a demonstration that the late administration has been universally odious.

The clergy of this province are a virtuous, sensible and learned set of men, and they don't take their sermons from news-papers but the bible, unless it be a few, who preach passive obedience. These are not generally curious enough to read Hobbes.

It is the duty of the clergy to accommodate their discourses to the times, to preach against such sins as are most prevalent, and recommend such virtues as are most wanted. For example, if exorbitant ambition and venality are predominant, ought they not to warn their hearers against these vices? If public spirit is much wanted, should they not inculcate this great virtue? If the rights and duties of Christian magistrates and subjects are disputed, should they not explain them, show their nature, ends, limitations, and restrictions, how much soever it may move the gall of Massachusettensis?

Let me put a supposition. Justice is a great Christian, as well as moral duty and virtue, which the clergy ought to inculcate and explain. Suppose a great man of a parish should for seven years together receive 600 sterling a year, for discharging the duties of an important office; but, during the whole time, should never do one act or take one step about it. Would not this be great injustice to the public? And ought not the parson of that parish to cry aloud and spare not, and show such a bold transgressor his sin? Show that justice was due to the public as well as to an individual, and that cheating the public of four thousand two hundred pounds sterling is at least as great a sin as taking a chicken from a private hen roost, or perhaps a watch from a fob!

Then we are told that newspapers and preachers have excited outrages disgraceful to humanity. Upon this subject I will venture to say, that there have been outrages in this province which I neither justify, excuse, nor extenuate; but these were not excited, that I know of, by newspapers or sermons. That, however, if we run through the last ten years and consider all the tumults and outrages that have happened, and at the same time recollect the insults, provocations, and oppressions which this people have endured; we shall find the two characteristicks of this people, religion and humanity, strongly marked on all their proceedings, not a life, nor that I have ever heard, a single limb has been lost thro' the whole. I will take upon me to say, there is not another province on this continent, nor in his majesty's dominions, where the people, under the same indignities, would not have gone greater lengths. Consider the tumults in the three kingdoms, consider the tumults in ancient Rome, in the most virtuous of her periods, and compare them with ours. It is a saying of Machiavel, which no wise man ever contradicted, which has been literally verified in this province, that "while the mass of the people is not corrupted, tumults do no hurt." By which he means, that they leave no lasting ill effects behind.

But let us consider the outrages committed by the Tories. Half a dozen men shot dead in an instant, in King Street, frequent resistance and affronts to civil officers and magistrates, officers, watchmen, citizens, cut and mangled in a most inhuman manner. Not to mention the shootings for desertion, and the frequent cruel whippings for other faults, cutting and mangling men's bodies before the eyes of citizens, spectacles which ought never to be introduced into populous places. The worst sort of tumults and outrages ever committed in this province were excited by the tories. But more of this hereafter.

We are then told, that the whigs erected a provincial democracy, or republic, in the province. I wish Massachusettensis knew what a democracy or republic is. But this subject must be considered another time.

[February 13, 1775]   Novanglus

V

We are at length arrived at the paper, on which I made a few strictures some weeks ago; these I shall not repeat, but proceed to consider the other part of it.

We are told "It is an universal truth, that he that would excite a rebellion, is at heart as great a tyrant as ever wielded the iron rod of oppression." Be it so. We are not exciting a rebellion. Opposition, nay open, avowed resistance by arms, against usurpation and lawless violence, is not rebellion by the law of God, or the land. Resistance to lawful authority makes rebellion. Hampden, Russell, Sidney, Somers, Holt, Tillotson, Burnet, Hoadly, &c. were no tyrants nor rebels, altho' some of them were in arms, and the others undoubtedly excited resistance, against the tories. Don't beg the question, Mr. Massachusettensis, and then give yourself airs of triumph. Remember the frank Veteran acknowledges, that "the word rebel is a convertible term."

This writer next attempts to trace the spirit of opposition, through the general court, and the courts of common law. "It was the policy of the whigs, to have their questions upon high matters determined by yea and nay votes, which were published in the gazettes." And ought not great questions to be so determined? In many assemblies, New-York particularly, they always are. What better way can be devised to discover the true sense of the people? It is extreamly provoking to courtiers that they can't vote, as the cabinet direct them, against their consciences, the known sense of their constituents, and the obvious good of the community, without being detected. Generally, perhaps universally, no unpopular measure in a free government, particularly the English, ought ever to pass. Why have the people a share in the legislature, but to prevent such measures from passing, I mean such as are disapproved by the people at large? But did not these yea and nay votes expose the whigs, as well as tories, to the impartial judgment of the public? If the votes of the former were given for measures injurious to the community, had not the latter an equal opportunity of improving them to the disadvantage of their adversaries in the next election? Besides, were not those few persons in the house, who generally voted for unpopular measures, near the governor, in possession of his confidence? Had they not the absolute disposal in their towns and counties of the favours of government? Were not all the judges, justices, sheriffs, coroners, and military officers in their towns, made upon their recommendation? Did not this give them a prodigious weight and influence? Had the whigs any such advantage? And does not the influence of these yea and nay votes, consequently prove to a demonstration the unanimity of the people, against the measures of the court?

As to what is said of "severe strictures, illiberal invectives, abuse, and scurrility, upon the dissentients," there was quite as much of all these published against the leading whigs. In truth, the strictures, &c. against the tories were generally nothing more than hints at the particular place or office, which was known to be the temptation to vote against the country. That "the dissentient was in danger of losing his bread and involving his family in ruin," is equally injurious. Not an instance can be produced, of a member, losing his bread, or injuring his business, by voting for unpopular measures. On the contrary, such voters never failed to obtain some lucrative employment, title or honorary office, as a reward from the court.

If "one set of members in committee, had always prepared the resolves," &c., which they did not, what would this prove but that this set was thought by the house the fittest for the purpose? Can it ever be otherwise? Will any popular assembly chuse its worst members for the best services? Will an assembly of patriots chuse courtiers to prepare votes against the court? No resolves against the claims of parliament or administration, or the measures of the governor, (excepting those against the Stamp Act, and perhaps the answers to Governor Hutchinson's speeches upon the supremacy of parliament) ever passed through the house, without meeting an obstacle. The governor had to the last hour of the house's existence, always some seekers and expectants in the house, who never failed to oppose, and offer the best arguments they could, and were always patiently heard. That the lips of the dissentients were sealed up; that they sat in silence, and beheld with regret, measures they dar'd not oppose, are groundless suggestions, and gross reflections upon the honour or courage of those members. The debates of this house were public, and every man who has attended the gallery knows there never was more freedom of debate, in any assembly.

Massachusettensis, in the next place, conducts us to the agent, and tells us "there cannot be a provincial agent without an appointment by the three branches of the assembly. The whigs soon found that they could not have such services rendered them, from a provincial agent as would answer their purposes."

The treatment this province has received, respecting the agency, since Mr. Hutchinson's administration commenced, is a flagrant example of injustice. There is no law, which requires the province to maintain any agent in England, much less is there any reason which necessarily requires, that the three branches should join in the appointment. In ordinary times, indeed, when a harmony prevails among the branches, it is well enough to have an agent constituted by all. But in times when the foundations of the constitution are disputed, and certainly attacked, by one branch or the other, to pretend that the house ought to join the governor in the choice, is a palpable absurdity.

It is equivalent to saying that the people shall have no agent at all; that all communication between them and their sovereign shall be cut off; and that there shall be no channel through which complaints and petitions may be conveyed to the royal ear: because a governor will not concur in an agent whose sentiments are not like his; nor will an agent of the governor's appointment be likely to urge accusations against him with any diligence or zeal, if the people have occasion to complain against him.

Every private citizen, much more every representative body, has an undoubted right to petition the king, to convey such petition by any agent, and to pay him for his service. Mr. Bernard, to do him justice, had so much regard to these principles, as to consent to the payment of the people's agents while he staid. But Mr. Hutchinson was scarcely seated in the chair as lieutenant-governor, before we had intelligence from England, that my Lord Hillsborough told Dr. Franklin, he had received a letter from Governor Hutchinson soliciting an instruction against consenting to the salary of the agent. Such an instruction was accordingly soon sent, and no agent for the board or house has received a farthing for services since that time, though Dr. Franklin and Mr. Bollan have taken much pains, and one of them expended considerable sums of money. There is a meanness in this play that would disgrace a gambler. A manifest fear that the truth should be known to the sovereign or the people. Many persons have thought that the province ought to have dismiss'd all agents from that time, as useless and nugatory; this behaviour amounting to a declaration, that we had no chance or hopes of justice from a minister.

But this province, at least as meritorious as any, has been long accustomed to indignities and injustice, and to bear both with unparalleled patience. Others, have pursued the same method before and since, but we have never heard that their agents are unpaid. They would scarcely have born it with so much resignation.

It is great assurance to blame the house for this, which was both their right and duty; but a stain in the character of his patron, which will not be soon worn out. Indeed this passage seems to have been bro't, in chiefly for the sake of a stroke or two, addressed to the lowest and meanest of the people; I mean the insinuation, that the two Agents doubled the Expense, which is as groundless as it is contracted; and that the ostensible agent for the province was only agent for a few individuals, that had got the art of wielding the house; and that several hundreds sterling a year, for attending levees and writing letters, were worth preserving. We, my friends, know that no members have the art of wielding us or our house, but by concurring in our principles, and assisting us in our designs. Numbers in both houses have turn'd about, and expected to wield us round with them; but they have been disappointed, and ever will be. Such apostates have never yet fail'd of our utter contempt, whatever titles, places, or pensions they might obtain.

The agent has never ecchoed back, or transmitted to America, any sentiments, which he did not give in substance to Governor Shirley, twenty years ago; and therefore this insinuation is but another slander. The remainder of what is said of the agency is levell'd at Dr. Franklin, and is but a dull appendix to Wedderburn's ribaldry, having all his malice without any of his wit or spirit. Nero murdered Seneca that he might pull up virtue by the roots, and the same maxim governs the scribblers and speechifyers, on the side of the minister. It is sufficient to discover that any man has abilities and integrity, a love of virtue and liberty; he must be run down at all events. Witness Pitt and Franklin and too many others.

My design in pursuing this malicious slanderer, concealed as he is under so soft and oily an appearance, through all the doublings of his tedious course, is to vindicate this Colony from his base aspersions; that strangers now among us, and the impartial public, may see the wicked arts which are still employed against us. After the vilest abuse upon the agent of the province and the house, that appointed him, we are brought to his Majesty's Council, and are told that the "whigs reminded them of their mortality. If any one opposed the violent measures, he lost his Election the next May. Half the whole number mostly men of the first families, note, abilities, attached to their native country, wealthy and independent, were tumbled from their seats in disgrace. Thus the board lost its weight, and the political balance was destroyed."

It is impossible for any man acquainted with this subject to read this zealous rant, without smiling, until he attends to the wickedness of it, which will provide his utmost indignation. Let us however consider it soberly.

From the date of our charter to the time of the Stamp Act, and indeed since that time, (notwithstanding the misrepresentations of our charter constitution, as too popular and republican) the council of this province have been generally on the side of the governor and the prerogative. For the truth of this, I appeal to our whole history and experience. The art and power of governors, and especially the negative, have been a stronger motive on the one hand, than the annual election of the two houses on the other. In disputes between the governor and the house, the council have generally adhered to the former, and in many cases have complied with his humour, when scarcely any council by mandamus, upon this continent, would have done it.

But in the time of the Stamp Act, it was found productive of many mischiefs and dangers, to have officers of the crown, who were dependent on the ministry, and judges of the superior court whose offices were thought incompatible with a voice in the legislature, members of council.

In May 1765, Lieutenant-Governor Hutchinson, Sec[retary] Oliver, and Mr. Belcher, were officers of the crown, the judges of the superior court, and some other gentlemen, who held commissions under the governor, were members of council. Mr. Hutchinson was chief justice, and a judge of probate for the first county, as well as lieutenant-governor, and a counsellor; too many offices for the greatest and best man in the world to hold, too much business for any man to do; besides, that these offices were frequently clashing and interfering with each other. Two other justices of the superior court were counsellors, and nearly and closely connected with him, by family alliances. One other justice was judge of admiralty during pleasure. Such a jumble of offices, never got together before in any English government. It was found in short, that the famous triumvirate, Bernard, Hutchinson, and Oliver, the ever-memorable, secret, confidential letter-writers, whom I call the junto, had by degrees, and before people were aware of it, erected a tyranny in the province. Bernard had all the executive, and a negative on the legislative; Hutchinson and Oliver, by their popular arts and secret intrigues, had elevated to the board, such a collection of crown officers and their own relations, as to have too much influence there; and they had three of a family on the superior bench, which is the supreme tribunal in all causes, civil and criminal, vested with all the powers of the king's bench, common pleas and exchequer, which gave them power over every act of this court. This junto, therefore, had the legislative and executive in their controul, and more natural influence over the judicial, than is ever to be trusted to any set of men in the world. The public accordingly found all these springs and wheels in the constitution set in motion to promote submission to the Stamp Act, and to discountenance resistance to it; and they thought they had a violent presumption, that they would forever be employed to encourage a compliance with all ministerial measures and parliamentary claims, of whatever character they might be.

The designs of the junto, however, were concealed as carefully as possible. Most persons were jealous; few were certain. When the assembly met in May 1766, after the Stamp Act was repealed, the whigs flattered themselves with hopes of peace and liberty for the future. Mr. Otis, whose abilities and integrity; whose great exertions, and most exemplary sacrifices of his private interest to the public service, had intitled him to all the promotion which the people could bestow, was chosen speaker of the house. Bernard negatived the choice. It can scarcely be conceived by a stranger, what an alarm this manoeuvre gave to the public. It was thought equivalent to a declaration, that although the people had been so successful as to obtain a repeal of the Stamp Act, yet they must not hope to be quiet long, for parliament, by the Declaratory Act, had asserted its supreme authority, and new taxations and regulations should be made, if the junto could obtain them; and every man who should dare to oppose such projects, let his powers, or virtues, his family or fortune be what they would, should be surely cut off from all hopes of advancement. The electors thought it high time to be upon their guard. All the foregoing reasons and motives prevailed with the electors; and the crown officers and justices of the supreme court were left out of council in the new choice. Those who were elected in their places were all negatived by Bernard, which was considered as a fresh proof, that the junto still persevered in their designs of obtaining a revenue, to divide among themselves.

The gentlemen elected anew, were of equal fortune and integrity, at least, and not much inferior in abilities to those left out, and indeed, in point of fortune, family, note or abilities, the councils which have been chosen from that time to this, taken on an average, have been very little inferior, if any, to those chosen before. Let Massachusettensis descend, if he will, to every particular gentleman by name through the whole period, and I will make out my assertion.

Every impartial person, will not only think these reasons a full vindication of the conduct of the two Houses, but that it was their indispensable duty, to their country, to act the part they did; and the course of time, which has develloped the dark intrigues of the junto before and since, has confirmed the rectitude and necessity of the measure. Had Bernard's Principles of

Polity been published and known at that time, no member of the house, who should have voted for any one of the persons then left out, if it was known to his constituents, would ever have obtained another election.

By the next step we rise to the chair. "With the board, the chair fell likewise," he says. But what a slander is this? Neither fell; both remained in as much vigour as ever. The junto, it is true, and some other gentlemen who were not in their secret, but however had been misled to concur in their measures, were left out of council. But the board had as much authority as ever. The board of 1766 could not have influenced the people to acknowledge the supreme, uncontroulable authority of parliament, nor could that of 1765, have done it. So that by the chair, and the board's falling, he means no more, if his meaning has any truth in it, than that the junto fell; the designs of taxing the colonies fell, and the schemes for destroying all the charters on the continent, and for erecting lordships fell. These it must be acknowledged fell very low indeed in the esteem of the people, and the two houses.

"The Governor," says our wily writer, "could do little or nothing without the council by the charter." "If he cal'd upon a military officer to raise the militia, he was answered they were there already," &c. The Council by the Charter, had nothing to do with the militia. The Governor alone had all authority over them. The council therefore are not to blame for their conduct. If the militia refused obedience to the Captain General, or his subordinate officers, when commanded to assist in carrying into execution the Stamp Act, or in dispersing those who were opposing it, does not this prove the universal sense and resolution of the people not to submit to it? Did not a regular army do more to James the second? If those, over whom the governor had the most absolute authority and decisive influence, refused obedience, does not this show how deeply rooted in all men's minds was the abhorrence of that unconstitutional power which was usurping over them? "If he called upon the Council for their assistance, they must first enquire into the cause." An unpardonable crime, no doubt! But is it the duty of a middle branch of legislature, to do as the first shall command them, implicitly, or to judge for themselves? Is it the duty of a privy council, to understand the subject before they give advice, or only to lend their names to any edict, in order to make it less unpopular? It would be a shame to answer such observations as these, if it was not for their wickedness. Our Council, all along, however, did as much as any Council could have done. Was the Mandamus Council at New York able to do more, to influence the people to a submission to the Stamp Act? Was the Chair, the Board, the Septennial House, with the assistance of General Gage and his troops, able to do more, in that city, than our branches did in this province? Not one iota. Nor could Bernard, his Council, and House, if they had been unanimous, have induced submission. The people would have spurned them all, for they are not to be wheedled out of their liberties by their own Representatives, any more than by strangers. "If he wrote to government at home to strengthen his hands, some officious person procured and sent back his letters." At last it seems to be acknowledged, that the governor did write for a military force, to strengthen government. For what? To enable it to enforce Stamp acts, Tea acts, and other internal regulations, the authority of which, the people were determined never to acknowledge.

But what a pity it was that these worthy gentlemen could not be allowed, from the dearest affection to their native country, to which they had every possible attachment, to go on in profound confidential secrecy, procuring troops to cut our throats, acts of parliament to drain our purses, destroy our charters and assemblies, getting estates and dignities for themselves and their own families, and all the while most devoutly professing to be friends to our charter, enemies to parliamentary taxation, and to all pensions, without being detected? How happy! if they could have annihilated all our charters, and yet have been beloved, nay deified by the people, as friends and advocates for their charters? What masterly politicians! to have made themselves nobles for life, and yet have been thought very sorry, that the two houses were deprived of the privilege of choosing the council? How sagacious, to get large pensions for themselves, and yet be thought to mourn, that pensions and venality were introduced into the country? How sweet and pleasant! to have been the most popular men in the community, for being stanch and zealous dissenters, true-blue Calvinists, and able advocates for public virtue and popular government, after they had introduced an American episcopate, universal corruption among the leading men, and deprived the people of all share in their supreme legislative council? I mention an episcopate, for although I don't know that Governors Hutchinson and Oliver ever directly solicited for Bishops, yet they must have seen, that these would have been one effect, very soon, of establishing the unlimited authority of parliament!

I agree with this writer, that it was not the persons of Bernard, Hutchinson, or Oliver, that made them obnoxious; but their principles and practices. And I will agree that, if Chatham, Campden, and St. Asaph, (I beg pardon for introducing these revered names into such company, and for making a supposition which is absurd) had been here, and prosecuted such schemes, they would have met with contempt and execration from this people. But when he says, "that had the intimations in those letters been attended to, we had now been as happy a people as good government could make us," it is too gross to make us angry. We can do nothing but smile. Have not these intimations been attended to? Have not fleets and armies been sent here whenever they requested? Have not governors, lieutenant governors, secretaries, judges, attorney generals, and sollicitor generals salaries been paid out of the revenue, as they solicited? Have not taxes been laid and continued? Have not English liberties been abridged, as Hutchinson desired? Have not "penalties of another kind" been inflicted, as he desired?

Has not our Charter been destroyed, and the Council put into the King's hands, as Bernard requested? In short, almost all the wild mock pranks of this desperate triumvirate have been attended to and adopted, and we are now as miserable as tyranny can well make us. That Bernard came here with the affections of New Jersey, I never heard nor read but in this writer. His abilities were considerable, or he could not have done such extensive mischief. His true British honesty and punctuality will be acknowledged by none, but such as owe all their importance to flattering him.

That Hutchinson was amiable and exemplary in some respects, and very unamiable and unexemplary in others, is a certain truth; otherwise he never would have retained so much popularity on one hand, nor made so pernicious a use of it, on the other. His behavior, in several important departments, was with ability and integrity, in cases which did not affect his political system, but he bent all his offices to that. Had he continued stedfast to those principles in religion and government, which in former life, he professed, and which alone had procured him the confidence of the people and all his importance, he would have lived and died, respected and beloved, and have done honor to his native country. But by renouncing these principles and that conduct, which had made him and all his ancestors respectable, his character is now considered by all America, and the best part of the three kingdoms, notwithstanding the countenance he receives from the ministry, as a reproach to the province that gave him birth as a man who by all his actions aimed at making himself great at the expense of the liberties of his native country. This gentleman was open to flattery, in so remarkable a degree, that any man who would flatter him was sure of his friendship, and every one who would not was sure of his enmity. He was credulous in a ridiculous degree, of every thing that favored his own plans, and equally incredulous of every thing which made against them. His natural abilities, which have been greatly exaggerated by persons whom he had advanced to power, were far from being of the first rate. His industry was prodigious. His knowledge lay chiefly in the laws and politicks and history of this province, in which he had a long experience. Yet, with all his advantages, he never was master of the true character of his native country, not even of New England and the Massachusetts Bay. Through the whole troublesome period since the last war, he manifestly mistook the temper, principles, and opinions of this people. He had resolved upon a system, and never could or would see the impracticability of it.

It is very true that all his abilities, virtues, interests, and connections were insufficient. But for what? To prevail on the people to acquiesce in the mighty claim of parliamentary authority. The constitution was not gone. The suggestion that it was is a vile slander. It had as much vigor as ever, and even the governor had as much power as ever, excepting in cases which affected that claim. "The spirit," says this writer, "was truly republican." It was not so in any one case whatever; any further than the spirit of the British constitution is republican. Even in the grand fundamental dispute, the people arranged themselves under their house of representatives and council, with as much order as ever, and conducted their opposition as much by the constitution as ever. It is true their constitution was employed against the measures of the junto, which created their enmity to it. However, I have not such an horror of a republican spirit, which is a spirit of true virtue and honest independence, I don't mean on the king, but on men in power. This spirit is so far from being incompatible with the British constitution, that it is the greatest glory of it, and the nation has always been most prosperous when it has most prevailed and been most encouraged by the crown. I wish it increased in every part of the world, especially in America; and I think the measures the Tories are now pursuing, will increase it to a degree that will insure us in the end redress of grievances, and an happy reconciliation with Great Britain.

"Governor Hutchinson strove to convince us, by the principles of government, our charters, and acknowledgments, that
our claims were inconsistent with the subordination due to
Great Britain," &c., says this writer.

Suffer me to introduce here a little history. In 1764, when the
system of taxing and new-modelling the colonies was first apprehended, Lieutenant Governor Hutchinson's friends strug-
gled in several successive sessions of the General Court, to get
him chosen agent for the province at the court of Great Britain.
At this time he declared freely, *that he was of the same sentiment with the people, that parliament had no Right to tax
them; but differed from the country party, only in his opinion
of the policy of denying that Right in their Petitions,* &c. I
would not injure him, I was told this by three gentlemen who
were of the committee of both houses, to prepare that petition
that he made this declaration explicitly before that committee.
I have been told by other gentlemen that he made the same
declaration to them. It is possible that he might make use of
expressions studied for the purpose, which would not strictly
bear this construction. But it is certain that they understood
him so, and that this was the general opinion of his sentiments
until he came to the chair.

The country party saw, that this aspiring genius, aimed at
keeping fair with the ministry, by supporting their measures,
and with the people, by pretending to be of our principles, and
between both to trim himself up to the chair. The only reason
why he did not obtain an election at one time, and was excused
from the service at another after he had been chosen by a small
majority, was because the members knew he would not openly
deny the right, and assure his majesty, the parliament, and
ministry, that the people never would submit to it. For the same
reason he was left out of council. But he continued to cultivate
his popularity and to maintain a general opinion among the
people, that he denied the right in his private judgment, and
this idea preserved most of those who continued their esteem
for him.

But upon Bernard's removal, and his taking the chair as lieutenant governor, he had no further expectations from the people nor complaisance for their opinions. In one of his first speeches he took care to advance the supreme authority of parliament. This astonished many of his friends. They were heard to say, we have been deceived. We thought he had been abused, but we now find what has been said of him is true. He is determined to join in the designs against this country. After his promotion to the government, finding that the people had little confidence in him, and showing that he had no interest at home to support him but what he had acquired by joining with Bernard in kicking up a durst, he determined to strike a bold stroke, and in a formal speech to both houses, became a champion for the unbounded authority of parliament over the colonies. This he thought would lay the ministry under an obligation to support him in the government, or else to provide for him out of it, not considering that starting that question before that assembly, and calling upon them as he did to dispute with him upon it, was scattering firebrands, arrows, and death in sport. The arguments he advanced were inconclusive indeed; but they shall be considered, when I come to the feeble attempt of Massachusettensis to give a colour to the same position.

The house, thus called upon, either to acknowledge the unlimited authority of parliament, or confute his arguments, were bound by their duty to God, their country and posterity, to give him a full and explicit answer. They proved incontestibly that he was out in his facts, inconsistent with himself, and in every principle of his law, he had committed a blunder. Thus the fowler was caught in his own snare; and altho' this country has suffered severe temporary calamities in consequence of this speech, yet I hope they will not be durable; but his ruin was certainly in part owing to it. Nothing ever opened the eyes of the people so much, to his designs, excepting his letters. Thus it is the fate of Massachusettensis to praise this gentleman, for those things which the wise part of mankind condemn in him, as the most insidious and mischievous of actions. If it was out of his power to do us any more injuries, I should wish to forget the part; but as there is reason to fear he is still to continue his malevolent labours against this country, altho' he is out of our sight, he ought not to be out of our minds. This country has every thing to fear, in the present state of the British court, while the lords Bute, Mansfield, and North have the principal conduct of affairs, from the deep intrigues of that artful man.

To proceed to his successor, whom Massachusettensis has been pleased to compliment with the epithet of "amiable." I have no inclination to detract from this praise, but have no panegyricks or invectives for any man, much less for any governor, until satisfied of his character and designs. This gentleman's conduct, although he came here to support the systems of his two predecessors, and instructed to throw himself into the arms of their connections, when he has acted himself, and not been teized by others much less amiable and judicious than himself, into measures, which his own inclination would have avoided, has been in general as unexceptionable as could be expected, in his very delicate, intricate and difficult situation.

We are then told, "that disaffection to Great Britain, was infused into the body of the people." The leading whigs, have ever, systematically, and upon principle, endeavoured to preserve the people from all disaffection to the king on the one hand, and the body of the people on the other, but to lay the blame where it is justly due on the ministry and their instruments.

We are next conducted into the superior court, and informed "that the judges were dependant on the annual grants of the general court; that their salaries were small in proportion to the salaries of other officers, of less importance; that they often petitioned the assembly to enlarge them, without success, and were reminded of their dependance; that they remained unshaken amid the raging tempests, which is to be attributed rather to their firmness than situation."

That the salaries were small, must be allowed but not smaller in proportion than those of other officers. All salaries in this Province have been and are small. It has been the policy of the country to keep them so, not so much from a spirit of parsimony, as an opinion, that the service of the public ought to be an honorary, rather than a lucrative employment; and that the great men ought to be obliged to set examples of simplicity and frugality before the people.

But, if we consider things maturely, and make allowance for all circumstances, I think the country may be vindicated. This province during the last war, had such overbearing burdens upon it, that it was necessitated to oeconomy in every thing. At the peace she was half a million sterling in debt, nearly. She thought it the best policy to get out of debt before she raised the wages of her servants, and if Great Britain had thought as wisely, she would not now have had 140 millions to pay, and she would never have thought of taxing America.

Low as the wages were, it was found that whenever a vacancy happened, the place was solicited with much more anxiety and zeal than the kingdom of heaven.

Another cause which had its effect was this. The judges of that court had almost always enjoyed some other office. At the time of the Stamp Act the chief justice was lieutenant governor, which yielded him a profit, and a judge of probate for the county of Suffolk, which yielded him another profit, and a counsellor, which if it was not very profitable, gave him an opportunity of promoting his family and friends to other profitable offices, an opportunity which the country saw he most religiously improved. Another justice of this court was a judge of admiralty, and another was judge of probate for the county of Plymouth. The people thought therefore, that as their time was not wholly taken up by their offices as judges of the superior court, there was no reason why they should be paid as much as if it had been.

Another reason was this. Those justices had not been bred to the bar, but taken from merchandize, husbandry and other occupations; had been at no great expense for education or libraries, and therefore the people thought that equity did not demand large salaries.

It must be confessed that another motive had its weight. The people were growing jealous of the chief justice and two other justices at least, and therefore thought it imprudent to enlarge their salaries, and by that means their influence.

Whether all these arguments were sufficient to vindicate the people for not enlarging their salaries, I shall leave to you, my friends, whose right it is to judge. But that the judges petition'd "often" to the assembly I don't remember. I knew it was suspected by many, and confidently affirmed by some, that Judge Russell carried home with him in 1766, a petition to his Majesty, subscribed by himself, and Chief Justice Hutchinson at least, praying his Majesty to take the payment of the judges into his own hands; and that this petition, together with the solicitations of Governor Bernard, and others, had the success to procure the act of parliament, to enable his Majesty to appropriate the revenue to the support of the administration of justice, &c., from whence a great part of the present calamities of America have flowed.

That the high whigs took *care* to get themselves chosen of the grand juries I don't believe. Nine tenths of the people were high whigs; and therefore it was not easy to get a grand jury without nine whigs in ten, in it. And the matter would not be much mended by the new act of parliament. The sheriff must return the same set of jurors, court after court, or else his juries would be nine tenths of them high whigs still. Indeed the tories are so envenom'd now with malice, envy, revenge and disappointed ambition, that they would be willing, for what I know, to be jurors for life, in order to give verdicts against the whigs. And many of them would readily do it, I doubt not, without any other law or evidence, than what they found in their own breasts. The suggestion of ledgerdemain, in drawing the names of petit jurors out of the box, is scandalous. Human wisdom cannot devise a method of obtaining petit jurors more fairly, and better secured against a possibility of corruption of any kind, than that established by our provincial law. They were drawn by chance out of a box, in open town meeting, to which the tories went, or might have gone, as well as the whigs, and have seen with their own eyes, that nothing unfair ever did or could take place. If the jurors consisted of whigs, it was because the freeholders were whigs, that is honest men. But now, it seems, if Massachusettensis can have his will, the sheriff who will be a person properly qualified for the purpose, is to pick a tory jury, if he can find one in ten, or one in twenty, of that character among the freeholders; and it is no doubt expected, that every newspaper that presumes to deny the right of parliament to tax us, or destroy our charter, will be presented as a libel, and every member of a committee of correspondence, or a congress, &c. &c. &c., are to be indicted for rebellion. These would be pleasant times to Massachusettensis and the junto, but they willl never live to see them.

"The judges pointed out seditious libels, on governors, magistrates, and the whole government to no effect." They did so. But the jurors thought some of these no libels, but solemn truths. At one time, I have heard that all the newspapers for several years, the Massachusetts Gazette, Evening Post, Boston Chronicle, Boston Gazette, and Massachusetts Spy, were laid before a grand jury at once. The jurors thought there were multitudes of libels written by the tories, and they did not know who they should attack, if they presented them; perhaps Governor Bernard, Lieutenant Governor Hutchinson, Secretary Oliver—possibly, the Attorney-General. They saw so many difficulties they knew not what to do.

As to the riots and insurrections, it is surprizing that this writer should say, "Scarce one offender was indicted, and I think not one convicted." Were not many indicted, convicted, and punished too, in the county of Essex? and Middlesex, and indeed, in every other county? But perhaps he will say, he means such as were connected with politicks. Yet this is not true, for a large number in Essex were punished for abusing an informer, and others were indicted and convicted in Boston, for a similar offence. None where indicted for pulling down the stamp office, because this was thought an honorable and glorious action, not a riot. And so it must be said of several other tumults. But was not this the case in royal as well as charter governments? Nor will this inconvenience be remedied by a sheriff's jury, if such a one should ever sit. For if such a jury should convict, the people will never bear the punishment. It is in vain to expect or hope to carry on government against the universal bent and genius of the people; we may whimper and whine as much as we will, but nature made it impossible, when she made men.

If causes of *meum* and *tuum* were not always exempt from party influence, the tories will get no credit by an examination into particular cases. Tho' I believe there was no great blame on either party in this respect, where the case was not connected with politics.

We are then told "the whigs once flattered themselves they should be able to divide the province between them." I suppose he means, that they should be able to get the honorable and lucrative offices of the province into their hands. If this was true, they would be chargeable with only designing what the tories have actually done; with this difference, that the whigs would have done it by saving the liberties and the constitution of the province, whereas the tories have done it by the destruction of both. That the whigs have ambition, a desire of profit, and other passions like other men, it would be foolish to deny. But this writer cannot name a set of men in the whole British empire, who have sacrificed their private interest to their nation's honour and the public good, in so remarkable a manner, as the leading whigs have done, in the two last administrations.

As to ["]cutting asunder the sinews of government and

breaking in pieces the ligament of social life," as far as this has been done, I have proved by incontestible evidence from Bernard's, Hutchinson's, and Oliver's letters, that the tories have done it, against all the endeavours of the whigs to preserve them from first to last.

The public is then amused with two instances of the weakness of our government, and these are with equal artifice and injustice, insinuated to be chargeable upon the whigs. But the whigs are as innocent of these as the tories. Malcolm was injured as much against the inclinations and judgment of the whigs as the tories. But the real injury he received is exaggerated by this writer. The cruelty of his whipping, and the danger of his life, are too highly coloured.

Malcolm was such an od[d]ity, as naturally to excite the curiosity and ridicule of the lowest class of people, wherever he went; had been active in battle against the Regulators in North Carolina, who were thought in Boston to be an injured people. A few weeks before, he had made a seizure at Kennebec River, 150 miles from Boston, and by some imprudence had excited the wrath of the people there, in such a degree, that they tar'd and feather'd him over his clothes. He comes to Boston to complain. The news of it was spread in town. It was a critical time, when the passions of the people were warm. Malcolm attacked a lad in the street, and cut his head with a cutlass in return for some words from the boy, which I suppose were irritating. The boy ran bleeding thro' the street to his relations, of whom he had many. As he passed the street, the people enquired into the cause of his wounds, and a sudden heat arose against Malcolm, which neither Whigs nor Tories, tho' both endeavour'd it, could restrain; and produced the injuries of which he justly complained. But such a coincidence of circumstances, might at any time, and in any place, have produced such an effect; and therefore it is no evidence of the weakness of government. Why he petitioned the General Court, unless he was advised to it by the Tories, to make a noise, I know not. That court had nothing to do with it. He might have bro't his action against the trespassers, but never did. He chose to go to England and get £200 a year, which would make his tar[r]ing the luckiest incident of his life.

The hospital at Marblehead is another instance, no more owing to the politicks of the times, than the burning of the temple at Ephesus. This hospital was newly erected, much against the will of the multitude. The patients were careless, some of them wantonly so, and others were suspected of designing to spread the smallpox in the town, which was full of people, who had not passed the distemper. It is needless to be particular, but the apprehension became general, the people arose and burnt the hospital. But the whigs are so little blameable for this, that two of the principle whigs in the province, gentlemen highly esteemed and beloved in the town, even by those who burnt the building, were owners of it. The principles and temper of the times had no share in this, any more than in cutting down the market in Boston, or in demolishing mills and dams in some parts of the country, in order to let the Alewives pass up the streams, forty years ago. Such incidents happen in all governments at times. And it is a fresh proof of the weakness of this writer's cause, that he is driven to such wretched shifts to defend it.

Towards the close of this lengthy speculation, Massachusetensis grows more and more splenetical, peevish, angry, and absurd.

He tells us, that in order to avoid the necessity of altering our provincial constitution, government at home made the judges independent of the grants of the general assembly. That is, in order to avoid the hazard of taking the fort by storm, they determined to take it by sap. In order to avoid altering our constitution, they changed it in the most essential manner; for surely by our charter the province was to pay the judges as well as the governor. Taking away this privilege, and making them receive their pay from the Crown, was destroying the charter so far forth, and making them dependent on the minister. As to their being dependent on the leading whigs, he means they were dependent on the province. And which is fairest to be dependent on, the province, or on the minister? In all this troublesome period, the leading whigs had never hesitated about granting their salaries, nor ever once moved to have them lessened, nor would the house have listened to them if they had. "This was done, he says, to make them steady." We know that very well. Steady to what? Steady to the plans of Bernard, Hutchinson, Oliver, North, Mansfield, and Bute; which the people thought was steadiness to their ruin, and therefore it was found, that a determined spirit of opposition to it, arose in every part of the province, like that to the Stamp Act.

The chief justice it is true was accused by the house of representatives, of receiving a bribe, a ministerial, not a royal bribe. For the king can do no wrong, altho' he may be deceived in his grant. The minister is accountable. The crime of receiving an illegal patent, is not the less for purchasing it, even of the king himself. Many impeachments have been for such offences.

He talks about attempts to strengthen government, and save our charter. With what modesty can he say this, when he knows that the overthrow of our charter was the very object which the junto had been invariably pursuing for a long course of years? Does he think his readers are to be deceived by such gross arts? But he says "the whigs subverted the charter constitution, abridged the freedom of the house, annihilated the freedom of the board, and rendered the governor a doge of Venice." The freedom of the house was never abridged, the freedom of the board was never lessened. The governor had as much power as ever. The house and board it is true, would do nothing in favour of parliamentary taxation. Their judgments and consciences were against it, and if they ever had done any thing in favour of it, it would have been through fear and not freedom. The governor found he could do nothing in favour of it, excepting to promote in every department in the state, men who hated the people and were hated by them. Eno' of this he did in all conscience and after filling offices with men who were despised, he wondered that the officers were not revered. ["]They, the whigs, engrossed all the power of the province into their own hands." That is, the house and board were whigs; the grand juries and petit juries were whigs; towns were whigs; the clergy were whigs; the agents were whigs; and wherever you found people you found all whigs excepting those who had commissions from the crown or the governor. This is almost true. And it is to the eternal shame of the tories, that they should pursue their ignis fatuus with such ungovernable fury as they have done, after such repeated and multiplied demonstrations, that the whole people were so universally bent against them. But nothing will satisfy them still, but blood and carnage. The destruction of the Whigs, Charters, English Liberties and all, they must and will have, if it costs the blood of tens of thousands of innocent people. This is the benign temper of the tories.

This influence of the Whigs he calls a democracy or repu[b]lic, and then a despotism; two ideas incompatible with each other. A democratical despotism is a contradiction in terms.

He then says, that the good policy of the act for regulating the government in this province will be the subject of some future paper. But that paper is still to come, and I suspect ever will be. I wish to hear him upon it, however.

With this, he and the junto ought to have begun. Bernard and the rest in 1764 ought to have published his objections to this government, if they had been honest men, and produced their arguments in favour of the alteration, convinced the people of the necessity of it, and proposed some constitutional plan for effecting it. But the same motives which induced them to take another course, will prevail with Massachusettensis to waive the good policy of the act. He will be much more cunningly employed in labouring to terrify women and children with the hor[r]ors of a civil war, and the dread of a division among the people. There lies your fort, Massachusettensis. Make the most of it.

[February 20, 1775]   Novanglus

VI

Such events as the resistance to the Stamp Act, and to the Tea Act, particularly the destruction of that which was sent by the ministry, in the name of the East India Company, have ever been cautiously spoken of by the Whigs, because they knew the delicacy of the subject, and they lived in continual hopes of a speedy restoration of liberty and peace. But we are now thrown into a situation, which would render any further delicacy upon this point criminal.

Be it remembered, then, that there are tumults, seditions, popular commotions, insurrections and civil wars, upon just occasions as well as unjust. . . . Surely Grotius, Pufendorf, Barbeyrac, Locke, Sidney, and Le Cler[c], are writers, of sufficient weight, to put in the scale against the mercenary scrib[b]lers in New-York and Boston, who have the unexampled impudence and folly, to call these which are revolution principles in question, and to ground their arguments upon passive obedience as a corner stone. What an opinion must these writers have of the principles of their patrons, the Lords Bute, Mansfield, and North, when they hope to recommend themselves by reviving that stupid doctrine, which has been infamous so many years. Dr. Sacheverel himself tells us that his sermons were burnt by the hands of the common hangman, by the order of the king, lords, and commons, in order to fix an eternal and indelible brand of infamy on that doctrine.

In the Gazette of January the 2d, Massachusettensis entertains you with an account of his own important self. This is a subject which he has very much at heart, but it is of no consequence to you or me, and therefore little need be said of it. If he had such a stand in the community, that he could have seen all the political manoeuvres, it is plain he must have shut his eyes, or he never could have mistaken so grossly, causes for effects, and effects for causes.

He undertakes to point out the principles and motives upon which the Blockade Act was made, which were according to him, the destruction of the East India Company's tea. He might have said more properly the Ministerial Tea; for such it was, and the company are no losers. They have received from the public treasury compensation for it.

Then we are amused with a long discourse about the nature of the British government, commerce, agriculture, arts, manufactures, regulations of trade, custom-house officers, which as it has no relation to the subject, I shall pass over.

The case is shortly this. The East India Company, by their contract with government, in their charter and statute, are bound, in consideration of their important profitable privileges, to pay to the public treasury, a revenue annually, of four hundred thousand pounds sterling, so long as they can hold up their dividends at twelve per cent, and no longer.

The mistaken policy of the ministry, in obstinately persisting in their claim of right to tax America, and refusing to repeal the duty on tea, with those on glass, paper and paint, had induced all America, except a few merchants in Boston, most of whom were closely connected with the junto, to refuse to import tea from Great Britain; the consequence of which was a kind of stagnation in the affairs of the company, and an immense accumulation of tea in their stores, which they could not sell. This, among other causes, contributed to affect their credit, and their dividends were on the point of falling below twelve per cent, and consequently the government was upon the point of losing 400,000£ sterling a year of revenue. The company solicited the ministry to take off the duty in America; but they adhering to their plan of taxing the colonies and establishing a precedent, framed an act to enable the company to send their tea directly to America. This was admired as a masterpiece of policy. It was tho't they would accomplish four great purposes at once: establish their precedent of taxing America; raise a large revenue there by the duties; save the credit of the company; and the 400,000£ to the government. The company however, were so little pleased with this, that there were great debates among the directors, whether they should risque it, which were finally determined by a majority of one only, and that one the chairman, being unwilling as it is said, to interfere in the dispute between the minister and the colonies, and uncertain what the result would be; and this small majority was not obtained, as it is said, until a sufficient intimation was given that the company should not be losers.

When these designs were made known, it appeared, that American politicans were not to be deceived; that their sight was as quick and clear as the minister's, and that they were as steady to their purpose as he was to his. This was tho't by all the colonies to be the precise point of time, when it became absolutely necessary to make a stand. If the tea should be landed, it would be sold; if sold the duties would amount to a large sum, which would be instantly applied to increase the friends and advocates for more duties, and to divide the people; and the company would get such a footing, that no opposition afterwards could ever be effectual. And as soon as the duties on tea should be established, they would be ranked among post-office fees, and other precedents, and used as arguments both of the right and expediency of laying on others, perhaps on all the necessaries, as well as conveniences and luxuries of life. The whole continent was united in the sentiment, that all opposition to parliamentary taxation must be given up forever, if this critical moment was neglected. Accordingly, New York and Philadelphia determined that the ships should be sent back; and Charlestown, that the tea should be stored and locked up. This

was attended with no danger in that city, because they are fully
united in sentiment and affection, and have no junto to perplex
them. Boston was under greater difficulties. The Consignees at
New York and Philadelphia most readily resigned. The consignees at Boston, the children, cousins, and most intimate connections of Governor Hutchinson, refused. I am very sorry that I
cannot stir a single step in developing the causes of my country's miseries, without stumbling upon this gentleman. But so
it is. From the near relation and most intimate connection of
the consignees with him, there is great cause of jealousy, if not
a violent presumption, that he was at the bottom of all this
business, that he had plann'd it, in his confidential letters with
Bernard, and both of them joined in suggesting and recommending it to the ministry. Without this supposition, it is difficult to account for the obstinacy with which the Consignees
refused to resign, and the governor to let the vessel go. However this might be, Boston is the only place upon the continent,
perhaps in the world, which ever breeds a species of misan-
thropos, who will persist in their schemes for their private interest, with such obstinacy, in opposition to the public good; diso-
blige all their fellow-citizens for a little pelf, and make
themselves odious and infamous, when they might be respected
and esteemed. It must be said, however, in vindication of the
town, that this breed is spawned chiefly by the junto. The Consignees would not resign; the custom-house refused clearances;
Governor Hutchinson refused passes by the castle. The question then was, with many, whether the governor, officers, and
consignees should be compelled to send the ships hence? An
army and navy was at hand, and bloodshed was apprehended.
At last, when the continent, as well as the town and province,
were waiting the issue of this deliberation with the utmost
anxiety, a number of persons, in the night, put them out of
suspense, by an oblation to Neptune. I have heard some gentlemen say, "this was a very unjustifiable proceeding," "that if
they had gone at noon-day, and in their ordinary habits, and

drowned it in the face of the world, it would have been a meritorious, a most glorious action. But to go in the night, and much more in disguise, they tho't very inexcuseable."

"The revenue was not the consideration before parliament," says Massachusettensis. Let who will, believe him. But if it was not, the danger to America was the same. I take no notice of the idea of a monopoly. If it had been only a monopoly, (tho' in this light it would have been a very great grievance) it would not have excited, nor in the opinion of any one, justified the step that was taken. It was an attack upon a fundamental principle of the Constitution, and upon that supposition was resisted, after multitudes of petitions to no purpose, and because there was no tribunal in the Constitution, from whence redress could have been obtained.

There is one passage so pretty, that I cannot refuse myself the pleasure of transcribing it. "A smuggler and a whig are cousin germans, the offspring of two sisters, avarice and ambition. They had been playing into each other's hands a long time. The smuggler received protection from the whig, and he in his turn received support from the smuggler. The illicit trader now demanded protection from his kinsman, and it would have been unnatural in him to have refused it; and beside, an opportunity presented of strengthening his own interest."

The wit, and beauty of the style in this place, seem to have quite enraptured the lively juvenile imagination of this writer. The truth of the fact he never regards, any more than the justice of the sentiment. Some years ago, the smugglers might be pretty equally divided between the whigs and the tories. Since that time, they have almost all married into the tory families, for the sake of dispensations and indulgences. If I were to let myself into secret history, I could tell very diverting stories of smuggling tories in New York and Boston. Massachusettensis is quarrelling with some of his best friends. Let him learn more discretion.

We are then told that the consignees offered to store the tea, under the care of the selectmen, or a committee of the town. This expedient might have answered, if none of the junto, nor any of their connections had been in Boston. But is it a wonder, that the selectmen declined accepting such a deposit? They supposed they should be answerable, and no body doubted that tories might be found who would not scruple to set fire to the store, in order to make them liable. Besides if the tea was landed, though only to be stored, the duty must be paid, which it was tho't was giving up the point.

Another consideration which had great weight, was, that the other colonies were grown jealous of Boston, and tho't it already deficient in point of punctuality, against the dutied articles; and if the tea was once stored, artifices might be used, if not violence, to disperse it abroad. But if through the continual vigilance and activity of the committee and the people, thro' a whole winter, this should be prevented; yet one thing was certain, that the tories would write to the other colonies and to England, thousands of falsehoods concerning it, in order to induce the ministry to persevere, and to sow jealousies and create divisions among the colonies.

Our acute logician then undertakes to prove the destruction of the tea unjustifiable, even upon the principle of the whigs, that the duty was unconstitutional. The only argument he uses is this, that "unless we purchase the tea, we shall never pay the duty." This argument is so frivolous, and has been so often confuted and exposed, that if the party had any other, I think they would relinquish this. Where will it carry us? If a duty was laid upon our horses, we may walk; if upon our butchers meat, we may live upon the produce of the dairy; and if that should be taxed, we may subsist as well as our fellow slaves in Ireland, upon Spanish potatoes and cold water. If a thousand pounds was laid upon the birth of every child, if children are not begotten, none will be born; if, upon every marriage, no duties will be paid, if all the young gentlemen and ladies agree to live bachelors and maidens.

In order to form a rational judgment of the quality of this transaction, and determine whether it was good or evil, we must go to the bottom of this great controversy. If parliament has a right to tax us, and legislate for us, in all cases, the destruction of the tea was unjustifiable; but if the people of America are right in their principle, that parliament has no such right, that the act of parliament is null and void, and it is lawful to oppose and resist it, the question then is, whether the destruction was necessary? for every principle of reason justice and prudence, in such cases, demands that the least mischief shall be done; the least evil among a number shall always be preferr'd.

All men are convinced that it was impracticable to return it, and rendered so by Mr. Hutchinson and the Boston consignees. Whether to have stored it would have answered the end, or been a less mischief than drowning it, I shall leave to the judgment of the public. The other colonies, it seems, have no scruples about it, for we find that whenever tea arrives in any of them, whether from the East India Company, or any other quarter, it never fails to share the fate of that in Boston. All men will agree that such steps ought not to be taken, but in cases of absolute necessity, and that such necessity must be very clear. But most people in America now think the destruction of the Boston tea, was absolutely necessary, and therefore right and just. It is very true, they say, if the whole people had been united in sentiment, and equally stable in their resolution, not to buy or drink it, there might have been a reason for preserving it; but the people here were not so virtuous or so happy. The British ministry had plundered the people by illegal taxes, and applied the money in salaries and pensions, by which devices, they had insidiously attached to their party, no inconsiderable number of persons, some of whom were of family, fortune, and influence, tho' many of them were of desperate fortunes, each of whom, however, had his circle of friends, connections, and dependents, who were determined to drink tea, both as evidence of their servility to administration, and their contempt and hatred of the people. These it was impossible to restrain without violence, perhaps bloodshed, certainly without hazarding more than the tea was worth. To this tribe of the wicked, they say, must be added another, perhaps more numerous, of the weak; who never could be brought to think of the consequences of their actions, but would gratify their appetites, if they could come at the means. What numbers are there in every community, who have no providence, or prudence in their private affairs, but will go on indulging the present appetite, prejudice, or passion, to the ruin of their estates and families, as well as their own health and characters! How much larger is the number of those who have no foresight for the public, or consideration of the freedom of posterity? Such an abstinence from the tea, as would have avoided the establishment of a precedent, depended on the unanimity of the people, a felicity that was unattainable. Must the wise, the virtuous and worthy part of the community, who constituted a very great majority, surrender their liberty, and involve their posterity in misery, in complaisance to a detestable, tho' small, party of knaves, and a despicable, tho' more numerous, company of fools?

If Boston could have been treated like other places, like New York and Philadelphia, the tea might have gone home from thence as it did from those cities. That inveterate, desperate junto, to whom we owe all our calamities, were determined to hurt us in this, as in all other cases, as much as they could. It is to be hoped they will one day repent and be forgiven, but it is very hard to forgive without repentance. When the news of this event arrived in England, it excited such passions in the minister as nothing could restrain; his resentment was inkindled into revenge, rage, and madness; his veracity was piqued, as his masterpiece of policy, proved but a bubble. The bantling was the fruit of a favorite amour, and no wonder that his natural affection was touched when he saw it despatched before his eyes. His grief and ingenuity, if he had any, were affected at the thought that he had misled the East India Company, so much nearer to destruction, and that he had rendered the breach between the kingdom and the colonies almost irreconcilable. His shame was excited because opposition had gained a triumph over him, and the three kingdoms were laughing at him for his obstinacy and his blunders; instead of relieving the company he had hastened its ruin; instead of establishing the absolute and unlimited sovereignty of parliament over the colonies, he had excited a more decisive denial of it, and resistance to it. An election drew nigh, and he dreaded the resentment even of the corrupted electors.

In this state of mind bordering on despair, he determines to strike a bold stroke. Bernard was near and did not fail to embrace the opportunity, to push the old systems of the junto. By attacking all the colonies together, by the Stamp Act, and the Paint and Glass Act, they had been defeated. The charter constitution of the Massachusetts Bay, had contributed greatly to both these defeats. Their representatives were too numerous, and too frequently elected, to be corrupted; their people had been used to consider public affairs in their town-meetings; their counsellors were not absolutely at the nod of a minister or governor, but were once a year equally dependent on the governor and the two houses. Their grand jurors were elective by the people, their petit jurors were returned merely by lot. Bernard and the junto rightly judged that by this constitution the people had a check, on every branch of power, and therefore as long as it lasted, parliamentary taxations, &c. could never be inforced.

Bernard publishes his select letters, and his principles of polity; his son writes in defence of the Quebec bill; hireling garretteers are employed to scribble millions of lies against us, in pamphlets and newspapers; and setters employed in the coffee-houses, to challenge or knock down all the advocates for the poor Massachusetts. It was now determined, instead of attacking the colonies together, tho' they had been all equally opposed to the plans of the ministry, and the claims of parliament, and therefore upon ministerial principles equally guilty, to handle them one by one; and to begin with Boston and the Massachusetts. The destruction of the tea was a fine event for scribblers and speechifiers to declaim upon; and there was an hereditary hatred of New England, in the minds of many in England, on account of their non-conforming principles. It was likewise thought there was a similar jealousy and animosity in the other colonies against New England; that they would therefore certainly desert her; that she would be intimidated and submit; and then the minister among his own friends, would acquire immortal honour, as the most able, skilful and undaunted statesman of the age.

The port bill, charter bill, murder bill, Quebec bill, making altogether such a frightful system, as would have terrified any people, who did not prefer liberty to life, were all concerted at once; but all this art and violence have not succeeded. This people under great trials and dangers, have discovered great abilities and virtues, and that nothing is so terrible to them as the loss of their liberties. If these arts and violences are persisted in, and still greater concerted, and carried on against them, the world will see that their fortitude, patience and magnanimity will rise in proportion.

"Had Cromwell," says our what shall I call him? "had the guidance of the national ire, your proud capital had been levell'd with the dust." Is it any breach of charity to suppose that such an event as this, would have been a gratification to this writer? Can we otherwise account for his indulging himself in a thought so diabolical? Will he set up Cromwell as a model for his deified lords, Bute, Mansfield, and North? If he should, there is nothing in the whole history of him so cruel as this. All his conduct in Ireland, as exceptionable as any part of his whole life, affords nothing that can give the least probability to the idea of this writer. The rebellion in Ireland, was most obstinate, and of many years duration; 100,000 Protestants had been murdered in a day, in cold blood, by papists, and therefore Cromwell might plead some excuse, that cruel severities were necessary, in order to restore any peace to that kingdom. But all this will not justify him; for as has been observed by an historian, upon his conduct in this instance, "men are not to divest themselves of humanity, and turn themselves into devils, because policy may suggest that they will succeed better as devils than as men!" But is there any parity or similitude between a rebellion of a dozen years standing, in which many battles had been fought, many thousands fallen in war, and 100,000 massacred in a day; and the drowning three cargoes of tea? To what strains of malevolence, to what flights of diabolical fury, is not tory rage capable of transporting men!

"The whigs saw their ruin connected with a compliance with the terms of opening the port." They saw the ruin of their country connected with such a compliance, and their own involved in it. But they might have easily voted a compliance, for they were undoubtedly a vast majority, and have enjoyed the esteem and affection of their fellow-slaves to their last hours. Several of them could have paid for the tea and never have felt the loss. They knew they must suffer, vastly more, than the tea was worth, but they thought they acted for America and posterity; and that they ought not to take such a step without the advice of the colonies. They have declared our cause their own; that they never will submit to a precedent in any part of the united colonies, by which Parliament may take away wharves and other lawful estates, or demolish Charters; for if they do, they have a moral certainty that in the course of a few years, every right of Americans will be taken away, and governors and councils, holding at the will of a Minister, will be the only legislatives, in the colonies.

A pompous account of the addressers of Mr. Hutchinson, then follows. They consisted of his relations, his fellow labourers in the tory vineyard, and persons whom he had raised in the course of four administrations, Shirley's, Pownal's, Bernard's, and his own to places in the province. Considering the industry that was used, and the vast number of persons in the province, who had received commissions under government upon his recommendation, the small number of subscribers that was obtained, is among a thousand demonstrations of the unanimity of this people. If it had been thought worth while to have procured a remonstrance against him, fifty thousand subscribers might have been easily found. Several gentlemen of property were among these addressers, and some of fair character, but their acquaintance and friendships lay among the junto and their subalterns entirely. Besides, did these addressers approve the policy or justice of any one of the bills, which were passed the last session of the late parliament? Did they acknowledge the unlimited authority of parliament? The Middlesex magistrates remonstrated against taxation; but they were flattered with hopes, that Mr. Hutchinson would get the Port Bill, &c. repealed, that is, that he would have undone all, which everybody but themselves knew he has been doing these fifteen years.

"But these patriotic endeavours, were defeated." By what? "By an invention of the fertile brain of one of our party agents, called a committee of correspondence. *This is the foulest, subtlest, and most venomous serpent that ever issued from the eggs of sedition.*"

I should rather call it the *ichneumon*, a very industrious, active, and useful animal, which was worshipped in Egypt as a divinity, because it defended their country from the ravages of the crocodiles. It was the whole occupation of this little creature to destroy those wily and ravenous monsters. It crushed their eggs, wherever they laid them, and with a wonderful address and courage, would leap into their mouths, penetrate their entrails, and never leave until it destroyed them.

If the honor of this invention is due to the gentleman, who is generally understood by the "party agent" or Massachusettensis, it belongs to one, to whom America has erected a statue in her heart, for his integrity, fortitude, and perseverance in her cause. That the invention itself is very useful and important, is sufficiently clear, from the unlimited wrath of the tories against it, and from the gall which this writer discharges upon it. Almost all mankind have lost their liberties thro' ignorance, inattention, and disunion. These committees are admirably calculated to diffuse knowledge, to communicate intelligence, and promote unanimity. If the high whigs are generally of such committees, it is because the freeholders who choose them, are such, and therefore prefer their peers. The tories, high or low, if they can make interest enough among the people, may get themselves chosen, and promote the great cause of parliamentary revenues, and the other sublime doctrines and mysteries of toryism. That these committees think themselves "amenable to none," is false; for there is not a man upon any one of them, who does not acknowledge himself to hold his place, at the pleasure of his constituents, and to be accountable to them, whenever they demand it. If the committee of the town of Boston, was appointed for a special purpose at first, their commission has been renewed from time to time; they have been frequently thanked by the town for their vigilance, activity, and disinterested labours in the public service. Their doings have been laid before the town, and approved of by it. The malice of the tories has several times swelled open their bosoms, and broke out into the most intemperate and illiberal invectives against it; but all in vain. It has only served to show the impotence of the tories, and increase the importance of the committee.

These committees cannot be too religiously careful of the exact truth of the intelligence they receive or convey; nor too anxious for the rectitude and purity of the measures they propose or adopt; they should be very sure that they do no injury to any man's person, property, or character; and they are generally persons of such worth, that I have no doubt of their attention to these rules; and therefore, that the reproaches of this writer are mere slanders.

If we recollect how many states have lost their liberties, merely from want of communication with each other, and union among themselves, we shall think that these committees may be intended by Providence to accomplish great events. What the eloquence and talents of negotiation of Demosthenes himself could not effect, among the states of Greece, might have been effected by so simple a device. Castile, Arragon, Valencia, Majorca, &c. all complained of oppression under Charles the fifth, flew out into transports of rage, and took arms against him. But they never consulted or communicated with each other. They resisted separately, and were separately subdued. Had Don Juan Padilla, or his wife, been possessed of the genius to invent a committee of correspondence, perhaps the liberties of the Spanish nation might have remained to this hour, without any necessity to have had recourse to arms. . . .

That it is owing to those committees that so many persons have been found to recant and resign, and so many others to fly to the army, is a mistake, for the same things would have taken place, if such a committee had never been in being, and such persons would probably have met with much rougher usage. This writer asks, "Have not these persons as good a right to think and act for themselves as the whigs?" I answer, yes. But if any man, whig or tory, shall take it into his head to think for himself, that he has a right to take my property without my consent, however tender I may be of the right of private judgment and the freedom of thought, this is a point in which I shall be very likely to differ from him, and to think for myself that I have a right to resist him. If any man should think, ever so conscientiously that the roman catholic religion is better than the protestant, or that the French government is preferable to the British constitution in [its] purity, Protestants and Britons, will not be so tender of that man's conscience as to suffer him to introduce his favorite religion and government. So the well bred gentlemen who are so polite as to think, that the charter constitution of this province, ought to be abolished, and another introduced wholly at the will of a minister or the crown, or that our ecclesiastical constitution is bad, and high church ought to come in, few people will be so tender of these consciences or complaisant to such polite taste, as to suffer the one or the other to be established. There are certain prejudices among the people, so strong, as to be irresistible. Reasoning is vain, and opposition idle. For example, there are certain popular maxims and precepts, call'd the ten commandments. Suppose a number of fine gentlemen, superior to the prejudices of education, should discover that these were made for the common people, and are too illiberal for gentlemen of refined taste to observe, and accordingly, should engage in secret confidential correspondences to procure an act of parliament, to abolish the whole decalogue, or to exempt them from all obligation to observe it; if they should succeed, and their letters be detected, such is the force of prejudice, and deep habits among the lower sort of people, that it is much to be questioned, whether those refined geniuses would be allowed to enjoy themselves in the latitude of their sentiments. I once knew a man, who had studied Jacob Beckman, and other mystics, until he conscienciously thought the millennium commenced, and all human authority at an end; that the saints only had a right to property; and to take from sinners any thing they wanted. In this persuasion, he very honestly stole a horse. Mankind pitied the poor man's infirmity, but thought it however their duty to confine him that he might steal no more.

The freedom of thinking was never yet extended in any country so far, as the utter subversion of all religion and morality, nor as the abolition of the laws and constitution of the country.

But "are not these persons as closely connected with the interest of their country as the whigs?" I answer, they are not; they have found an interest in opposition to that of their country, and are making themselves rich and their families illustrious, by depressing and destroying their country. But "do not their former lives and conversations appear to have been regulated by principles, as much as those of the whigs?" A few of them, it must be acknowledged, until seduced by the bewitching charms of wealth and power, appeared to be men of principle. But taking the Whigs and Tories on an average, the balance of principle, as well as genius, learning, wit, and wealth, is infinitely in favour of the former. As to some of these fugitives, they are known to be men of no principles at all in religion, morals or government.

But the "policy" is questioned, and you are asked if you expect to make converts by it? As to the policy or impolicy of it, I have nothing to say; but we don't expect to make converts of most of those persons by any means whatever, as long as they have any hopes that the ministry will place and pension them. The instant these hopes are extinguished, we all know they will be converted of course. Converts from places and pensions are only to be made by places and pensions, all other reasoning is idle; these are the *Penultima Ratio* of the Tories, as field-pieces are the *ultima.*

That we are not "unanimous" is certain. But there are nineteen on one side to one on the other, through the province. And ninety-nine out of an hundred of the remaining twentieth part, can be fairly shown to have some sinister private view, to induce them to profess his opinion.

Then we are threatened high, that "this is a changeable world, and time's rolling wheel may e'er long bring them uppermost, and in that case we should not wish to have them fraught with resentment."

To all this we answer, without ceremony, that they always have been uppermost, in every respect, excepting only the esteem and affection of the people; that they always have been fraught with resentment, (even their cunning and policy have not restrained them,) and we know they always will be. That they have indulged their resentment and malice, in every instance in which they had power to do it; and we know that their revenge will never have other limits than their power.

Then this consistent writer, begins to flatter the people, "he appeals to their good sense, he knows they have it." The same people, whom he has so many times represented as mad and foolish.

"I know you are loyal and friends to good order." This is the same people that in the whole course of his writings, he has represented as continuing for ten years together in a continual state of disorder, demolishing the Chair, Board, Supreme Court, and encouraging all sorts of riots, insurrections, treason and rebellion. Such are the shifts to which a man is driven when he aims at carrying a point not at discovering truth.

The people are then told that "they have been insidiously taught to believe that Great Britain is rapacious, cruel and vindictive, and envies us the inheritance purchased by the sweat and blood of our ancestors." The people do not believe this; they will not believe it. On the contrary, they believe if it was not for scandals constantly transmitted from this province by the Tories, the nation would redress our grievances. Nay as little as they reverence the Ministry, they even believe that the Lords North, Mansfield, and Bute, would relieve them, and would have done it long ago, if they had known the truth. The moment this is done "long live our gracious king and happiness to Britain," will resound from one end of the province to the other; but it requires a very little foresight to determine, that no other plan of governing the province and the colonies, will ever restore a harmony between the two countries, but desisting from the plan of taxing them and interfering with their internal concerns, and returning to that system of colony administration which nature dictated, and experience for one hundred and fifty years found useful.

[February 27, 1775]   Novanglus

VII

Our rhetorical magician, in his paper of January the 9th, continues to wheedle. "You want nothing but to know the true state of facts, to rectify whatever is amiss." He becomes an advocate for the poor of Boston! Is for making great allowance for the whigs. "The whigs are too valuable a part of the community to lose. He would not draw down the vengeance of Great Britain. He shall become an advocate for the leading whigs," &c. It is in vain for us to enquire after the *sincerity* or *consistency* of all this. . . .

After a long discourse, which has nothing in it but what has been answered already, he comes to a great subject indeed, the British constitution; and undertakes to prove that "the authority of parliament extends to the colonies."

Why will not this writer state the question fairly? The whigs allow that from the necessity of a case not provided for by common law, and to supply a defect in the British dominions, which there undoubtedly is, if they are to be governed only by that law, America has all along consented, still consents, and ever will consent, that parliament being the most powerful legislature in the dominions, should regulate the trade of the dominions. This is founding the authority of parliament to regulate our trade, upon *compact* and *consent* of the colonies, not upon any principle of common or statute law, not upon any original principle of the English constitution, not upon the principle that parliament is the supream and sovereign legislature over them in all cases whatsoever.

The question is not therefore, whether the authority of parliament extends to the colonies in any case; for it is admitted by the whigs that it does in that of commerce. But whether it extends in all cases.

We are then detained with a long account of the three simple forms of government; and are told that "the British constitution consisting of king, lords and commons, is formed upon the principles of monarchy, aristocracy and democracy, in due proportion; that it includes the principled excellencies, and excludes the principal defects of the other kinds of government—the most perfect system that the wisdom of ages has produced, and Englishmen glory in being subject to, and protected by it."

Then we are told "that the colonies are a part of the British empire." But what are we to understand by this? Some of the colonies, most of them indeed, were settled before the kingdom of Great Britain was brought into existence. The union of England and Scotland, was made and established by act of parliament in the reign of Queen Anne, and it was this union and statute which erected the kingdom of Great Britain. The colonies were settled long before, in the reigns of the James's and Charles's. What authority over them had Scotland? Scotland, England and the colonies were all under one king before that; the two crowns of England and Scotland, united on the head of James the first, and continued united on that of Charles the first, when our first charter was granted. Our charter being granted by him who was king of both nations, to our ancestors, most of whom were *post nati*, born after the union of the two crowns, and consequently, as was adjudged in Calvin's case, free natural subjects of Scotland, as well as England, had not the king as good a right to have governed the colonies by his Scottish, as by his English parliament, and to have granted our charters under the seal of Scotland, as well as that of England?

But to waive this. If the English parliament were to govern us, where did they get the right, without our consent to take the Scottish parliament, into a participation of the government over us? When this was done, was the American share of the democracy of the constitution consulted? If not, were not the Americans deprived of the benefit of the democratical part of the constitution? And is not the democracy as essential to the English constitution as the monarchy or aristocracy? Should we have been more effectually deprived of the benefit of the British or English constitution, if one or both houses of parliament, or if our house and council, had made this union with the two houses of parliament in Scotland, without the king?

If a new constitution was to be formed for the whole British dominions, and a supream legislature coextensive with it, upon the general principles of the English constitution, and equal mixture of monarchy, aristocracy and democracy, let us see what would be necessary. England have six millions of people we will say; America had three. England has five hundred members in the house of commons we will say; America must have two hundred and fifty. Is it possible she should maintain them there, or could they at such a distance know the state, the sense or exigences of their constituents? Ireland too must be incorporated, and send another hundred or two of members. The territory in the East Indies and West India Islands must send members. And after all this, every navigation act, every act of trade must be repealed. America and the East and West Indies and Africa too, must have equal liberty to trade with all the world, that the favoured inhabitants of Great Britain have now. Will the ministry thank Massachusettensis for becoming an advocate for such an union and incorporation of all the dominions of the king of Great Britain. Yet without such an union, a legislature which shall be sovereign and supream in all cases whatsoever, and coextensive with the empire, can never be established upon the general principles of the English constitution, which Massachusettensis lays down, viz. an equal mixture of monarchy, aristocracy and democracy. Nay further, in order to comply with this principle, this new government, this mighty Colossus which is to bestride the narrow world, must have an house of lords consisting of Irish, East and West Indian, African, American, as well as English and Scottish noblemen; for the nobility ought to be scattered about all the dominions, as well as the representatives of the commons. If in twenty years more America should have six millions of inhabitants, as there is a boundless territory to fill up, she must have five hundred representatives. Upon these principles, if in forty years, she should have twelve millions, a thousand; and if the inhabitants of the three kingdoms remain as they are, being already full of inhabitants, what will become of your supream legislative? It will be translated, crown and all, to America. This is a sublime system for America. It will flatter those ideas of independency which the tories impute to them, if they have any such, more than any other plan of independency, that I have ever heard projected.

"The best writers upon the law of nations tell us, that when a nation takes possession of a distant country and settles there, that country though separated from the principal establishment, or mother country, naturally becomes a part of the state, equal with its ancient possessions." We are not told who these "best writers" are. I think we ought to be introduced to them. But their meaning may be no more than that it is best they should be incorporated with the ancient establishment by contract, or by some new law and institution, by which the new country shall have equal right, powers and privileges, as well as equal protection; and be under equal obligations of obedience with the old. Has there been any such contract between Britain and the Colonies? Is America incorporated into the realm? Is it a part of the realm? Is it a part of the kingdom? Has it any share in the legislative of the realm? The constitution requires that every foot of land should be represented, in the third estate, the democratical branch of the constitution. How many millions of acres in America, how many thousands of wealthy landholders, have no representatives there?

But let these "best writers" say what they will, there is nothing in the law of nations, which is only the law of right reason, applied to the conduct of nations, that requires that emigrants from a state should continue, or be made a part of the state.

The practice of nations has been different. The Greeks planted colonies, and neither demanded nor pretended any authority over them but they became distinct independent commonwealths.

The Romans continued their colonies under the jurisdiction of the mother commonwealth; but, nevertheless, she allowed them the privileges of cities. Indeed that sagacious city seems to have been aware of the difficulties similar to those under which Great Britain is now labouring; she seems to have been sensible of the impossibility of keeping colonies planted at great distances, under the absolute control of her *senatus consulta.* Harrington tells us, Oceana p. 43, that "the commonwealth of Rome, by planting colonies of its citizens within the bounds of Italy, took the best way of propagating itself, and naturalizing the country; whereas, if it had planted such colonies without the bounds of Italy, it would have alienated the citizens, and given a root to liberty abroad, that might have sprung up foreign, or savage and hostile to her; *wherefore it never made any such dispersion of itself, and its strength,* till it was under the yoke of the emperors, who disburdening themselves of the people, as having less apprehension of what they could do abroad than at home, took a contrary course." But these Italian cities, altho' established by decrees of the senate of Rome, to which the colonists was always party, either as a Roman citizen about to emigrate, or as a conquered enemy treating upon terms; were always allow'd all the rights of Roman citizens, and were go-vern'd by senates of their own. It was the policy of Rome to conciliate her colonies, by allowing them equal liberties with her citizens. . . .

The practice of free nations only can be adduced, as prece-dents of what the law of nature has been thought to dictate upon this subject of colonies. Their practice is different. The senate and people of Rome did not interfere commonly in making laws for their colonies, but left them to be ruled by their governors and senates. Can Massachusettensis produce from the whole history of Rome, or from the Digest, one example of a *Senatus consultum*, or a *Plebiscitum*, laying taxes on a colony?

Having mentioned the wisdom of the Romans in not planting colonies out of Italy, and their reasons for it; I cannot help recollecting an observation of Harrington, Oceana, p. 44, "For the colonies in the Indies, says he, they are yet babes, that cannot live without sucking the breasts of their mother cities; but such as I mistake, if when they come of age, they do not wean themselves, which causes me to wonder at princes that delight to be exhausted in that way." This was written 120 years ago; the colonies are now nearer manhood than even Harrington foresaw they would arrive in such a period of time. Is it not astonishing then, that any British minister should ever have considered this subject so little as to believe it possible for him to new model all our governments, to tax us by an authority that never taxed us before, and subdue us to an implicit obedience to a legislature, that millions of us scarcely ever tho't any thing about?

I have said that the practice of free governments alone can be quoted with propriety, to show the sense of nations. But the sense and practice of nations is not enough. Their practice must be reasonable, just and right, or it will not govern Americans.

Absolute monarchies, whatever their practice may be, are nothing to us. Or as Harrington observes, "Absolute monarchy, as that of the Turks, neither plants its people at home nor abroad, otherwise than as tenants for life or at will; wherefore its national and provincial government is all one."

I deny therefore that the practice of free nations, or the opinions of the best writers upon the law of nations, will warrant the position of Massachusettensis, that, when a nation takes possession of a distant territory, that becomes a part of the state equally with its ancient possessions. The practice of free nations and the opinions of the best writers, are in general on the contrary.

I agree, that "two supreme and independent authorities cannot exist in the same state," any more than two supream beings in one universe. And therefore I contend, that our provincial legislatures are the only supream authorities in our colonies. Parliament, notwithstanding this, may be allowed an authority supream and sovereign over the ocean, which may be limited by the banks of the ocean, or the bounds of our charters; our charters give us no authority over the high seas. Parliament has our consent to assume a jurisdiction over them. And here is a line fairly drawn between the rights of Britain and the rights of the colonies, viz. the banks of the ocean, or low water mark. The line of division between common law and civil, or maritime law. If this is not sufficient,—if parliament are at a loss for any principle of natural, civil, maritime, moral or common law, on which to ground any authority over the high seas, the Atlantic especially, let the colonies be treated like reasonable creatures, and they will discover great ingenuity and modesty. The acts of trade and navigation might be confirmed by provincial laws, and carried into execution by our own courts and juries, and in this case, illicit trade would be cut up by the roots forever. I knew the smuggling tories in New York and Boston would cry out against this, because it would not only destroy their profitable game of smuggling, but their whole place and pension system. But the whigs, that is a vast majority of the whole continent, would not regard the smuggling tories. In one word, if public principles and motives and arguments were alone to determine this dispute between the two countries, it might be settled forever, in a few hours; but the everlasting clamours of prejudice, passion and private interest, drown every consideration of that sort, and are precipitating us into a civil war.

"If then we are a part of the British empire, we must be subject to the supreme power of the state, which is vested in the estates in parliament."

Here again we are to be conjured out of our senses by the magic in the words "British empire," and "supreme power of the state." But however it may sound, I say we are not a part of the British empire. Because the British government is not an empire. The governments of France, Spain, &c. are not empires, but monarchies, supposed to be governed by fixed fundamental laws, tho' not really. The British government, is still less entitled to the style of an empire. It is a limited monarchy. If Aristotle, Livy and Harrington, knew what a republic was, the British constitution is much more like a republic than an empire. They define a republic to be *a government of laws, and not of men.* If this definition is just, the British constitution is nothing more nor less than a republic, in which the king is first magistrate. This office being hereditary, and being possessed of such ample and splendid prerogatives, is no objection to the government's being a republic, as long as it is bound by fixed laws, which the people have a voice in making, and a right to defend. An empire is a despotism, and an emperor a despot, bound by no law or limitation, but his own will; it is a stretch of tyranny beyond absolute monarchy. For altho' the will of an absolute monarch is law, yet his edicts must be registered by parliaments. Even this formality is not necessary in an empire. There the maxim is *quod principi placuit, legis habet vigorem,* even without having that will and pleasure recorded. There are but three empires now in Europe, the German, or Holy Roman, the Russian and the Ottoman.

There is another sense indeed in which the word empire is used, in which it may be applied to the government of Geneva, or any other republic, as well as to monarchy, or despotism. In this sense it is synonimous with government, rule or dominion. In this sense we are within the dominion, rule or government of the king of Great Britain.

The question should be, whether we are a part of the kingdom of Great Britain. This is the only language, known in English laws. We are not then a part of the British kingdom, realm or state; and therefore the supreme power of the kingdom, realm or state is not upon these principles, the supreme power over us. That "supreme power over America is vested in the estates in parliament," is an affront to us; for there is not an acre of American land represented there; there are no American estates in parliament.

To say, that we "must be" subject, seems to betray a consciousness that we are not by any law or upon any principles but those of mere power; and an opinion that we ought to be, or that it is necessary that we should be. But if this should be admitted, for argument sake only, what is the consequence? The consequences that may fairly be drawn are these. That Britain has been imprudent enough to let Colonies be planted, until they are become numerous and important, without ever having wisdom enough to concert a plan for their government, consistent with her own welfare. That now it is necessary to make them submit to the authority of parliament; and because there is no principle of law or justice, or reason, by which she can effect it, therefore she will resort to war and conquest—to the maxim, *delenda est Carthago*. These are the consequences, according to this writer's ideas. We think the consequences are, that she has after 150 years, discovered a defect in her government, which ought to be supplied by some just and reasonable means, that is, by the consent of the Colonies; for metaphysicians and politicians may dispute forever, but they will never find any other moral principle or foundation of rule or obedience, than the consent of governors and governed. She has found out that the great machine will not go any longer without a new wheel. She will make this herself. We think she is making it of such materials and workmanship as will tear the whole machine to pieces. We are willing, if she can convince us of the necessity of such a wheel, to assist with artists and materials, in making it, so that it may answer the end. But she says, we shall have no share in it; and if we will not let her patch it up as she pleases, her Massachusetten-sises and other advocates tell us, she will tear it to pieces herself, by cutting our throats. To this kind of reasoning we can only answer, that we will not stand still to be butchered. We will defend our lives as long as providence shall enable us.

"It is beyond doubt, that it was the sense both of the *Parent Country* and *our Ancestors*, that they were to remain subject to parliament."

This has been often asserted, and as often contradicted, and fully confuted. The confutation, may not, however, have come to every eye which has read this newspaper.

The public acts of kings and ministers of state, in that age, when our ancestors emigrated, which were not complained of, remonstrated and protested against by the commons, are look'd upon as sufficient proof of the "sense" of the parent country.

The charter to the treasurer and company of Virginia, 23 March 1609, grants ample powers of government, legislative, executive and judicial, and then contains an express covenant "to and with the said treasurer and company, their successors, factors, and assigns, that they, and every of them, shall be free from all taxes and impositions forever, upon any goods or merchandises, at any time or times, hereafter, either upon importation thither, or exportation from thence, into our realm of England, or into any other of our realms or dominions."

I agree with this writer that the authority of a supreme legislature includes the right of taxation. Is not this quotation then an irresistible proof, that it was not the sense of King James or his ministers, or of the ancestors of the Virginians, "that they were to remain subject to parliament as a supreme legislature?"

After this, James issued a proclamation, recalling this patent, but this was never regarded. Then Charles issued another proclamation, which produced a remonstrance from Virginia, which was answered by a letter from the lords of the privy council, 22d July 1634 containing the royal assurance that "all their estates, trade, freedom, and privileges should be enjoyed by them, in as extensive a manner, as they enjoyed them before those proclamations."

Here is another evidence of the sense of the king and his ministers.

Afterwards parliament sent a squadron of ships to Virginia; the colony rose in open resistance, until the parliamentary commissioners granted them conditions, that they should enjoy the privileges of Englishmen; that their assembly should transact the affairs of the colony; that they should have a free trade to all places and nations, as the people of England; and 4thly, that "Virginia shall be free from all *taxes,* customs, and impositions whatever, and none to be imposed on them without consent of their general assembly; and that neither forts nor castles be erected, or garrisons maintained, without their consent."

One would think this was evidence enough of the sense both of the parent country, and our ancestors.

After the acts of navigation were passed, Virginia sent agents to England, and a remonstrance against those acts. Charles in answer, sent a declaration under the privy seal, 19 April 1676, affirming, "that taxes ought not be laid upon the inhabitants and proprietors of the colony, but by the common consent of the general assembly; except such impositions as the parliament should lay on the commodities imported into England from the colony." And he ordered a charter under the great seal, to secure this right to the Virginians.

What becomes of the "sense" of the parent country and our ancestors? for the ancestors of the Virginians are our ancestors, when we speak of ourselves as Americans. From Virginia let us pass to Maryland. Charles 1st, in 1633, gave a charter to the Baron of Baltimore, containing ample powers of government, and this express covenant, "to and with the said Lord Baltimore, his heirs and assigns, that we, our heirs and successors, shall at no time hereafter, set or make, or cause to be set, any imposition, custom, or other taxation, rate, or contribution whatsoever, in and upon the dwellings and inhabitants of the aforesaid province, for their lands, tenements, goods or chattels, within the said province; or to be laden or unladen, within the ports or harbors of the said province."

What then was the "sense" of the parent country and the ancestors of Maryland? But if by "our ancestors," he confines his idea to New England or this province, let us consider. The first planters of Plymouth were "our ancestors" in the strictest sense. They had no charter or patent for the land they took possession of and derived no authority from the English Parliament or Crown to set up their government. They purchased land of the Indians, and set up a government of their own, on the simple principle of nature, and afterwards purchased a patent for the land of the council at Plymouth, but never purchased any charter for government, of the Crown, or the King, and continued to exercise all the powers of government, legislative, executive and judicial, upon the plain ground of an original contract among independent individuals for 68 years, i.e. until their incorporation with Massachusetts by our present charter. The same may be said of the colonies which emigrated to Say-Brook, New-Haven, and other parts of Connecticut. They seem to have had no idea of dependence on Parliament, any more than on the Conclave. The Secretary of Connecticut has now in his possession, an original letter from Charles 2d. to that colony, in which he considers them rather as friendly allies, than as subjects to his English Parliament, and even requests them to pass a law in their assembly, relative to piracy.

The sentiments of your ancestors in the Massachusetts may be learned from almost every ancient paper and record. It would be endless to recite all the passages, in which it appears that they thought themselves exempt from the authority of parliament, not only in the point of taxation, but in all cases whatsoever. Let me mention one. Randolph, one of the predecessors of Massachusettensis, in a representation to Charles 2d, dated 20 September 1676, says, "I went to visit the governor at his house, and among other discourse, I told him, I took notice of several ships that were arrived at Boston, some since my being there, from Spain, France, Straits, Canaries, and other parts of Europe, contrary to your Majesty's laws for encouraging Navigation and regulating the trade of the plantations. He freely declared to me, that the law made by your Majesty and your parliament, obligeth them in nothing but what consists with the interest of that colony, that the legislative power is and abides in them solely to act and make laws by virtue of a Charter from your Majesty's royal father." Here is a positive assertion of an exemption from the authority of parliament, even in the case of the regulation of trade.

Afterwards in 1677, the General Court passed a law, which shows the sense of our ancestors in a very strong light. It is in these words: "This court being informed, by letters received this day from our messengers, of his Majesty's expectation that the acts of Trade and Navigation be exactly and punctually observed by this his Majesty's colony, his pleasure therein not having before now, [been] signified unto us, either by express from his Majesty or any of his ministers of state. It is therefore hereby ordered, and by the authority of this court enacted, that henceforth, all masters of ships, ketches, or other vessels, of greater or lesser burthen, arriving in, or sailing from any of the ports in this jurisdiction, do, without coven, or fraud, yield faithful and constant obedience unto, and observation of, all the said acts of navigation and trade, on penalty of suffering such forfeitures, loss and damage, as in the said acts are particularly expressed. And the governor and council, and all officers, commissionated and authorized by them, are hereby ordered and required to see to the strict observation of the said acts." As soon as they had passed this law, they wrote a letter to their agent, in which they acknowledge they had not conformed to the acts of trade; and they say, they "apprehended them to be an invasion of the rights, liberties and properties of the subjects of his Majesty in the colony, they not being represented in parliament, and according to the usual sayings of the learned in the law, *the laws of England were bounded within the four seas, and did not reach America.* However, as his Majesty had signified his pleasure, that these acts should be observed in the Massachusetts, they had made provision, by a law of the colony, that they should be strictly attended from time to time, although it greatly discouraged trade, and was a great damage to his Majesty's plantation."

Thus it appears, that the ancient Massachusettensians and Virginians, had precisely the same sense of the authority of parliament, viz. that it had none at all; and the same sense of the necessity, that by the voluntary act of the colonies, their free chearful consent, it should be allowed the power of regulating trade; and this is precisely the idea of the late Congress at Philadelphia, expressed in the fourth proposition in their Bill of Rights.

But this was the sense of the parent country too, at that time; for K[ing] Charles II. in a letter to the Massachusetts, after this law had been laid before him, has these words, "We are informed that you have lately made *some good provision* for observing the acts of trade and navigation, which is well pleasing unto us." Had he, or his ministers an idea that parliament was the sovereign legislative over the Colony? If he had, would he not have censured this law as an insult to that legislature?

I sincerely hope, we shall see no more such round affirmations, that it was the sense of the parent country and our ancestors, that they were to remain subject to parliament.

So far from thinking themselves subject to parliament, that during the Interregnum, it was their desire and design to have been a free commonwealth, an independent Republic; and after the restoration, it was with the utmost reluctance, that in the course of 16 or 17 years, they were bro't to take the oaths of allegiance; and for some time after this, they insisted upon taking an oath of fidelity to the country, before that of allegiance to the King.

That "it is evident, from the Charter itself," that they were to remain subject to parliament, is very unaccountable, when there is not one word in either Charter concerning parliament.

That the authority of parliament has been exercised almost ever since the settlement of the country, is a mistake; for there is no instance, until the first Navigation Act, which was in 1660, more than 40 years after the first settlement. This act was never executed or regarded, until 17 years afterwards, and then it was not executed as an act of parliament, but as a law of the colony, to which the king agreed.

"This has been expressly acknowledged by our Provincial Legislatures." There is too much truth in this. It has been twice acknowledged by our House of Representatives, that parliament was the supreme legislative; but this was directly repugnant to a multitude of other votes by which it was denied. This was in conformity to the distinction between taxation and legislation, which has since been found to be a distinction without a difference.

When a great question is first started, there are very few, even of the greatest minds, which suddenly and intuitively comprehend it, in all its consequences.

It is both "our interest and our duty to continue subject to the authority of parliament," as far as the regulation of our trade, if it will be content with that, but no longer.

"If the colonies are not subject to the authority of parliament, Great Britain and the colonies must be distinct states, as compleatly so as England and Scotland were before the union, or as Great Britain and Hanover are now." There is no need of being startled at this consequence. It is very harmless. There is no absurdity at all in it. Distinct states may be united under one king. And those states may be further cemented and united together, by a treaty of commerce. This is the case. We have by our own express consent contracted to observe the Navigation Act, and by our implied consent, by long usage and uninterrupted acquiescence, have submitted to the other acts of trade, however grievous some of them may be. This may be compared to a treaty of commerce, by which those distinct states are cemented together, in perpetual league and amity. And if any further ratifications of this pact or treaty are necessary, the colonies would readily enter into them, provided their other liberties were inviolate.

That the colonies owe "no allegiance" to any imperial crown, provided such a crown involves in it a house of lords and a house of commons, is certain. Indeed we owe no allegiance to any crown at all. We owe allegiance to the person of his majesty, King George the third, whom God preserve. But allegiance is due universally, both from Britons and Americans to the person of the king, not to his crown; to his natural, not his politic capacity, as I will undertake to prove hereafter, from the highest authorities, and most solemn adjudications, which were ever made within any part of the British Dominions.

If his Majesty's title to the crown, is "derived from an act of parliament made since the settlement of these Colonies," it was not made since the date of our charter. Our charter was granted by King William and Queen Mary, three years after the revolution. And the oaths of allegiance are established by a law of the province. So that our allegiance to his majesty is not due by virtue of any act of a British parliament, but by our own charter and province laws. It ought to be remembered, that there was a revolution here, as well as in England, and that we made an original, express contract with King William, as well as the people of England.

If it follows from thence, that he appears king of the Massachusetts, king of Rhode Island, king of Connecticut, &c. This is no absurdity at all. He will appear in this light, and does appear so, whether parliament has authority over us or not. He is king of Ireland, I suppose, although parliament is allowed to have authority there. As to giving his Majesty those titles, I have no objection at all; I wish he would be graciously pleased to assume them.

The only proposition in all this writer's long string of pretended absurdities, which he says follow from the position, that we are distinct states, is this. That "as the king must govern each state by its parliament, those several parliaments would pursue the particular interest of its own state and however well disposed the king might be to pursue a line of interest that was common to all, the checks and controul that he would meet with would render it impossible." Every argument ought to be allowed its full weight; and therefore candor obliges me to acknowledge, that here lies all the difficulty that there is in this whole controversy. There has been, from first to last, on both sides of the Atlantic, an idea, an apprehension that it was necessary there should be some superintending power, to draw together all the wills, and unite all the strength of the subjects in all the dominions, in case of war, and in the case of trade. The necessity of this, in case of trade, has been so apparent, that, as has often been said, we have consented that parliament should exercise such a power. In case of war, it has by some been thought necessary. But in fact and experience, it has not been found so. What tho' the proprietary colonies, on account of disputes with the proprietors, did not come in so early to the assistance of the general cause in the last war, as they ought, and perhaps one of them not at all! The inconveniences of this were small, in comparison of the absolute ruin to the liberties of all which must follow the submission to parliament, in all cases, which would be giving up all the popular limitations upon the government. These inconveniences fell chiefly upon New England. She was necessitated to greater exertions But she had rather suffer these again and again than others infinitely greater. However, this subject has been so long in contemplation that it is fully understood now, in all the colonies; so that there is no danger in case of another war, of any colony['s] failing of its duty.

But admitting the proposition in its full force, that it is absolutely necessary there should be a supreme power, coextensive with all the dominions, will it follow that parliament as now constituted has a right to assume this supream jurisdiction? By no means.

A union of the colonies might be projected, and an American legislature; or if America has 3,000,000 people, and the whole dominions twelve, she ought to send a quarter part of all the members to the house of commons, and instead of holding parliaments always at Westminister, the haughty members for Great Britain, must humble themselves, one session in four, to cross the Atlantic, and hold the parliament in America.

There is no avoiding all inconveniences in human affairs. The greatest possible or conceivable, would arise from ceding to parliament all power over us, without a representation in it. The next greatest, would accrue from any plan that can be devised for a representation there. The least of all arise from going on as we begun, and fared well for 150 years, by letting parliament regulate trade, and our own assemblies all other matters.

As to "the prerogatives not being defined or limited," it is as much so in the Colonies as in G[reat] Britain, and as well understood, and as cheerfully submitted to in the former as the latter.

But "where is the British constitution, that we all agree we are intitled to?" I answer, if we enjoy, and are intitled to more liberty than the British constitution allows, where is the harm? Or if we enjoy the British constitution in greater purity and perfection than they do in England, as is really the case, whose fault is this? Not ours.

We may find all the blessings "of this constitution in our Provincial Assemblies." Our Houses of Representatives have, and ought to exercise, every power of the house of Commons. The first Charter to this colony is nothing to the present argument; but it did grant a power of taxing the people, implicitly, tho' not in express terms. It granted all the rights and liberties of Englishmen, which include the power of taxing the people.

"Our Council Boards," in the royal governments, "are destitute of the noble independence and splendid appendages of peerages." Most certainly. They are the meerest creatures and tools in the political creation. Dependent every moment for their existence on the tainted breath of a prime minister. But they have the authority of the house of lords, in our little models of the English constitution. And it is this which makes them so great a grievance. The crown has really, two branches of our legislatures in its power. Let an act of parliament pass at home, putting it in the power of the king, to remove any peer from the house of lords at his pleasure, and what will become of the British constitution? It will be overturned from the foundation. Yet we are perpetually insulted, by being told, that making our council by mandamus, brings us nearer to the British constitution. In this province, by charter, the council certainly hold their seats for the year, after being chosen and approved, independent of both the other branches. For their creation, they are equally obliged to both the other branches; so that there is little or no bias in favour of either, if any, it is in favour of the prerogative. In short, it is not easy without an hereditary nobility, to constitute a council more independent, more nearly resembling the House of Lords than the council of this province has ever been by Charter. But perhaps it will be said, that we are to enjoy the British constitution in our supreme legislature, the Parliament, not in our provincial legislatures.

To this I answer, if parliament is to be our supreme legislature, we shall be under a compleat oligarchy or aristocracy, not the British constitution, which this writer himself defines a mixture of monarchy, aristocracy, and democracy. For king, lords and commons, will constitute one great oligarchy, as they will stand related to America, as much as the Decemvirs did in Rome. With this difference for the worse, that our rulers are to be three thousand miles off. The definition of an oligarchy, is a government by a number of grandees, over whom the people have no controul. The States of Holland were once chosen by the people frequently. Then chosen for life. Now they are not chosen by the people at all. When a member dies, his place is filled up not by the people he is to represent, but by the States. Is not this depriving the Hollanders of a free constitution, and subjecting them to an aristocracy, or oligarchy? Will not the government of America be like it? Will not representatives be chosen for them by others, whom they never saw nor heard of?

If our provincial constitutions are in any respect imperfect, and want alteration, they have capacity enough to discern it, and power enough to effect it, without the interposition of parliament. There never was an American constitution attempted by parliament, before the Quebec Bill and Massachusetts Bill. These are such *samples* of what they may and probably will be, that few Americans are in love with them. However, America will never allow that parliament has any authority to alter their constitution at all. She is wholly penetrated with a sense of the necessity of resisting it, at all hazards. And she would resist it, if the constitution of the Massachusetts had been altered as much for the *better*, as it is for the worse. The question we insist on most, is not whether the alteration is for the better or not, but whether parliament has any right to make any alteration at all. And it is the universal sense of America, that it has none.

We are told that "the provincial constitutions have no principle of stability within themselves." This is so great a mistake, that there is not more order or stability in any government upon the globe, than there ever has been in that of Connecticut. The same may be said of the Massachusetts and Pennsylvania, and indeed, of the others, very nearly. "That these constitutions in turbulent times would become wholly monarchial or wholly republican." They must be such times as would have a similar effect upon the constitution at home. But in order to avoid the danger of this, what is to be done. Not give us an English constitution, it seems, but make sure of us at once, by giving us constitutions wholly monarchical, annihilating our houses of representatives first, by taking from them the support of government, &c. and then making the council and judges wholly dependent on the crown.

That a representation in parliament is impracticable we all agree; but the consequence is, that we must have a representation in our supreme legislatures here. This was the consequence that was drawn by kings, ministers, our ancestors, and the whole nation, more than a century ago, when the colonies were first settled, and continued to be the general sense until the last peace and it must be the general sense again soon, or Great Britain will lose her colonies.

"This is apparently the meaning of that celebrated passage in Gov[ernor] Hutchinson's letter, that rung through the continent, viz. 'There must be an abridgment of what is called English liberties.' " But all the art and subtlety of Massachusettensis will never vindicate or excuse that expression. According to this writer, it should have been "there is an abridgment of English liberties, and it can't be otherwise." But every candid reader must see that the letter-writer had more than that in his *view* and in his *wishes*. In the same letter, a little before, he says, "What marks of resentment the parliament will show, whether they will be upon the province in general or particular persons, is extremely uncertain; but that they will be placed somewhere is most certain, and I add, *because I think it ought to be so.*" Is it possible to read this without thinking of the Port Bill, the Charter Bill, and the resolves for sending persons to England by the statute of H[enry] 8, to be tried! But this is not all: "This is most certainly a crisis," says he, &c. "If no measure shall have been taken to secure this dependence, (i.e., the dependence which a colony ought to have upon the parent state) it is all over with us." "The friends of government will be utterly disheartened, and the friends of anarchy will be afraid of nothing, be it ever so extravagant." But this is not all. "I never think of the measures necessary for the peace and good order of the colonies without pain." "There must be an abridgment of what are called English liberties." What could he mean? Any thing less than depriving us of trial by jury? Perhaps he wanted an act of parliament to try persons here for treason by a court of admiralty. Perhaps an act that the province should be governed by a governor and a mandamus council, without a house of representatives. But to put it out of all doubt that his meaning was much worse than Massachusettensis endeavours to make it, he explains himself in a subsequent part of the letter, "I wish," says he, "the good of the colony, *when I wish to see some further restraint of liberty."* Here it is rendered certain, that he is pleading for a further restraint of liberty, not explaining the restraint, he apprehended the constitution had already laid us under.

My indignation at this letter, has sometimes been softened by compassion. It carries on the face of it, evident marks of *madness.* It was written in such a transport of passions, *ambition,* and *revenge* chiefly, that his reason was manifestly overpowered. The vessel was tost in such a hurricane, that she could not feel her helm. Indeed he seems to have had a confused consciousness of this himself. "Pardon me this excursion, says he, it really proceeds from the state of mind into which our perplexed affairs often throws me."

"It is our highest interest to continue a part of the British empire, and equally our duty to remain subject to the authority of parliament," says Massachusettensis.

We are a part of the British dominions, that is of the King of Great Britain, and it is our interest and duty to continue so. It is equally our interest and duty to continue subject to the authority of parliament, in the regulation of our trade, as long as she shall leave us to govern our internal policy, and to give and grant our own money, and no longer.

This letter concludes with an agreeable flight of fancy. The time may not be so far off, however, as this writer imagines, when the colonies may have the balance of numbers and wealth in her favour. But when that shall happen, if we should attempt to rule her by an American parliament, without an adequate representation in it, she will infallibly resist us by her arms.

[March 6, 1775]   Novanglus

VIII

It has often been observed by me, and it cannot be too often repeated, that *colonization* is *casus omissus* at common law. There is no such title known in that law. By common law, I mean that system of customs, written and unwritten, which was known and in force in England, in the time of king Richard the first. This continued to be the case, down to the reign of Elizabeth and king James the first. In all that time, the laws of England were confined to the realm, and within the four seas. There was no provision made in this law for governing colonies, beyond the Atlantic, or beyond the four seas, by authority of parliament, no nor for the king to grant charters to subjects to settle in foreign countries. It was the king's prerogative to prohibit the emigration of any of his subjects, by issuing his writ *Ne exeat Regno.* And therefore it was in the king's power to permit his subjects to leave the kingdom. . . . "It is a high crime to disobey the king's lawful commands or prohibitions, as not returning from beyond sea upon the king's letters to that purpose; for which the offender's lands shall be seized 'til he return; and when he does return, he shall be fined, &c.; or going beyond sea against the king's will, expressly signified, either by the writ *Ne exeat Regno,* or under the great or privy seal, or signet, or by proclamation." When a subject left the kingdom by the king's permission, and if the nation did not remonstrate against it, by the nation's permission too, at least connivance, he carried with him, as a man, all the rights of nature. His allegiance bound him to the king and intitled him to protection.

But how? Not in France; the King of England was not bound to protect him in France. Nor in America. Not in the dominions of Lewis nor of Passichus, or Massachusetts. He had a right to protection, and the liberties of England, upon his return there, not otherwise. How then do we New Englandmen derive our laws? I say, not from parliament, not from common law, but from the law of nature and the compact made with the king in our charters. Our ancestors were intitled to the common law of England, when they emigrated, that is, to just so much of it as they pleased to adopt, and no more. They were not bound or obliged to submit to it, unless they chose it. By a positive principle of the common law, they were bound, let them be in what part of the world they would, to do nothing against their allegiance to the king. But no kind of provision was ever made by common law, for punishing or trying any man even for treason, committed out of the realm. He must be tried in some county of the realm, by that law, the county where the overt act was done, or he could not be tried at all. Nor was any provision ever made, until the reign of Henry the Eighth, for trying treasons committed abroad, and the acts of that reign were made on purpose to catch Cardinal Pole.

So that our ancestors, when they emigrated, having obtained permission of the king to come here, and being never commanded to return into the realm, had a clear right to have erected in this wilderness a British constitution, or a perfect democracy, or any other form of government they saw fit. They indeed, while they lived, could not have taken arms against the king of England, without violating their allegiance, but their children would not have been born within the king's allegiance, would not have been natural subjects, and consequently not intitled to protection, or bound to the king.

Massachusettensis, Jan. 16, seems possessed of these ideas, and attempts in the most awkward manner, to get rid of them. He is conscious that America must be a part of the realm, before it can be bound by the authority of parliament; and therefore is obliged to suggest, that we are annexed to the realm, and to endeavour to confuse himself and his readers, by confounding the realm, with the empire and dominions.

But will any man soberly contend, that America was ever annexed to the realm? To what realm? When New England was settled, there was a realm of England, a realm of Scotland, and a realm of Ireland. To which of these three realms was New England annexed? To the realm of England, it will be said. But by what law? No territory could be annexed to the realm of England, but by an act of parliament. Acts of parliament have been passed to annex Wales, &c. &c. to the realm. But none ever passed to annex America. But if New England was annexed to the realm of England, how came she annexed to the realm of or kingdom of Great Britain? The two realms of England and Scotland were by the act of union incorporated into one kingdom, by the name of Great Britain. But there is not one word about America in that act.

Besides, if America was annexed to the realm, or a part of the kingdom, every act of parliament that is made, would extend to it, named or not named. But everybody knows that every act of parliament, and every other record, constantly distinguishes between this kingdom and his Majesty's other dominions. Will it be said that Ireland is annex'd to the realm, or a part of the kingdom of Great Britain? Ireland is a distinct kingdom or realm by itself, notwithstanding British parliament claims a right of binding it in all cases, and exercises it in some. And even so the Massachusetts is a realm, New York is a realm, Pennsylvania another realm, to all intents and purposes, as much as Ireland is, or England or Scotland ever were. The King of Great Britain is the sovereign of all these realms.

This writer says, "that in denying that the colonies are annexed to the realm, and subject to the authority of parliament, individuals and bodies of men, subvert the fundamentals of government, deprive us of British liberties, and build up absolute monarchy in the colonies."

This is the first time that I ever heard or read that the colonies are annexed to the realm. It is utterly denied that they are, and that it is possible they should be, without an act of parliament, and acts of the colonies. Such an act of parliament cannot be produced, nor any such law of any one colony. Therefore as this writer builds the whole authority of parliament upon this fact, viz.—that the colonies are annexed to the realm; and as it is certain they never were so annexed, the consequence is, that his whole superstructure falls.

When he says, that they subvert the fundamentals of government, he begs the question. We say that the contrary doctrines subvert the fundamentals of government. When he says, that they deprive us of British liberties, he begs the question again. We say that the contrary doctrine deprives us of English Liberties; as to British Liberties, we scarcely know what they are, as the liberties of England and Scotland are not precisely the same to this day. English liberties are but certain rights of nature reserved to the citizen, by the English constitution, which rights cleaved to our ancestors when they crossed the Atlantic, and would have inhered in them, if instead of coming to New England, they had gone to Outaheite, or Patagonia, even altho' they had taken no patent or charter from the king at all. These rights did not adhere to them the less, for their purchasing patents and charters, in which the king expressly stipulates with them, that they and their posterity should forever enjoy all those rights and liberties.

The human mind is not naturally the clearest atmosphere; but the clouds and vapours which have been raised in it, by the artifices of temporal and spiritual tyrants, have made it impossible to see objects in it distinctly. Scarcely any thing is involved in more systematical obscurity, than the rights of our ancestors, when they arrived in America. How, in common sense, came the dominions of King Philip, King Massachusetts, and twenty other sovereigns, independent princes here, to be within the allegiance of the king of England, James and Charles? America was no more within the allegiance of those princes, by the common law of England, or by the law of nature, than France and Spain were. Discovery, if that was incontestible, could give no title to the English king, by common law, or by the law of nature, to the lands, tenements and hereditaments of the native Indians here. Our ancestors were sensible of this, and therefore honestly purchased their lands of the natives. They might have bought them to hold allodially, if they would.

But there were two ideas, which confused them, and have continued to confuse their posterity, one derived from the feudal, the other from the canon law. By the former of these systems, the prince, the general, was supposed to be sovereign lord of all the lands conquered by the soldiers in his army; and upon this principle, the king of England was considered in law as Sovereign Lord of all the land within the realm. If he had sent an army here to conquer king Massachusetts, and it had succeeded, he would have been sovereign lord of the land here upon these principles; but there was no rule of the common law that made the discovery of a country by a subject, a title to that country in the prince. But conquest would not have annexed the country to the realm, nor have given any authority to the parliament. But there was another mist cast before the eyes of the English nation from another source. The pope claimed a sovereign propriety in, as well as authority over the whole earth. As head of the Christian church, and vicar of God, he claimed this authority over all Christendom; and in the same character he claimed a right to all the countries and possessions of heathens and infidels; a right divine to exterminate and destroy them at his discretion, in order to propagate the Catholic faith. When King Henry the eighth and his parliament, threw off the authority of the pope, stripped his holiness of his supremacy, and invested it in himself by an act of parliament, he and his courtiers seemed to think that all the right[s] of the holy see, were transferred to him; and it was a union of these two the most impertinent and fantastical ideas that ever got into an human pericranium, viz. that as feudal sovereign and supream head of the church together, a king of England had a right to all the land their subjects could find, not possessed by any Christian state or prince, tho' possessed by heathen or infidel nations, which seems to have deluded the nation about the time of the settlement of the colonies. But none of these ideas gave or inferred any right in parliament, over the new countries conquered or discovered; and therefore denying that the colonies are a part of the realm, and that as such they are subject to parliament, by no means deprives us of English liberties. Nor does it "build up absolute monarchy in the colonies." For admitting these notions of the common and feudal law to have been in full force, and that the king was absolute in America, when it was settled; yet he had a right to enter into a contract with his subjects, and stipulate that they should enjoy all the rights and liberties of Englishmen forever, in consideration of their undertaking to clear the wilderness, propagate Christianity, pay a fifth part of ore, &c. Such a contract as this has been made with all the colonies, royal governments as well as charter ones. For the commissions to the governors contain the plan of the government, and the contract between the king and subject, in the former, as much as the charters in the latter.

Indeed, this was the reasoning, and upon these feudal and *catholic* principles in the time of some of the predecessors of Massachusettensis. This was the meaning of Dudley, when he asked, "Do you think that English liberties will follow you to the ends of the earth?" His meaning was, that English liberties were confined to the realm, and out of that the king was absolute. But this was not true, for an English king had no right to be absolute over Englishmen, out of the realm, any more than in it, and they were released from their allegiance, as soon as he deprived them of their liberties.

But "our charters suppose regal authority in the grantor." True they suppose it, whether there was any or not. "If that authority be derived from the British (he should have said English) crown, it presupposes this territory to have been a part of the British (he should have said English) dominion, and as such subject to the imperial sovereign." How can this writer show this authority to be derived from the English crown, including in the idea of it Lords and Commons? Is there the least colour for such an authority but in the popish and feudal ideas before mentioned? And do these popish and feudal ideas, include parliament? Was parliament, were Lords and Commons, parts of the head of the church or was parliament, that is, Lords and Commons, part of the sovereign feudatory? Never. But why was this authority derived from the English, any more than the Scottish or Irish crown? It is true, the land was to be held in socage like the manor of East Greenwich, but this was compact, and it might have been as well to hold, as they held in Glasgow or Dublin.

But says this writer, "if that authority was vested in the person of the king in a different capacity, the British constitution and laws are out of the question, and the king must be absolute as to us, as his prerogatives have never been limited." Not the prerogative limited in our charters, when in every one of them all the rights of Englishmen are secured to us! Are not the rights of Englishmen sufficiently known, and are not the prerogatives of the king's among those rights?

As to those colonies which are destitute of charters, the commissions to their governors have ever been considered as equivalent securities both for property, jurisdiction and privileges, with charters; and as to the power of the crown being absolute in those colonies, it is absolute nowhere. There is no fundamental or other law, that makes a king of England absolute anywhere, except in conquered countries, and an attempt to assume such a power, by the fundamental laws, forfeits the prince's right even to the limited crown.

As to "the charter governments reverting to absolute monarchy, as their charters may happen to be forfeited, by the grantees not fulfilling the conditions of them," I answer, if they could be forfeited, and were actually forfeited, the only consequence would be, that the king would have no power over them at all. He would not be bound to protect the people, nor, that I can see, would the people here, who were born here, be, by any principle of common law, bound even to allegiance to the king. The connection would be broken between the crown and the natives of the country.

It has been a great dispute whether charters granted within the realm, can be forfeited at all. It was a question debated with infinite learning, in the case of the charter of London. It was adjudged forfeited, in an arbitrary reign; but afterwards, after the revolution, it was declared in parliament, not forfeited, and by an act of parliament made incapable of forfeiture. The charter of Massachusetts was declared forfeited too. So were other American charters. The Massachusetts alone, were tame enough to give it up. But no American charter will ever be decreed forfeited again, or if any should, the decree will be regarded no more, than a vote of the lower house of the robbinhood society. The court of chancery has no authority without the realm; by common law, surely it has none in America. What! the privileges of millions of Americans depend on the discretion of a lord chancellor? God forbid! The passivity of this colony in receiving the present charter in lieu of the first, is in the opinion of some the deepest stain upon its character. There is less to be said in excuse for it than the witchcraft, or hanging the Quakers. A vast party in the province were against it at the time, and thought themselves betrayed by their agent. It has been a warning to their posterity, and one principal motive with the people, never to trust any agent with power to concede away their privileges again. It may as well be pretended that the people of Great Britain can forfeit their privileges, as the people of this province. If the contract of state is broken, the people and king of England, must recur to nature. It is the same in this province. We shall never more submit to decrees in chancery, or acts of parliament, annihilating charters, or abridging English liberties.

Whether Massachusettensis was born, as a politician, in the year 1764, I know not; but he often writes as if he knew nothing of that period. In his attempt to trace the denial of the supreme authority of the parliament, he commits such mistakes, as a man of age at that time ought to blush at. He says, that "when the Stamp Act was made, the authority of parliament to impose external taxes, or in other words, to lay duties upon goods and merchandize was admitted," and that when the Tea Act was made, "a new distinction was set up, that parliament had a right to lay duties upon merchandize for the purpose of regulating trade, but not for the purpose of raising a revenue." This is a total misapprehension of the declared opinions of people at those times. The authority of parliament to lay taxes for a revenue, has been always generally denied. And their right to lay duties to regulate trade, has been denied by many, who have ever contended that trade should be regulated only by prohibitions.

The act of parliament of the 4 George the third, passed in the year 1764, was the first act of the British parliament that ever was passed, in which the design of raising a revenue was expressed. Let Massachusettensis name any statute before that in which the word revenue is used, or the thought of raising a revenue, is expressed. This act is intitled "An act for granting certain duties in the British colonies and plantations in America," &c. The word revenue, in the preamble of this act instantly ran through the colonies, and rang an alarm, almost as much as if the design of forging chains for the Colonists had been expressed in words. I have now before me a pamphlet, written and printed in the year 1764, intitled, "The Sentiments of a British American," upon this act. . . .

The first objection to this act, which was made in that pamphlet, by its worthy author, OXENBRIDGE THACHER, Esq.; who died a Martyr to that amity for this country, which the conduct of the junto gave him, is this, "The first objection is, that a tax is thereby laid on several commodities, to be raised and levied in the plantations, and to be remitted home to England. This is esteemed a grievance, inasmuch as the same are laid, without the consent of the representatives of the colonists. It is esteemed an essential British right, that no person shall be subject to any tax; but what in person, or by his representative, he hath a voice in laying." Here is a tax unquestionably external, in the sense in which that word is used in the distinction that is made by some between external and internal taxes, and unquestionably laid in part for the regulation of trade; yet called a grievance, and a violation of an essential British right, in the year 1764, by one who was then at the head of the popular branch of our constitution, and as well acquainted with the sense of his constituents, as any man living. And it is indisputable that in those words he wrote, the almost universal sense of this colony.

There are so many egregious errors in point of fact, and respecting the opinions of the people, in this writer, that it is difficult to impute to wilful misrepresentation, that I sometimes think he is some smart young gentleman, come up, into life, since this great controversy was opened; if not, he must have conversed wholly with the junto, and they must have deceived him, respecting their own sentiments.

This writer sneers at the distinction between a right to lay the former duty of a shilling on the pound of tea, and the right to lay the three pence. But is there not a real difference between laying a duty to be paid in England upon exportation, and to be paid in America upon importation? Is there not a difference between parliament's laying on duties within their own realm, where they have undoubtedly jurisdiction, and laying them out of their realm, nay, laying them on in our realm, where we say they have no jurisdiction? Let them lay on what duties they please in England, we have nothing to say against that.

"Our patriots most heroically resolved to become independent states, and flatly denied that parliament had a right to make any laws whatever, that should be binding upon the colonies."

Our scribbler, more heroically still, is determined to show the world that he has courage superior to all regard to modesty, justice or truth. Our patriots have never determined or desired to be independent states, if a voluntary cession of a right to regulate their trade can make them dependent even on parliament; though they are clear in theory that, by the common law and the English constitution, parliament has no authority over them. None of the patriots of this province, of the present age, have ever denied that parliament has a right, from our voluntary cession, to make laws which shall bind the colonies, so far as their commerce extends.

"There is no possible medium between absolute independence and subjection to the authority of parliament." If this is true, it may be depended upon, that all North America are as fully convinced of their independence, their absolute independence, as they are of their own existence; and as fully determined to defend it at all hazards, as Great Britain is to defend her independence against foreign nations. But it is not true. An absolute independence on parliament, in all internal concerns and cases of taxation, is very compatible with an absolute dependence on it in all cases of external commerce.

"He must be blind indeed that cannot see our dearest interest, in the latter (that is, in an absolute subjection to the authority of parliament) notwithstanding many pant after the former," (that is absolute independence). The man who is capable of writing, in cool blood, that our interest lies in an absolute subjection to parliament, is capable of writing or saying any thing for the sake of his pension. A legislature that has so often discovered a want of information concerning us, and our country; a legislature interested to lay burdens upon us; a legislature, two branches of which, I mean the Lords and Commons, neither love nor fear us! Every American of fortune and common sense, must look upon his property to be sunk downright one half of its value, the moment such an absolute subjection to parliament is established.

That there are any who pant after "independence," (meaning by this word, a new plan of government over all America, unconnected with the crown of England, or meaning by it an exemption from the power of parliament to regulate trade) is as great a slander upon the province as ever was committed to writing. The patriots of this province desire nothing new; they wish only to keep their old privileges. They were for 150 years allowed to tax themselves, and govern their internal concerns, as they tho't best. Parliament governed their trade as they tho't fit. This plan, they wish may continue forever. But it is honestly confessed, rather than become subject to the absolute authority of parliament, in all cases of taxation and internal polity, they will be driven to throw off that of regulating trade.

"To deny the supreme authority of the state, is a high misdemeanor; to oppose it by force, an overt act of treason." True; and therefore Massachusettensis, who denies the king represented by his governor, his majesty's council, by charter, and house of representatives, to be the supreme authority of this province, has been guilty of a high misdemeanour; and those ministers, governors, and their instruments, who have brought a military force here, and employed it against that supreme authority, are guilty of—, and ought to be punished with—. I will be more mannerly than Massachusettensis.

"The realm of England is an appropriate term for the ancient realm of England, in contradistinction to Wales and other territories, that have been annexed to it."

There are so many particulars in the case of Wales, analogous to the case of America, that I must beg leave to enlarge upon it.

[March 13, 1775]   Novanglus

IX

Wales was a little portion of the island of Great-Britain, which the Saxons were never able to conquer. The Britons had reserved this tract of land to themselves and subsisted wholly by pasturage among their mountains. Their princes however, during the Norman period, and until the reign of King Edward the first, did homage to the crown of England, as their feudal sovereign, in the same manner as the prince of one independent state in Europe frequently did to the sovereign of another. This little principality of shepherds and cowherds, had however maintained their independence through long and bloody wars against the omnipotence of England, for 800 years. It is needless to enumerate the causes of the war between Lewellyn and Edward the first. It is sufficient to say that the Welch prince refused to go to England to do homage, and Edward obtained a new aid of a fifteenth from his parliament, to march with a strong force into Wales. Edward was joined by David and Roderic, two brothers of Lewellyn, who made a strong party among the Welch themselves, to assist and second the attempts to enslave their native country. The English monarch however, with all these advantages, was afraid to put the valour of his enemies to a trial, and trusted to the *slow effects of famine* to subdue them. Their pasturage, with such an enemy in their country, could not subsist them, and Lewellyn 19 Nov. 1277 at last submitted; and bound himself to pay a reparation of damages, to do homage to the crown of England, and almost to surrender his independence as a Prince by permitting all the other Barons of Wales, excepting four, to swear fealty to the same crown. But fresh complaints soon arose. The English grew insolent on their bloodless victory, and oppressed the inhabitants, many insults were offered, which at last raised the indignation of the Welch, so that they determined again to take arms, rather than bear any longer the oppression of the haughty victors. The war raged, some time, until Edward summoned all his military tenants, and advanced with an army too powerful for the Welch to resist. Lewellyn was at last surprized, by Edward's General Mortimer, and fighting at a great disadvantage was slain with two thousand of his men. David, who succeeded in the principality, maintained the war for some time, but at last was betrayed to the enemy, sent in chains to Shrewsbury, brought to a formal trial before the peers of England, and altho' a sovereign prince, ordered by Edward to be hanged, drawn and quartered, as a traitor, for defending by arms the liberties of his native country! All the Welch nobility submitted to the conqueror. The laws of England, sheriffs, and other ministers of justice, were established in that principality, which had maintained its liberties and independency, 800 years.

Now Wales was always part of the dominions of England. "Wales was always feudatory to the kingdom of England." It was always held of the crown of England, or the kingdom of England; that is, whoever was king of England, had a right to homage, &c. from the prince of Wales. But yet Wales was not parcel of the realm or kingdom, nor bound by the laws of England. I mention and insist upon this because it shows, that altho' the colonies are bound to the crown of England or in other words, owe allegiance to whomsoever is king of England; yet it does not follow that the colonies are parcel of the realm or kingdom, and bound by its laws. As this is a point of great importance, I must beg pardon, however unentertaining it may be, to produce my authorities. . . .

Here is the most certain evidence that Wales was subject to the kings of England by the feudal law before the conquest, tho' not bound by any laws but their own. 2. That the conquest was considered, in that day, as conferring the property as well as jurisdiction of Wales, to the English crown. 3. The conquest was considered as annexing and uniting Wales to the English crown, both in point of property and jurisdiction, as a part of one body. Yet notwithstanding all this, parliament was not considered as acquiring any share in the government of Wales by this conquest. If then, it should be admitted that the colonies are all annexed and united to the crown of England, it will not follow that Lords and Commons have any authority over them.

This statutum Walliae, as well as the whole case and history of that principality, is well worthy of the attention and study of Americans, because it abounds, with evidence, that a country may be subject to the crown of England, without being subject to the Lords and Commons of that realm, which entirely overthrows the whole argument of Governor Hutchinson and of Massachusettensis in support of the supreme authority of parliament, over all the dominions of the imperial crown. . . .

Here is then a conquered people submitting to a system of laws framed by the mere will of the conqueror, and agreeing to be forever governed by his mere will. This absolute monarch then might afterwards govern this country, with or without the advice of his English lords and commons.

To shew that Wales was held before the conquest of Lewellyn, of the King of England, altho' governed by its own laws, hear Lord Coke, 2 Inst. 194, in his commentary on the statute of Westminster. "At this time viz. in 3 Edward I, Lewellyn was a Prince or King of Wales, who held the *same of the King of England as his superior lord, and owed him liege homage, and fealty;* and this is proved by our act, viz. that the King of England was *superior dominus,* i.e., sovereign lord of the kingdom or principality of Wales."

Lord Coke in 4 Inst. 239, says "Wales was sometime a realm, or kingdom (realm from the French word royaume, and both a regno) and governed *per suas regulas,*" and afterwards, "but *jure feudali,* the kingdom of Wales was holden of the *crown of England,* and thereby as Bracton saith, was *sub potestate regis.* And so it continued until the 11 year of King Edward I., when he subdued the Prince of Wales, rising against him, and executed him for treason." "The next year, viz. in the 12 year of King Edward I, by authority of parliament, it is declared thus, speaking in the person of the king (as ancient statutes were wont to do) *divina providentia,"* &c., as in the statute *Walliae* before recited. But here is an inaccuracy for the *statutum Walliae* was not an act of parliament, but made by the king with the advice of his officers of the army, by his sole authority, as the statute itself sufficiently shows. "Note," says Lord Coke, "divers monarchs hold their kingdoms of others *jure feudali,* as the Duke of Lombardy, Cicill, Naples, and Bohemia of the empire, Granado, Leons, of Aragon, Navarre, Portugal of Castile; and so others."

After this the Welsh seem to have been fond of the English laws, and desirous of being incorporated into the realm, to be represented in parliament, and enjoy all the rights of Englishmen, as well as to be bound by the English laws. But kings were so fond of governing this principality by their discretion alone, that they never could obtain these blessings until the reign of Henry the Eighth, and then they only could obtain a statute, which enabled the king to alter their laws at his pleasure . . . . Yet we see they could not obtain any security for their liberties, for Lord Coke tells us, "in the act of 34 Henry 8 it was enacted, that the king's most royal majesty should, from time to time change, &c. all manner of things in that act rehearsed, as to his most excellent wisdom and discretion should be thought convenient and also to make laws and ordinances for the commonwealth of his said dominion of Wales at his majesty's pleasure. But for that the subjects of the dominion of Wales, &c. had lived in all dutiful subjection to the crown of England, &c., the said branch of the said statute of 34 Henry 8 is repealed and made void, by 21 Jac. c. 10."

But if we look into the statute itself, of 27 Henry 8 c. 26, we shall find the clearest proof, that being subject to the imperial crown of England did not intitle Welchmen to the liberties of England, nor make them subject to the laws of England. . . .

Upon this statute let it be observed, 1. That the language of Massachusettensis, "imperial crown" is used in it; and Wales is affirmed to have *ever* been annexed and united to that imperial crown, as a very member and joint; which shows that being annexed to the imperial crown does not annex a country to the realm, or make it subject to the authority of parliament; because Wales, certainly before the conquest of Lewellyn never was pretended to be so subject, nor afterwards ever pretended to be annexed to the realm, at all, nor subject to the authority of parliament any otherwise than as the king claimed to be absolute in Wales, and therefore to make laws for it, by his mere will, either with the advice of his proceres or without. 2. That Wales never was incorporated with the realm of England until this statute was made, nor subject to any authority of English lords and commons. 3. That the king was so tenacious of his exclusive power over Wales that he would not consent to this statute, without a clause in it, to retain the power in his own hands of giving it what system of law he pleased. 4. That knights and burgesses, i.e. representatives, were considered as *essential* and *fundamental* in the constitution of the new legislature, which was to govern Wales. 5. That since this statute, the distinction between the realm of England and the realm of Wales has been abolished, and realm of England, now, and ever since, comprehends both; so that Massachusettensis is mistaken, when he says, that the realm of England is an appropriate term for the ancient realm of England, in contradistinction from Wales, &c. 6. That this union and incorporation was made by the consent, and upon the supplication of the people of Wales as Lord Coke, and many other authors inform us so that here was an express contract between the two bodies of people. To these observations let me add a few questions.

Was there ever any act of parliament, annexing, uniting, and consolidating any one of all the colonies to and with the realm of England or the kingdom of Great Britain? 2. If such an act of parliament should be made, would it upon any principles of English laws and government, have any validity, without the consent, petition or supplication of the colonies? 3. Can such a union and incorporation, ever be made, upon any principles of English laws and government, without admitting representatives for the colonies in the house of commons, and American lords into the house of peers? 4. Would not representatives in the house of commons, unless they were numerous in proportion to the numbers of people in America, be a snare rather than a blessing? 5. Would Britain ever agree to a proportionable number of American members, and if she would, could America support the expense of them? 6. Could American representatives, possibly know the sense, the exigencies, &c. of their constituents, at such a distance, so perfectly as it is absolutely necessary legislators should know? 7. Could Americans ever come to the knowledge of the behaviour of their members, so as to dismiss the unworthy? 8. Would Americans in general, ever submit to septennial elections? 9. Have we not sufficient evidence, in the general frailty and depravity of human nature, and especially the experience we have had of Massachusettensis and the junto, that a deep, treacherous plausible, corrupt minister would be able to seduce our Members to betray us, as fast as we could send them? . . .

From the conquest of Lewellyn to this statute of James is near three hundred and fifty years, during all which time the Welch were very fond of being incorporated and enjoying the English laws, the English were desirous that they should be; yet the crown would never suffer it to be compleatly done, because it claimed an authority to rule it by discretion. It is conceived, therefore that there cannot be a more compleat and decisive proof of any thing, than this instance is, that a country may be subject to the crown of England, the imperial crown; and yet not annexed to the realm, or subject to the authority of parliament.

The word crown, like the word throne, is used in various figurative senses, sometimes it means the kingly office, the head of the commonwealth, but it does not always mean the political capacity of the king; much less does it include in the idea of it, lords and commons. It may as well be pretended that the house of commons includes or implies a king. Nay it may as well be pretended that the mace includes the three branches of the legislature.

By the feudal law, a person or a country might be subject to a king, a feudal sovereign three several ways.

1. It might be subject to his person, and in this case, it would continue so subject, let him be where he would, in his dominions or without. 2. To his crown, and in this case subjection was due, to whatsoever person or family, wore that crown, and would follow it, whatever revolutions it underwent. 3. To his crown and realm or state, and in this case it was incorporated, as one body with the principal kingdom, and if that was bound by a parliament, diet, or cortes, so was the other.

It is humbly conceived, that the subjection of the colonies by compact, and law is of the second sort. . . .

[March 20, 1775]   Novanglus

X

Massachusettensis, in some of his writings has advanced, that
our allegiance is due to the political capacity of the King, and
therefore involves in it obedience to the British parliament.
Governor Hutchinson in his memorable speech laid down the
same position. I have already shown from the case of Wales, that
this position is groundless, and that allegiance was due from the
Welch to the king, *jure feodali*, before the conquest of Lewellyn, and after that to the Crown, until it was annexed to the
realm, without being subject to acts of parliament any more
than to acts of the King without parliament. I shall hereafter
show from the case of Ireland, that subjection to the Crown
implies no obedience to parliament. But before I come to this,
I must take notice of a pamphlet intitled, "A candid examination of the mutual claims of Great Britain and the colonies, with
a plan of accommodation on constitutional principles." This
author, p. 8, says—"to him, (i.e. the King) in this representative
capacity, and as supreme executor of the laws, made by a joint
power of him and others, the oaths of allegiance are taken," and
afterwards, "Hence these professions (i.e., of allegiance) are not
made to him either in his legislative, or executive capacities; but
yet it seems they are made to the King. And into this distinction,
which is nowhere to be found, either in the constitution of the
government, in reason or common sense, the ignorant and
thoughtless have been deluded ever since the passing of the
Stamp Act, and they have rested satisfied with it without the
least examination." And in p. 9, he says, "I do not mean to offend

the inventers of this refined distinction, when I ask them is this acknowledgment made to the king, in his politick capacity as king of Great Britain &c. If so, it includes a promise of obedience to the British laws." There is no danger of this gentleman's giving offence to the inventers of this distinction, for they have been many centuries in their graves. This distinction is to be found everywhere, in the case of Wales, Ireland and elsewhere, as I shall show most abundantly before I have done. It is to be found in two of the greatest cases and most deliberate and solemn judgments, that were ever passed. One of them is Calvin's case, 7 Rep. which as Lord Coke tells us, was as elaborately, substantially, and judiciously argued as he ever heard, or read of any. After it had been argued in the court of king's bench, by learned counsel, it was adjourned to the exchequer chamber, and there argued again, first by council on both sides and then by the lord chancellor and all the twelve judges of England; and among these were the greatest men, that Westminster Hall ever could boast. Ellismore, Bacon, Hide, Hobart, Crook, and Coke, were all among them. And the chancellor and judges were unanimous in resolving. What says the book? 7 Rep. 10 "Now, seeing the king hath but one person, and several capacities, and one politick capacity for the realm of England, and another for the realm of Scotland, it is necessary to be considered, to which capacity *ligeance* is due. *And it was resolved* that it was due to the *natural person* of the king, (which is ever accompanied with the politick capacity, and the politick capacity as it were appropriated to the natural capacity) and it is not due to the politick capacity only, that is, to the crown or kingdom, distinct from his natural capacity." And further on, 7 Rep. 11. "But it was clearly resolved by all the judges, that presently by the descent his majesty was compleatly and absolutely king, &c." and that coronation was but a royal ornament! [7 Rep.]6. "In the reign of Ed[ward] 2d, the Spencers, to cover the treason hatched in their hearts, invented this damnable and damned opinion, that homage and oath of allegiance was more by reason of the king's crown (that is of his politick capacity) than by reason of the person of the king, upon which opinion they inferred execrable and detestable consequences." And afterwards, [7 Rep.] 12. "Where books and acts of parliament speak of the ligeance of *England*, &c. speaking briefly in a vulgar manner, are to be understood of the ligeance due by the people of England to the King; for no man will affirm, that England itself, taking it for the continent thereof, doth owe any ligeance or faith, or that *any faith or ligeance should be due to it;* but it manifestly appeareth, that the ligeance or faith of the subject is *proprium quarto modo* to the king, *omni, soli, et semper.* And oftentimes in the reports of our book cases and in acts of parliament also, the crown or kingdom is taken for the king himself," &c. "Tenure *in capite* is a tenure of the Crown, and is a *seigniorie in grosse,* that is of the person of the King." And afterwards [7 Rep.]6.—"For special purposes *the law makes him a body politick, immortal and invisible, whereunto our allegiance cannot appertain.*" I beg leave to observe here, that these words in the foregoing adjudication, that "the natural person of the King is ever accompanied with the politick capacity, and the politick capacity as it were appropriated to the natural capacity," neither imply nor infer allegiance or subjection to the politick capacity, because in the case of King James the first, his natural person was "accompanied" with three politick capacities at least, as King of England, Scotland and Ireland; yet the allegiance of an Englishman to him did not imply or infer subjection, to his politick capacity as King of Scotland.

Another place in which this distinction is to be found is in Moore's Reports, p. 700. "The case of the union of the realm of Scotland with England." And this deliberation, I hope was solemn enough. This distinction was agreed on by commissioners of the Englsih lords and commons in a conference with commissioners of the Scottish parliament, and after many arguments and consultations by the lord chancellor and all the judges, and afterwards adopted by the lords and commons of both nations. . . .

Indeed allegiance to a sovereign lord, is nothing more than fealty to a subordinate lord, and in neither case, has any relation to, or connection with laws or parliaments, lords or commons. There was a reciprocal confidence between the lord and vassal. The Lord was to protect the vassal in the enjoyment of his land. The vassal was to be faithful to his lord, and defend him against his enemies. This obligation on the part of the vassal, was his fealty, *fidelitas.* The oath of fealty, by the feudal law to be taken by the vassal or tenant, is nearly in the very words as the ancient oath of allegiance. But neither fealty, allegiance, or the oath of either implied any thing about laws, parliaments, lords or commons.

The fealty and allegiance of Americans then is undoubtedly due to the person of King George the third, whom God long preserve and prosper. It is due to him, in his natural person, as that natural person is intituled to the crown, the kingly office, the royal dignity of the realm of England. And it becomes due to his natural person, because he is intituled to that office. And because by the charters, and other express and implied contracts made between the Americans and the kings of England, they have bound themselves to fealty and allegiance to the natural person of that prince, who shall rightfully hold the kingly office in England, and no otherwise.

"With us in England," says Blackstone, v. 1, 367, "it becoming a settled principle of tenure, that all lands in the kingdom are holden of the king as their sovereign and lord paramount, &c. the oath of allegiance was necessarily confined to the Person of the king alone. By an easy analogy, the term of allegiance was soon brought to signify all other engagements, which are due from subjects to their prince, as well as those duties which were simply and merely territorial. And the oath of allegiance, as administered for upwards of six hundred years, contained a promise to be true and faithful to the king and his heirs, and truth and faith to bear of life and limb and terrene honor, and not to know, or hear of any ill or damage intended him, without defending him therefrom." But at the revolution, the terms of this oath, being thought perhaps to favour too much the notion of non resistance, the present form was introduced by the convention parliament, which is more general and indeterminate than the former, the subject only promising "that he will be faithful and bear true allegiance to the king, without mentioning his heirs, or specifying in the least wherein that allegiance consists."

Thus, I think, that all the authorities in law, coincide, exactly with the observation which I have heretofore made upon the case of Wales, and show that subjection to a king of England, does not necessarily imply subjection to the crown of England; and that subjection to the crown of England, does not imply subjection to the parliament of England, for allegiance is due to the person of the king, and to that alone, in all three cases, that is, whether we are subject to his parliament and crown, as well as his person, as the people in England are, whether we are subject to his crown and person, without parliament, as the Welch were after the conquest of Lewellyn, and before the union, or as the Irish were after the conquest and before Poyning's law, or whether we are subject to his person alone, as the Scots were to the king of England, after the accession of James 1st, being not at all subject to the parliament or crown of England.

We do not admit any binding authority in the decisions and adjudications of the court of king's bench or common pleas, or the court of chancery over America; but we quote them as the opinions of learned men. In these we find a distinction between a country conquered and a country discovered. Conquest, they say gives the crown an absolute power; discovery only gives the subject a right to all the laws of England. They add, that all the laws of England are in force there. I confess I do not see the reason of this. . . .

Upon this case I beg leave to make a few observations. 1. That Shower's reasoning, that we are not bound by statutes, because not represented in parliament, is universal, and therefore his exception "unless specially named," altho' it is taken from analogy to the case of Ireland, by Lord Coke and others, yet it is not taken from the common law, but is merely arbitrary and groundless, as applied to us. Because if the want of representation could be supplied by "expressly naming" a country, the right of representation might be rendered null and nugatory. But of this more another time. 2d. That by the opinion of Holt and the whole court, the laws of England, common and statute, are in force in a vacant country, discovered by Englishmen. But American was not a vacant country, it was full of inhabitants; our ancestors purchased the land; but if it had been vacant, his lordship has not shown us any authority at common law, that the laws of England would have been in force there. On the contrary, by that law it is clear they did not extend beyond seas, and therefore could not be binding there, any further than the free will of the discoverers should make them. The discoverers had a right by nature, to set up those laws, if they liked them, or any others, that pleased them better, provided they were not inconsistent with their allegiance to their king. 3d. The court held that a country must be parcel of the kingdom of England, before the laws of England could take place there; which seems to be inconsistent with what is said before, because discovery of a vacant country does not make it parcel of the kingdom of England, which shows, that the court, when they said that all laws in *force* in England are in *force* in the discovered country, meant no more than that the discoverers had a right to all such laws, if they chose to adopt them. 4. The idea of the court, in this case, is exactly conformable to, if not taken from the case of Wales. They consider a conquered country as Edward I. and his successors did Wales, as by the conquest annexed to the crown, as an absolute property, possession, or revenue, and therefore to be disposed of at its will; not intitled to the laws of England, although bound to be govern'd by the king's will, in parliament or out of it, as he pleased. 5. The Isle of Man, and Ireland, are considered like Wales, as conquered countries, and part of the possessions (by which they mean property or revenue) of the crown of England, yet have been allowed by the king's will to retain their ancient laws. 6. That the case of America differs totally from the case of Wales, Ireland, Man, or any other case, which is known at common law or in English history. There is no one precedent in point, in any English history. There is no one precedent in point, in any English records, and therefore it can be determined only by eternal reason and the law of nature. But yet that the analogy of all these cases of Ireland, Wales, Man, Chester, Durham, Lancaster, &c. clearly concur with the dictates of reason and nature, that Americans are entitled to all the liberties of Englishmen, and that they are not bound by any acts of parliament whatever, by any law known in English records of history, excepting those for the regulation of trade, which they have consented to and acquiesced in. 7. To these let me add, that as the laws of England and the authority of parliament, were by common law confined to the realm and within the four seas, so was the force of the great seal of England. Salk. 510. "The great seal of England is appropriated to England, and what is done under it has relation to England, and to no other place." So that the king, by common law, had no authority to create peers or governments, or any thing out of the realm, by his great seal; and therefore our charters and commissions to governors, being under the great seal, gives us no more authority, nor binds us to any other duties, than if they had been given under the privy seal, or without any seal at all. Their binding force, both upon the crown and us, is wholly from compact and the law of nature. . . .

[March 27, 1775]   Novanglus

XI

Give me leave now to descend from these general matters, to Massachusettensis. He says "Ireland, who has perhaps the greatest possible subordinate legislature, and send no members to the British parliament, is bound by its acts, when expressly named." But if we are to consider what ought to be, as well as what is, why should Ireland have the greatest possible subordinate legislature? Is Ireland more numerous and more important to what is called the British empire, than America? Subordinate as the Irish legislature is said to be, and a conquered country as undoubtedly it is, the parliament of Great Britain, altho' they claim a power to bind Ireland by statutes, have never laid one farthing of a tax upon it. They knew it would occasion resistance if they should. But the authority of parliament to bind Ireland at all, if it has any, is founded upon a different principle entirely from any that takes place in the case of America. It is founded on the consent and compact of the Irish by Poyning's law to be so governed, if it has any foundation at all; and this consent was given and compact made in consequence of a conquest. . . .

Thus, I have cursorily mentioned every law made by the King of England, whether in parliament or out of it, for the government of Ireland, from the conquest of it by Henry the 2nd, in 1172, down to the reign of Henry the 7th, when an express contract was made between the two kingdoms, that Ireland should for the future be bound by English acts of parliament, in which it should be specially named. This contract was made in 1495, so that upon the whole it appears, beyond dispute, that for more than 300 years, tho' a conquered country, and annexed to the crown of England; yet was so far from being annexed to or parcel of the realm, that the king's power was absolute there, and he might govern it without his English parliament, whose advice concerning it, he was under no obligation to ask or pursue.

The contract I here allude to, is what is called Poyning's law, the history of which is briefly this. Ireland revolted from England, or rather adhered to the partisans of the house of York, and Sir Edward Poyning was sent over about the year 1495, by King Henry the 7th, with very extensive powers, *over the civil as well as military administration.* On his arrival he made severe inquisition about the disaffected, and in particular attacked the Earls of Dismond and Kildare. The first stood upon the defensive, and eluded the power of the deputy; but Kildare was sent prisoner to England; *not to be executed it seems, nor to be tried upon the statute of Henry 8,* but to be dismissed as he actually was, to his own country, with marks of the king's esteem and favour; Henry judging that, at such a juncture, he should gain more by clemency and indulgence, than by rigour and severity. In this opinion he sent a commissioner to Ireland with a formal amnesty, in favour of Desmond and all his adherents, whom the tools of his ministers did not fail to call traitors and rebels with as good a grace and as much benevolence, as Massachusettensis discovers.

Let me stop here and enquire, whether Lord North has more wisdom than Henry the 7th, or whether he took the hint from the history of Poyning's, of sending General Gage, with his civil and military powers? If he did, he certainly did not imitate Henry, in his blustering menaces, against certain "ringleaders and forerunners."

While Poyning resided in Ireland, he called a parliament, which is famous in history for the acts which it passed in favour of England, and Englishmen settled in Ireland. By these, which are still called Poyning's laws, all the former laws of England

were made to be of force in Ireland, and no bill can be introduced into the Irish parliament, unless it previously receive the
sanction of the English privy council; and by a construction if
not by the express words of these laws, Ireland is still said to be
bound by English statutes in which it is specially named. Here
then let Massachusettensis pause and observe the original of the
notion that countries might be bound by acts of parliament, if
"specially named," tho' without the realm. Let him observe too,
that this notion is grounded entirely on the voluntary act, the
free consent of the Irish nation, and an act of an Irish parliament, called Poyning's law. Let me ask him, has any colony in
America ever made a Poyning's act? Have they ever consented
to be bound by acts of parliament, if specially named? Have
they ever acquiesced in, or implicitly consented to any acts of
parliament, but such as are *bona fide* made for the regulation
of trade? This idea of binding countries without the realm, "by
specially naming" them, is not an idea taken from the common
law. There was no such principle, rule, or maxim, in that law,
it must be by statute law then, or none. In the case of Wales and
Ireland, it was introduced by solemn compact, and established
by statutes to which the Welch and Irish were parties, and
expressly consented. But in the case of America there is no such
statute, and therefore Americans are bound by statutes in
which they are "named," no more than by those in which they
are not.

The principle upon which Ireland is bound by English statutes in which it is named, is this, that being a conquered country, and subject to the mere will of the king, it voluntarily
consented to be so bound. This appears in part already, and
more fully in 1. Blackstone, 99, 100, &c. who tells us, "that
Ireland is a distinct, tho' a dependent, subordinate kingdom."
But how came it dependent and subordinate? He tells us "that
king John, in the twelfth year of his reign, after the conquest,
went into Ireland, carried over with him many able sages of the
law; and there *by his letters patent, in right of the dominion of*

conquest, is said to have ordained and established, that Ireland should be governed by the laws of England; which letters patent Sir Edward Coke apprehends to have been there confirmed in parliament." "By the same rule that no laws made in England, between King John's time and Poyning's law, were then binding in Ireland, it follows that no acts of the English parliament, made since the tenth of Henry the 7th, do now bind the people of Ireland, unless specially named or included under general words. And on the other hand it is equally clear, that where Ireland is particularly named, or is included under general words, they are bound by such acts of parliament; for it follows from the very nature and constitution of a dependent state; dependence being very little else but an obligation to conform to the will or law of that superior person or state, upon which the inferior depends. The original and true ground of this superiority in the present case, is what we usually call, tho' somewhat improperly, *the right of conquest;* a right allowed by the law of nations, if not by that of nature; but which in reason and civil policy can mean nothing more, than that, in order to put an end to hostilities, *a compact* is either expressly or tacitly made between the conqueror and the conquered, that if they will acknowledge the *victor* for their *master,* he will treat them for the future as subjects, and not as enemies."

These are the principles upon which the dependence and subordination of Ireland are founded. Whether they are just or not, is not necessary for us to enquire. The Irish nation have never been entirely convinced of their justice; have been ever discontented with them, and ripe and ready to dispute them. Their reasonings have ever been answered by the *ratio ultima and penultima* of the tories, and it requires to this hour, no less than a standing army of 12,000 men to confute them. As little as the British parliament exercises the right, which it claims of binding them by statutes, and altho' it never once attempted or presumed to tax them, and altho' they are so greatly inferior to Britain in power, and so near in situation.

But thus much is certain, that none of these principles take place, in the case of America. She never was conquered by Britain. She never consented to be a state dependent upon, or subordinate to the British parliament, excepting only in the regulation of her commerce; and therefore the reasonings of British writers, upon the case of Ireland, are not applicable to the case of the colonies, any more than those upon the case of Wales.

Thus I have rambled after Massachusettensis through Wales and Ireland, but have not reached my journey's end. I have yet to travel through Jersey, Guernsey, and I know not where. At present I shall conclude with one observation. In the history of Ireland and Wales, though undoubtedly conquered countries, and under the very eye and arm of England, the extreme difficulty, the utter impracticability, of governing a people who have any sense, spirit, or love of liberty, without incorporating them into the state, or allowing them in some other way equal priviledges may be clearly seen. Wales was forever revolting for a thousand years, until it obtained that mighty blessing. Ireland, has been frequently revolting, altho' the most essential power of a supreme legislature, that of imposing taxes has never been exercised over them, and it cannot now be kept under, but by force, and it would revolt forever, if parliament should tax them. What kind of an opinion then must the ministry entertain of America. When her distance is so great, her territory so extensive, her commerce so important, not a conquered country, but dearly purchased and defended? When her trade is so essential to the navy, the commerce, the revenue, the very existence of Great Britain, as an independent state? They must think America inhabited by three million fools and cowards.

[April 3, 1775]   Novanglus

XII

The cases of Wales and Ireland are not yet exhausted. They afford such irrefragable proofs, that there is a distinction between the crown and realm, and that a country may be annexed and subject to the former, and not to the latter, that they ought to be thoroughly studied and understood.

The more these cases, as well as those of Chester, Durham, Jersey, Guernsey, Calais, Gascoine, Guienne, &c. are examined, the more clearly it will appear, that there is no precedent in English records, no rule of common law, no provision in the English constitution, no policy in the English or British government, for the case of the colonies; and therefore that we derive our laws and government solely from our own compacts with Britain and her kings, and from the great legislature of the universe.

We ought to be cautious of the inaccuracies of the greatest men, for these are apt to lead us astray. . . .

I have been at the pains of transcribing this long passage, for the sake of a variety of important observations that may be made upon it. 1. That exuberance of proof that is in it, both that Ireland is annexed to the crown, and that it is not annexed to the realm of England. 2. That the reasoning in the year book, that Ireland has a parliament, and makes laws, and our statutes don't bind them, because they don't send knights to parliament, is universal, and concludes against these statutes binding in which Ireland is specially named, as much as against these in which it is not, and therefore Lord Coke's parenthesis, *(which is to be understood unless they be specially named)* is wholly arbitrary and groundless, unless it goes upon the supposition that the king is absolute in Ireland, it being a conquered country, and so has power to bind it at his pleasure, by an act of parliament, or by an edict; or unless it goes upon the supposition of Blackstone, that there had been an express agreement and consent of the Irish nation to be bound by acts of the English parliament; and in either case it is not applicable even by analogy to America, because that is not a conquered country, and most certainly never consented to be bound by all acts of parliament, in which it should be named. 3. That the *instance, request and consent* of the Irish is stated, as a ground upon which King John, and his discreet law-sages, first established the laws of England in Ireland. 4. The resolution of the judges in the cases of O'Rurke and Perrot, is express that Ireland was *without the realm of England,* and the late resolutions of both houses of parliament and the late opinion of the judges, that Americans may be sent to England upon the same statute to be tried for treason, is also express that America is *out of the realm of England.* So that we see what is to become of us, my friends. When they want to get our money by taxing us, our privileges by annihilating our charters, and to screen those from punishment who shall murder us at their command, then we are told that we are within the realm; but when they want to draw, hang and quarter us, for honestly defending those liberties which God and compact have given and secured to us, oh then we are clearly out of the realm. 5. In Stowell's case it is resolved that Ireland is out of this land, that is, the land of England. The consequence is, that it was out of the reach and extent of the *law of the land,* that is the common law. America surely is still further removed from that *land,* and therefore is without the jurisdiction of that law which is called the law of the land in England. I think it must appear by this time, that America is not parcel of the *realm, state, kingdom, government, empire or land* of England, or Great Britain, in any sense which can make it subject universally to the supreme legislature of that island. . . .

After all I believe there is no evidence of any express contract of the Irish nation to be governed by the English parliament, and very little of an implied one; that the notion of binding it by acts in which it is expressly named is merely arbitrary. And that this nation which has ever had many and great virtues, has been most grievously oppressed; and it is to this day so greatly injured and oppressed, that I wonder American committees of correspondence and congresses, have not attended more to it than they have. Perhaps in some future time they may. But I am running beyond my line.

We must now turn to Burrows's Reports, vol. 2, 834. Rex vs. Cowle. Lord Mansfield has many observations upon the case of Wales, which ought not to be overlooked. Page 850. He says, "Edward 1st conceived the great design of annexing all other parts of the island of Great Britain to the realm of England. The better to effectuate his idea, as time should offer occasion, he mentioned, 'that all the parts thereof, not in his own hands or possession, were holden of his crown.' " . . . The 27 H. 8. c. 26, adheres to the same plan, and recites that "Wales ever hath been incorporated, annexed, united, and subject to, and under the imperial crown of this realm, as a very member, and joint of the same." Edward I. having succeeded as to Wales maintained likewise that Scotland was holden of the crown of England. This opinion of the court was delivered by Lord Mansfield in the year 1759. In conformity to the *system* contained in these words, my Lord Mansfield, and my Lord North, together with their little friends, Bernard and Hutchinson, have "conceived the great design of annexing" all North America "to the realm of England," and "the better to effectuate this idea, they all maintain, that North America is holden of the crown."

And (no matter upon what foundation) they all maintained that America is dependent on the imperial crown and parliament of Great Britain; and they are all very eagerly desirous of treating the Americans as rebellious vassals, to subdue them and take possession of their country. And when they do, no doubt America will come back as parcel of the realm of England, from which (by fiction of law at least) or by virtual representation, or by some other dream of a shadow of a shade, they had been originally severed.

But these noblemen and ignoblemen ought to have considered that Americans understand the laws and the politicks as well as themselves, and that there are 600,000 men in it, between 16 and 60 years of age, and therefore it will be very difficult to chicane them out of their liberties by "fictions of law," and "no matter upon what foundation."

Methinks I hear his lordship upon this occasion, in a soliloquy somewhat like this. "We are now in the midst of a war, which has been conducted with unexampled success and glory. We have conquered a great part, and shall soon complete the conquest of the French power in America. His majesty is near 70 years of age, and must soon yield to nature. The amiable, virtuous, and promising successor, educated under the care of my nearest friends, will be influenced by our advice. We must bring the war to a conclusion, for we have not the martial spirit and abilities of the great commoner; but we shall be obliged to leave upon the nation an immense debt. How shall we manage that? Why, I have seen letters from America, proposing that parliament should bring America to a closer dependence upon it, and representing that if it does not, she will fall a prey to some foreign power, or set up for herself. These hints may be improved, and a vast revenue drawn from that country and the East Indies, or at least the people here may be flattered and quieted with the hopes of it. It is the duty of a judge to declare law, but under this pretence, many we know have given law or made law, and none in all the records of Westminster Hall more than of late. Enough has been already made, if it is wisely improved by others, to overturn this constitution. Upon this occasion I will accommodate my expressions, to such a design upon America and Asia, and will so accommodate both law and fact, that they may hereafter be improved to admirable effect in promoting our design." This is all romance, no doubt, but it has as good a moral as most romances. For first, it is an utter mistake that Edward 1st conceived the great design of annexing all to England, as one state, under one legislature. He conceived the design of annexing Wales, &c. to his crown. He did not pretend that it was before subject to the crown but to him. *"Nobis jure feodali"* are his words. And when he annexes it to his crown, he does it by an edict of his own, not an act of parliament; and he never did in his whole life allow, that his parliament, that is his lords and commons, had any authority over it, or that he was obliged to take or ask their advice in any one instance concerning the management of it, nor did any of his successors for centuries. It was not Edward I., but Henry 7, who first conceived the great design of annexing it to the realm, and by him and Henry 8 it was done, in part, but never completed until Jac. I. There is a sense indeed in which annexing a territory to the crown, is annexing it to the realm as putting a crown upon a man's head, is putting it on the man, but it does not make it part of the man. 2d. His lordship mentions the statute of Rutland but this was not an act of parliament, and therefore could not annex Wales to the realm if the king had intended it, for it never was in the power of the king alone to annex a country to the realm. This cannot be done, but by act of parliament. As to Edward's treating the Prince of Wales as a "rebellious vassal," this was arbitrary, and is spoken of by all historians as an infamous piece of tyranny.

Edward I and Henry 8 both considered Wales, as the *property* and *revenue* of the crown, not as a part of the realm, and the expressions *"coronae regni Angliae, tanquam partem corporis ejusdem,"* signified "as part of the same body," that is of the same "crown," not "realm" or "kingdom;" and the expressions in 27 H. 8, under the imperial crown of this realm, as a very member "and joint of the same," mean, as a member and joint of the "imperial crown," not of the realm. For the whole history of the principality, the acts of kings, parliaments, and people show, that Wales never was intituled by this annexation to the laws of England, nor bound to obey them. The case of Ireland is enough to prove that the crown and realm are not the same. For Ireland is certainly annexed to the crown of England, and it certainly is not annexed to the realm.

There is one paragraph in the foregoing words of Lord Mansfield, which was quoted by his admirer Governor Hutchinson in his dispute with the house, with a profound compliment. "He did not know a greater authority," &c. But let the authority be as great as it will, the doctrine will not bear the test.

"If the principality was feudatory, the conclusion necessarily follows, that it was under the government of the king's laws." Ireland is feudatory to the crown of England, but would not be subject to the king's English laws without its consent and compact. An estate may be feudatory to a lord, a country may be feudatory to a sovereign lord, upon all possible variety of conditions; it may be only to render homage; it may be to render a rent, it may be to pay a tribute, if his lordship by feudatory means, the original notion of feuds it is true that the king, the general imperator, was absolute, and the tenant held his estate only at will, and the subject not only his estate but his person and life, at his will. But this notion of feuds had been relaxed in an infinite variety of degrees, in some the estate is held at will, in others for life, in others for years, in others forever, to heirs, &c.; in some to be governed by prince alone, in some by prince and nobles, and in some by prince, nobles, and commons, &c. So that being feudatory by no means proves that English lords and commons have any share in the government over us. As to counties palatine; these were not only holden of the king and crown, but were exerted by express acts of parliament, and therefore were never exempted from the authority of parliament. The same parliament, which erected the county palatine, and gave it its *jura regalia* and complete jurisdiction, might unmake it, and take away those regalia and jurisdiction. But American governments and constitutions were never erected by parliament, their *regalia* and jurisdiction were not given by parliament, and therefore parliament have no authority to take them away.

But if the colonies are feudatory to the kings of England, and subject to the government of the king's laws, it is only to such laws as are made in their general assemblies, their provincial legislatures.

[April 10, 1775]   Novanglus

XIII

We now come to Jersey and Guernsey, which Massachusettensis says "are no part of the realm of England, nor are they represented in parliament, but are subject to its authority." A little knowledge of this subject will do us no harm, and as soon as we shall acquire it, we shall be satisfied how these islands came to be subject to the authority of parliament. It is either upon the principle that the king is absolute there, and has a right to make laws for them by his mere will, and therefore may express his will by an act of parliament or an edict at his pleasure, or it is an usurpation. If it is an usurpation, it ought not to be a precedent for the colonies, but it ought to be reformed, and they ought to be incorporated into the realm, by act of parliament, and their own act. Their situation is no objection to this. Ours is an insurmountable obstacle.

Thus we see that in every instance which can be found, the observation proves to be true, that by the common law, the laws of England, the authority of parliament and the limits of the realm, were confined within seas. That the kings of England had frequently foreign dominions, some by conquest, some by marriage, and some by descent. But in all those cases the kings were either absolute in those dominions, or bound to govern them according to their own respective laws, and by their own legislative and executive councils. That the laws of England did not extend there, and the English parliament pretended no jurisdiction there, nor claimed any right to controul the king in his government of those dominions. And from this extensive survey of all the foregoing cases, there results a confirmation of what has been so often said, that there is no provision in the common law, in English precedents, in the English government or constitution, made for the case of the colonies. It is not a conquered, but a discovered country. It came not to the king by descent, but was explored by the settlers. It came not by marriage to the king, but was purchased by the settlers of the savages. It was not granted by the king of his grace, but was dearly, very dearly earned by the planters, in the labour, blood, and treasure which they expended to subdue it to cultivation. It stands upon no grounds then of law or policy, but what are found in the law of nature, and their express contracts in their charters, and their implied contracts in the commission to governors and terms of settlement.

The cases of Chester and Durham, counties palatine within the realm, shall conclude this fatiguing ramble. Chester was an earldom and a county; and in 21st year of King R[ichard] 2, A.D. 1397, it was by an act of parliament, erected into a principality, and several castles and towns, were annexed to it, saving to the king the rights of his crown. This was a county palatine, and had *jura regalia* before this erection of it, into a principality. . . .

I have before recited all the acts of parliament, which were ever made to meddle with Chester, except the 51 H[enry] 3 st[at]. 5, in 1266, which only provides that the justices of Chester, and other bailiffs shall be answerable in the exchequer, for wards, escheats, and other bailiwicks; yet Chester was never severed from the crown or realm of England, nor ever expressly exempted from the authority of parliament; yet as they had generally enjoyed an exemption from the exercise of the authority of parliament, we see how soon they complain of it as grievous, and claim a representation, as a right; and we see how readily it was granted. America, on the contrary, is not in the realm, never was subject to the authority of parliament, by any principle of law, is so far from Great Britain, that she never can be represented; yet she is to be bound in all cases whatsoever.

The first statute, which appears in which Durham is named, is 27 H[enry] 8 c.24, [par.] 21. Cuthbert, Bishop of Durham, and his successors, and their temporal chancellor of the county palatine of Durham, are made justices of the peace. The next is 31 Eliz[abeth] c.9, [and] recites, that Durham is, and of long time hath been, an ancient county palatine, in which the Queen's writ, hath not, and yet doth not run; enacts that a writ of proclamation upon an exigent, against any person dwelling in the bishoprick, shall run there for the future. And [par.] 5 confirms all the other liberties of the bishop and his officers.

And after this, we find no other mention of that bishoprick in any statute until 25 Char[les] 2. c.9. This statute recites, "whereas the inhabitants of the county palatine of Durham, have not hitherto had the liberty and privilege of electing and sending any knights and burgesses to the high court of parliament, altho' the inhabitants of the said county palatine *are liable to all payments, rates, and subsidies granted by parliament*, equally with the inhabitants of other counties, cities, and boroughs, in this kingdom, who have their knights and burgesses in the parliament, and are therefore *concerned equally with others*, the inhabitants of this kingdom, to have knights and burgesses in the said high court of parliament *of their own election*, to present the condition of their county, as the inhabitants of other counties, and boroughs of this kimgdom have.["] Enacts two knights for the county, and two burgesses for the city. Here it should be observed, that, altho' they acknowledge that they had been *liable* to all *rates*, &c. granted by parliament, yet none had actually been laid upon them before this statute.

Massachusettensis then comes to the first charter of this province, and he tells us, that in it "we shall find irresistible evidence, that our being a part of the empire subject to the supreme authority of the state, bound by its laws, and subject to its protection, was the very terms and conditions by which our ancestors held their lands and settled the province." This is roundly and warmly said, but there is more zeal in it than knowledge. As to our being part of the empire, it could not be the British empire, as it is called, because that was not then in being, but was created seventy or eighty years afterwards. It must be the English empire then, but the nation was not then polite enough to have introduced into the language of the law, or common parlance any such phrase or idea. Rome never introduced the terms Roman empire until the tragedy of her freedom was completed. Before that, it was only the republic, or the city. In the same manner the realm or the kingdom, or the dominions of the king, were the fashionable style in the age of the first charter. As to being subject to the supreme authority of the state, the prince who granted that charter thought it resided in himself, without any such troublesome tumults as lords and commons; and before the granting that charter, had dissolved his parliament, and determined never to call another, but to govern without. It is not very likely then, that he intended our ancestors should be governed by parliament, or bound by its laws. As to being subject to its protection, we may guess what ideas king and parliament had of that, by the protection they actually afforded to our ancestors. Not one farthing was ever voted or given by the king or his parliament, or any one resolution taken about them. As to holding their lands, surely they did not hold their lands of lords and commons. If they agreed to hold their lands of the king, this did not subject them to English lords and commons, any more than the inhabitants of Scotland holding their lands of the same king, subjected them. But there is not a word about the empire, the supreme authority of the state, being bound by its laws, or obliged for its protection in that whole charter. But "our charter is in the royal style." What then? Is that the parliamentary style? The style is, this: "Charles, by the grace of God, King of England, Scotland, France, and Ireland, defender of the faith, &c." Now in which capacity did he grant that charter? as King of France, or Ireland, or Scotland, or England? He govern'd England by one parliament, Scotland by another. Which parliament, were we to be governed by? And Ireland by a third, and it might as well be reasoned that America was to be governed by the Irish parliament as by the English. But it was granted "under the great seal of England." True. But this seal runneth not out of the realm, except to mandatory writs, and when our charter was given, it was never intended to go out of the realm. The charter and the corporation were intended to abide and remain within the realm, and be like other corporations there. But this affair of the seal is a mere piece of imposition.

In Moore's Reports, in the case of the union of the realm of Scotland with England, it is resolved by the judges that "the seal is alterable by the king at his pleasure, and he might make one seal for both kingdoms (of England and Scotland), for seals, coin, and leagues are of absolute prerogative to the king without parliament, nor restrained to any assent of the people," and in determining how far the great seal doth command out of England, they made this distinction. "That the great seal was current for remedials, which groweth on complaint of the subject, and thercupon writs are addressed under the great seal of England, which writs are limited, their precinct to be within the places of the jurisdiction of the court, that was to give the redress of the wrong. And therefore writs are not to go into Ireland, or the Isles, nor Wales, nor the counties palatine, because the king's courts here have not power to hold pleas of lands or things there. But the great seal hath a power preceptory to the person, which power extendeth to any place where the person may be found," &c. This authority plainly shows that the great seal of England, has no more authority out of the realm, except to mandatory or preceptory writs, (and surely the first charter was no preceptory writ) than the privy seal, or the great seal of Scotland, or no seal at all. In truth, the seal and charter were intended to remain within the realm, and be of force to a corporation there; but the moment it was transferred to New England, it lost all its legal force, by the common law of England; and as this translation of it was acquiesced in by all parties, it might well be considered as good evidence of a contract between the parties, and in no other light, but not a whit the better or stronger for being under the great seal of England. But "the grants are made by the king for his heirs and successors." What then? So the Scots held their lands of him who was then king of England, his heirs and successors, and were bound to allegiance to him, his heirs and successors, but it did not follow from thence that the Scots were subject to the English parliament. So the inhabitants of Aquitain, for ten descents, held their lands, and were tied by allegiance to him who was king of England, his heirs and successors, but were under no subjection to English lords and commons.

Heirs and *successors* of the king are supposed to be the same persons, and are used as synonymous words in the English law. There is no positive, artificial provision made by our laws or the British constitution, for revolutions. All our positive laws suppose that the royal office will descend to the eldest branch of the male line, or in default of that to the eldest female, &c. forever, and that the succession will not be broken. It is true that nature, necessity, and the great principles of self-preservation, have often overruled the succession. But this was done without any positive instruction of law. Therefore the grants being by the king for his heirs and successors, and the tenures being of the king his heirs and successors, and the preservation being to the king his heirs and successors, are so far from proving that we were to be part of an empire as one state subject to the supreme authority of the English or British state, and subject to its protection, that they don't so much as prove that we are annexed to the English crown. And all the subtilty of the writers on the side of the ministry, has never yet proved that America is so much as annexed to the crown, much less to the realm. "It is apparent the king acted in his royal capacity as king of England." This I deny. The laws of England gave him no authority to grant any territory out of the realm. Besides, there is no colour for his thinking that he acted in that capacity, but his using the great seal of England; but if the king is absolute in the affair of the seal, and may make or use any seal that he pleases, his using that seal which had been commonly used in England, is no certain proof that he acted as king of England; for it is plain, he might have used the English seal in the government of Scotland, and in that case it will not be pretended that he would have acted in his royal capacity as king of England. But his acting as king of England "necessarily supposes the territory granted to be a part of the English dominions, and holden of the crown of England." Here is the word "dominions," systematically introduced instead of the word "realm." There was no English dominions but the realm. And I say that America was not any part of the English realm or dominions. And therefore, when the king granted it, he could not act as king of England by the laws of England. As to the "territory being holden of the crown," there is no such thing in nature or art. Lands are holden according to the original notion of feuds of the natural person of the lord. Holding lands, in feudal language, means no more than the relation between lord and tenant. The reciprocal duties of these are all personal. Homage, fealty, &c., and all other services, are personal to the lord; protection, &c., is personal to the tenant. And therefore no homage, fealty, or other services, can ever be rendered to the body politick, the political capacity, which is not corporated, but only a frame in the mind, an idea. No lands here or in England, are held of the crown, meaning by it, the political capacity; they are all held of the royal person, the natural person of the king. Holding lands, &c. of the crown, is an impropriety of expression, but it is often used, and when it is, it can have no other sensible meaning than this, that we hold lands of that person, whoever he is, who wears the crown; the law supposes he will be a right, natural heir of the present king forever.

Massachusettensis then produces a quotation from the first

charter, to prove several points. It is needless to repeat the whole, but the parts chiefly relied on, are italicized. It makes the company a body politick in fact and name, &c. and enables it ["] to sue and be sued." Then the writer asks, "whether this looks like a distinct state or independent empire?" I answer no. And that it is plain and uncontroverted, that the first charter was intended only to erect a corporation within the realm, and the governor and company were to reside within the realm, and their general courts were to be held there. Their agents, deputies and servants only were to come to America. And if this had taken place, nobody ever doubted but they would have been subject to parliament. But this intention was not regarded on either side, and the company came over to America, and brought their charter with them. And as soon as they arrived here, they got out of the English realm, dominions, states, empire, call it by what name you will, and out of the legal jurisdiction of parliament. The king might by his writ or proclamation, have commanded them to return, but he did not.

[April 17, 1775]   Novanglus

XIV*

Another clause in the Charter, quoted by this writer, contains the power *"to make* laws and ordinances for the good and welfare of the sd. Co., and for ye gov[ern]m[en]t and ordering of ye sd. lands and plantations, and ye people inhabiting the same; So as such laws and ordinances be not contrary or repugnant to the laws and Statutes of this Our Realm *of England."* This is the usual clause inserted in the *Charters* of all Corporations in England, and it is intended to restrain these *bodies politick* within the limits of the Constitution and ye laws; it expresses no more, however, than the Law would imply. For ye K[ing] could not erect a Corporation within the Realm, and give it power to supersede or overrule the general laws of ye Kingdom. A similar clause is inserted in the Laws of this province, which impowers Towns to make Byelaws, "so as they be not repugnant to the Laws of the province." I suppose this clause was inserted in that Charter to restrain the Corporation from setting up any form of government different from the English Constitution in general, and perhaps was intended to subject them to the Common Law [and to such statutes as were then in force. But if we allow it the utmost latitude of construction and suppose that it meant to confine them to obedience to Common Law] and all statutes which were then in force and to all others which should thereafter be made, this is no more than they would have been bound to if no such clause had been in the Charter, so long as they and their Charter had remained in England, which both Grantor and Grantees then intended; *but the moment* the Charter and the Company were removed to New England, beyond the four seas, out of the Realm, out of the extent and local limit of the laws of England, *that moment* they were discharged from all obligation of obedience to the Laws of England. The Charter lost all force which it ever had by the law of England as a legal instrument and became only evidence of a Contract. The whole plan and design of all parties was effectually changed. If a charter granted in England, to be used there, can be forfeited by the Laws of England; the translation of that Charter and Company to America and setting up a government here, under it, was a forfeiture of it. What the consequences of this forfeiture were, is another question. The king might have commanded the adventurers to return, and upon their refusal, might have seized their estates in England, if they had any; that is all, but he did not. But it did not bring our ancestors under the authority of parliament, nor under the absolute power of ye king. Nay, what is more, this Charter was decreed forfeited and void for these very reasons in the King's bench, Trin. 11. Car. I.; yet our ancestors continued to enjoy their privileges and carry on government, according to that charter, from that time, until the reign of James the 2d.; nay, until the Revolution. In a collection of original papers, relative to the history of the Colony of Massachusetts, p. 101, 102, 103, 104, 105, 106, you will find the evidence of all this. "A quo warranto brought against the Company of the Massachusetts Bay by Sir John Banks, Attorney General". This quo warranto goes upon the principle upon which I have all along proceeded, viz, that the common law had made no provision for erecting governments or colonies out of the Realm, and therefore any Royal Charter, out of the Realm was void. The quo warranto begins, "That Sir Henry Roswell and all the Massachusetts Company &c in several parts beyond the Seas, *out of* this Kingdom of England, without any warrant or Royal Grant (meaning that quoad hoc, the *royal grant* was void) the Liberties, privileges and Franchises following &c. 1. To be a body politick &c. 8. To appoint councell Houses in England and beyond Seas and *there,* when they please, to hold a Court of such of said Company as they please, and in such Courts to make such Laws and Statutes concerning the Lands, goods and chattels of that Company and other persons, beyond Seas, against the Laws and Customs of England &c. 9. To transport out of England, beyond the Seas, his Majesty's subjects and others, and them, at their wills to govern on the Seas and on parts beyond the seas. 14. To examine on oath any person, in any cause touching life and member and to proceed to tryal and sentence, judgment and execution touching life and member, lands and tenements, goods and chattels, against the law and customs of England. All which Franchises Liberties &c. the said Sir Henry Roswell and others of the said Company have for all that time, and still do usurp &c."

This quo warranto, manifestly, is grounded on the principle, that the laws of England did not extend beyond seas and therefore that the Charter, when translated beyond seas, was void. In Mich. term Car. 1., Eaton, and in Hil. 11. Car. 1. Roswell, and, in Pasc. 13. Car. 1. Young, and in Hil. 12. Car. 1., Saltonstall, and, Mich. 11. Car. 1. Ven, came in and pleaded, that they never usurped any of the said liberties &c. nor doth use or claim any of the same, but wholly disclaim them. Whereupon the Court gave judgment, that they shall not, for the future intermeddle with any the liberties &c. aforesaid, but shall be forever excluded from all use and claim of the same, &c.; Cradock made default and was convicted of the usurpation &c. and had judgment against him; Harwood, Perry, Wright, Vassall, Goffe, Adams, Brown and Foxcraft, pleaded and had judgment as Eaton. The rest of the patentees *(being in New England)* stood outlawed, and no judgment was entred up against them. In consequence of these proceedings, an order of the Privy Council, 4th April 1638, to Mr. Winthrop, in his Majesty's name, "requiring and enjoining the said Winthrop, or any other, in whose power the said Letters patent were, that they fail not to transmit the said Patent hither by the return of the ship, it being resolved, in case of any further neglect &c., their Lordships will move his Majesty to reassume into his hands, the whole plantation."

The intent of this *Order*, was, that the Patent should be sent over, that the government of [the] Colony might be under a Corporation in England, according to the Original and true meaning of the Patent. But did Mr. Winthrop or any other of the adventurers return the Patent? No; young as the plantation was, they had the courage and the wisdom to keep their patent in their own power. But as this translation of the Patent to New England, instead of using it within the Realm, as was at first intended, is of great importance in this controversy, we must be a little more particular. The Charter as I have said, shews upon the face of it, that it was intended to erect a Corporation within the Realm. The first Governor, Deputy Governor and Assistants were chosen in England, 13 May 1628. Cradock was chosen Governor, and Goffe Deputy Governor in England, and as soon as the Election was over, they, with the assistants, appointed Mr. Endicott their Governor in the plantation. This shews that they had one Governor in England, who was the head of the Corporation, and another Governor in America, who was only principal agent or manager for the Company. And in this manner the affairs of the Company were conducted until July 1629; when the Company in England projected a much larger embarkation of adventurers and a translation of the Patent itself to New England. *A Committee* was appointed to consider of it and advise with Council. The Company had been at great Expence, without any returns or rational prospect of profit. Johnson, Winthrop, Dudley and others (not the rascally rabble of Romulus, but) Gentlemen of family, fortune, education and figure, offered to go over with their families, upon condition, that the Patent and charter should go with them. The objection against it was a doubt whether the transfer was legal. The report of the committee is not on record; but a Mr. White, a counsellor at law, was of the Company, and his opinion was taken, and the Company concurred with it, "That the government and Patent should be settled in New England." It is much to be wished that this important opinion of Mr. White was preserved. It might discover "Arcana." It was certainly a wise and judicious opinion in point of prudence and policy, and has been vastly successful; for the plantation probably had dwindled away, but for that advice. However, Governor Winthrop himself, who knew very well that the Laws of England were confined within ye four seas, must have been sensible that there could be no provision in that Law for the translation of the Company beyond seas, and indeed they seem to have been all sensible of this and to have considered the Charter only as a Licence to their people to go abroad. On the 20th of October, at a general Court in England, Mr. Winthrop was chosen Governor, and the Deputy Governor and assistants chosen, were all such as proposed to go over with the Charter. They went over accordingly, and the existence of the English power in America, is entirely owing to this manifest departure from the first intent of the Charter. For, at this critical time, Rich[e]lieu and De Monts were upon the point of making settlements here, which would have excluded the English forever.

Massachusettensis says that this clause in the Charter, "So as such laws be not contrary or repugnant to the laws and statutes of this our realm of England" is as evident a recognition of the authority of Parliament over this Province as if the words "acts of Parliament" had been inserted &c. But there is no such clause in the first Charter or the second, and if there had been in the first Charter, it would have been void; for, by an express clause in the first Charter, every part of it was to be expounded most favorably for the Grantees; and therefore, if there had been two contradictory clauses in it, that must have been taken which was most in favor of the Grantees. Now they think that any clause obliging them to obedience to Parliament, would have been directly repugnant to the clause under consideration, which gives them the liberties and immunities of natural born subjects.

Soon after we are struck with a smart remark indeed, "if we are not annext to the Realm we are Aliens. . . ." But unfortunately, all history and law are against it. Lord Coke observed, what a Concurrence of judgments, resolutions and rules there be in our books, in all ages, concerning this case, as if they had been prepared for deciding this point; and that which never fell out in any doubtful case, no one opinion in all our books is against this judgment in Calvin's case, who was not of the Realm, but yet was no Alien, because born within the allegiance of the King. . . .

[April 19, 1775]   [Novanglus]